What makes churches grow?

What makes churches grow?

Vision and practice in effective mission

Bob Jackson

Church House Publishing
Church House
Great Smith Street
London SW1P 3AZ

Published 2015 by Church House Publishing

British Library Cataloguing in Publication Data

A catalogue record for this book is available from the British Library

ISBN 978 0 7151 4474 9

Typeset by Regent Typesetting
Printed and bound in Great Britain by
CPI Group (UK) Ltd, Croydon

Contents

List of tables vii
List of figures ix
Foreword xi
Introduction – new hope xiii

Part 1 How is the growth project getting on? 1

1 Growth in numbers – what is church growth and how do you measure it? 3
2 Measuring growth in depth and vitality 10
3 Growth initiatives 27
4 Growth in patterns 39
5 Growth in total? 47

Part 2 What is working on the ground today? 71

6 Intending to grow 73
7 Leading to grow 92
8 Training to grow 114
9 Inviting to grow 127
10 Families to grow 140
11 Planting to grow 159
12 Changing to grow 177
13 Spending to grow 196
14 Cathedrals to grow 208
15 Dioceses to grow 222

Part 3 What is working under the surface? 245

16 Angels and growth 247
17 Guidance, prayer and growth 256
18 The Holy Spirit and growth 269

Notes 284
Index 289

List of tables

4.1 UK church membership by denomination (thousands) 41
4.2 Average all-age weekly attendance in October 42
4.3 Electoral roll increases 42
4.4 Adult uSa change in Church of England single church benefices 43

5.1 Decline in church numbers, 1980–90 and 1990–2000 48
5.2 Number of churches in the Church of England 49
5.3 Numbers of active clergy 52
5.4 Infant and child baptisms (thousands) 53
5.5 Adult baptisms 53
5.6 Marriages (thousands) 54
5.7 Funerals (thousands) 55
5.8 Confirmations 55
5.9 PCC total income 56
5.10 Easter attendance (thousands) 57
5.11 Christmas attendance on Christmas Eve and Christmas Day (thousands) 58
5.12 Usual Sunday attendance (thousands) 59
5.13 Average attendance in October 60
5.14 Usual Sunday attendance as percentage of electoral rolls 62
5.15 Joiners and leavers 2013 (thousands) 65
5.16 Statistics for Mission figures on church growth and decline 67
5.17 Indicators in church growth 69
5.18 Summary of indicators in church growth 70

7.1 The range of benefices 96
7.2 Numbers of active clergy 107

8.1 Church attendance before and after LyCiG 124
8.2 The effectiveness of LyCiG on the mission of the parish 125

9.1 Getting the welcome right 139

10.1 Percentage of adults aged under 45 147
10.2 Focus of fresh expressions 149

13.1 Giving to churches (real terms in 2011 purchasing power) 198
13.2 Annual average increase in giving in real terms (real terms in 2011 purchasing power) 199

14.1 Cathedral statistics 211

15.1 Population growth by diocese, 2001–11 230

List of figures

2.1	The nine core qualities of church life	14
4.1	Percentage change in adult uSa in 3,000 single church benefices in the Church of England, 2001–11	43
5.1	The proportion of Church of England churches showing growth and decline in child weekly attendance, 2013	51
5.2	Attendance frequency census, October 2014 (% attending)	63
6.1	The effects of MAP on the electoral roll in London, 1972–2013	78
6.2	MAP and the halted decline in Blackburn, 2004–11	79
6.3	Higher quality of MAP: better growth trend of the church	79
6.4	Growth with MAP higher than growth without MAP	80
6.5	Relative growth between a good MAP and an inadequate MAP	81
6.6	MAP and change in attendance and joiners/leavers in Derby, 2010–12	82
6.7	MAP, or a written mission statement, and church growth	83
7.1	Change in all-age uSa in 2008–12 in groups of dioceses with different falls in clergy numbers	97

8.1 Attendance change from the year before a vacancy to a year after it ends by length of vacancy 122
8.2 Numbers of churches growing and shrinking before and after their leader(s) attended LyCiG 124

10.1 Percentage with religious affiliation by decade of birth 142
10.2 Children in Britain attending Sunday school 143
10.3 UK Sunday school scholars by denomination, 1900–2000 143
10.4 Age at which 1,242 people became Christians 145
10.5 Pattern of church growth in Leicester, 2013 148
10.6 Fresh expressions attendance in Liverpool Diocese, 2010 (3,410 people, 17 per cent of uSa) 149

11.1. Number of registered Messy Churches in February each year 174

12.1 Percentage change in adult attendance, 2010–13 184
12.2 Percentage change in child attendance, 2010–13 184
12.3 Diocese of St Davids numbers of congregations 187
12.4 Diocese of St Davids numbers of congregations, 2010–13 187

14.1 Total attendance at English cathedral services 210
14.2 Attendance trends at cathedral services (numbers of services) 213

15.1 Percentage change in groups of dioceses with different rates of population growth, 2001–11 231
15.2 St Davids' bookmark with logo 233

16.1 The church handicap hurdles 252

18.1 Adult (13+) baptisms in the Church of England 276

Foreword

For years we have been aware of the seriousness of the situation facing the Church of England; the task ahead cannot be overestimated. However, we have also been aware of the dynamic life of the Spirit of God bringing new life and hope as well as strategy to the Church of Jesus Christ.

This book is a wind-sock to point out the direction in which the Spirit is blowing. For those who are charged with catching the wind, there can be few more important books for taking stock. I believe attendance to Bob Jackson's work will help all of us do what we desire to do above all: see where God is at work and join in.

✠ Justin
Archbishop of Canterbury

Foreword

Introduction – new hope

> 'For I know the plans I have for you,' declares the Lord, 'plans to prosper you and not to harm you, plans to give you hope and a future.' (Jeremiah 29.11)

This is a book about new life. It's about how the new Church of England is growing under the radar of the media, the critics and, sometimes, the bishops. There will be lots of statistics, trends and principles about how churches are growing but I will try to make them so interesting you will not be able to resist reading them. And there will be some real-life church stories along the way.

Jeremiah got his pessimistic reputation from his dire warnings about the sins of God's people, the fall of Jerusalem and the exile in Babylon. However, once the exile had begun, his message changed. In his letter to the exiles in chapter 29 Jeremiah is full of hope not gloom. Provided that the people sort themselves out, he now promises a bright future and return from exile.

Today I feel a bit like the Jeremiah of chapter 29. When I wrote two earlier books, *Hope for the Church* (2002)[1] and *The Road to Growth* (2005),[2] it was obvious from all the evidence that the Church of England was still suffering serious decline. We had in fact been shrinking for most of the last hundred years and, in that time, we had rarely thought about trying to combat our decline. I argued that it was high time the Church adopted a strategy for growth, rather than one for managed decline. This was perfectly possible because we were starting to see how new hope and growth could be generated. Such strategy should come from prayer and guidance. However, the human element should be based not on anecdote, hunch or a piece of contentious theology but on evidence and research. Neither denial nor fatalism were adequate responses to the decline of the Church – better would be a new, widespread and soundly based determination to first face the facts and then develop growing, flourishing churches suited to our fast-changing world.

Rather to my surprise, this call for a new focus on growing the Church has been heeded at national, diocesan and local church levels. No longer do I need to argue that turning decline into growth should be a priority. Rather, the task has become to put good tools for growth into the hands of the willing. So I've spent some time developing courses such as *Everybody Welcome* (2009),[3] *Growing through a Vacancy* (2013)[4] and *Leading Your Church into Growth – Local* (2014).[5] These are intended to resource whole churches, not just the clergy, for it is the whole people of God who will grow the future churches. That's why I'm rather hoping this new book will be read by lots of lay people as well as clergy!

Back in the early years of the century when I wrote the previous two books, the Church of England was still obviously shrinking numerically. I argued then that if enough individual churches and diocesan leaderships tried to grow, then overall, in the grace of God, the whole Church of England would start to expand again. If the Church of England was still obviously shrinking in 2014 despite everyone's best efforts then I would have been proved wrong.

Mercifully, the balance of the evidence in 2014 suggests that the Church of England has probably stopped shrinking numerically and, on some measures, may even be growing overall.

Part 1 of this book reviews how the growth project is getting on, checks out the growth patterns and trends that are emerging, and charts our developing understanding and consensus about the nature of growth itself. So Part 1 describes the hope that is growing in the churches.

Part 2 reviews the main ingredients identified by the evidence that are helping to generate new growth in the churches. It charts the role of intentionality, leadership, training, invitation and welcome, families, planting and fresh expressions, money, change, cathedrals and dioceses. So Part 2 is about how we can actively grow hope for the future.

Part 3 goes behind the scenes to explore the spiritual realities of the angels of the churches, prayer and the Holy Spirit that govern the possibilities of new growth. The development and flourishing of churches depends on a cooperative effort between God and humans. So Part 3 is about the God of hope giving hope to the churches.

I hope the book will give you a clearer idea of how your own church can flourish and grow in the future within the context of a resurgent Church overall.

We live in north Derbyshire in the village of Eyam, famous for its plague story in the 1660s. Led by the vicar the people decided to stay put and risk plague themselves rather than run away and infect surrounding areas. Many of them died. One of the villages saved from the plague by the heroism of Eyam was Baslow, now part of our benefice. As I drove down to take the morning service on Easter Sunday this year I was expecting the usual 30 faithful and delightful people, most of whom would be even older than myself. But I had reckoned without the Messy Church the rector had started a few months earlier based on his contacts at the excellent Church of England primary school in the village. There was now a monthly Messy Church congregation of around 70, but Easter Sunday was not a Messy Church week. So some of the new families had decided to turn up to the traditional Easter Sunday service and I was confronted with a congregation of 75, including lots of children. So I scrapped the prepared sermon and did some family service stuff, involved the children and had lots of fun. What a joy!

I tell this story of being surprised by resurrection at Easter not because the story at Baslow is spectacular or novel but because it isn't. Easter Sunday was just one step along the way in a middle-of-the-road village church that has turned a corner, begun to grow and started to attract families and young people again. It is an ordinary, low-key, story being repeated the length and breadth of the land.

So, what is going on, how is God renewing our ancient Church of England and how can we join in with what God is doing? If you are interested in these questions then please read on.

Part 1

How is the growth project getting on?

1

Growth in numbers – what is church growth and how do you measure it?

> They devoted themselves to ... prayer ... All the believers were together ... they gave to anyone as he had need ... And the Lord added to their number daily those who were being saved. (Acts 2.42, 44, 45, 47)

Growth in three dimensions

How do you measure a lake? Your eye is drawn to the surface area. But a broad, shallow lake might hold less water than a narrow, deep one. A small lake high in the mountains might possess more hydro-power potential than a large lake in the flatlands. A large, polluted lake may have less life in it than a small, healthy one brimming with fish and frogspawn.

It's the same when measuring a church. The circumference of the church, the number of people in it, is an important measure of its size. But if the faith and spirituality of the people is only skin deep then the church is not as voluminous as it looks. And sometimes a small church does more good in the world than a large one.

So we should assess the size and growth of a church in three ways – by the number of its people, the depth of its faith, and the power of its ministry. When Archbishop Rowan spelled out his priorities for the next five years in his presidential address to General Synod in November 2010 they were, 'To take forward the spiritual and numerical growth of the Church of England, including the growth of its capacity to serve the whole community of this country.' This threefold growth aim has been reaffirmed by Archbishop Justin.

When the Diocese of Lichfield adopted a 'Going for Growth' strategy in 2004 it penned a prayer which began: 'God our creator and redeemer, help your church to grow in holiness, unity, effectiveness and numbers' – healthy churches don't grow in one dimension only. Gimmicks might grow a church numerically but will do nothing for its spiritual depth or effectiveness. Churches that stay numerically small are likely to stay weak in their ability to change the world. Churches that simply try to deepen their own spirituality can just be self-serving. Depth is quarried out of evangelism and service. Healthy growth comes in holiness, effectiveness and numbers all together. And health needs unity – a squabbling church puts people off from joining it, neglects its own spirituality and wastes the energy it needs to serve the world.

This is a book unashamedly about the numerical growth of the Church but this inevitably means it is about every dimension of healthy, holistic growth in the body of Christ.

Church is a community not an attendance event

We once thought we knew what church was and how to measure it numerically. Church happened when we gathered for a public act of worship with a priest in a consecrated building on a Sunday. We measured the church by the number of people who attended the public act of worship. Until the year 2000 we used an estimate of average attendance on Sundays. Now we also count average weekly attendance across four weeks in October including weekdays. You may be all too familiar with the annual 'Statistics for Mission' form, the source of these statistics.

But the church of the Bible is not a culturally fixed form of activity. The essence of the church we find there is not meeting-format but human relationships. The church is the community of the followers of Christ. As Archbishop Rowan put it in the foreword to *Mission-Shaped Church*: 'Church is what happens when people encounter the Risen Jesus and commit themselves to sustaining and deepening that encounter in their encounter with each other' (2004, p. vii).

We thought we could measure the size of the church by counting numbers at particular attendance events. We were wrong. Church is not one type of attendance event to the exclusion of others. We are no less church in a small group than we are at Evening Prayer. Church is community, not event. It is the eternal Bride of Christ, a group of people committed to Christ and bound to each other, trying to go deeper, seeking to serve, attempting to grow.

The people of God in the Bible

The Old Testament has two different words for the people of God. Amazingly, the scholars seem to disagree on their exact meanings but we won't let that spoil a good story.

'Edhah' describes the whole community of Israel that God assembled to take through the wilderness into the Promised Land. Edhah is a single community, a living, breathing entity surviving the death of every individual, imperfect, experiencing crises and setbacks, yet walking with God down the centuries. It is the Edhah about which God says through Hosea, 'When Israel was a child, I loved him, and out of Egypt I called my son' (11.1).

'Qahal' is the word mostly used for an actual meeting of the people of God, the edhah. The qahal is summoned to form a gathering that constitutes God's people for that moment even though not all the edhah may be present. In the Greek Bible, it is qahal rather than edhah that translates as 'ekklesia'.

Ekklesia (the main NT word for church) derives from the gathering of the citizens of the Greek city state so it sounds more like qahal than edhah. At first this did not matter as the whole edhah more or less lived together, edhah and qahal being the same thing – 'All the believers were together and had everything in common' (Acts 2.44). But the church quickly expanded and spread over the ancient world. Ekklesia soon began to mean the whole circle of believers irrespective of whether or not they were assembled for worship. See, for example, 1 Corinthians 16.1, 'Now about the collection for God's people: Do what I told the Galatian churches to do.'

In Acts 9.31 Luke summarizes the situation: 'Then the church throughout Judea, Galilee and Samaria enjoyed a time of peace. It was strengthened; and encouraged by the Holy Spirit, it grew in numbers.' It was the community of Christians that formed the church and grew in numbers.

When the afterglow of the first white heat of Pentecost was fading, the writer of Hebrews felt he had to rally the troops: 'Let us consider how we may spur one another on towards love and good deeds. Let us not give up meeting together, as some are in the habit of doing, but let us encourage one another' (10.24–25). The people were not meeting together as regularly as they should, but they were still the church!

Using appropriate measures

If the church is composed of all who participate in its life then average attendance no longer measures the size of the church because we never all gather together at one time.

But the electoral roll, our traditional membership measure, is of little use either. Some join the electoral roll for purposes other than to signify active belonging – to get married, to get their children into a church school, or to show support for the church without ever taking part. Others belong to the church community but never join the roll. Many postmoderns are uncomfortable joining a formal membership list. New forms of church (fresh expressions) may never ask new members to join the electoral roll for fear of putting them off with an inappropriate demand. And electoral rolls exclude children. Yet the Bible clearly treats children as members of the people of God. Paul writes to the Ephesians in 1.1: 'To the saints in Ephesus, the faithful in Christ Jesus'. Then in 6.1 he specifically addresses those saints who are children – 'Children obey your parents in the Lord'. Children were part of the ekklesia in Ephesus and are part of the church today.

In fact the health and future of the church are in large part determined by its child members. The church with many children is likely to project health and joy, to flourish and grow. The childless church faces a dreary inevitable demise. So, far from being excluded from membership, the children are the Christian Church's most crucial members. It is inconceivable to count the Christian community and miss out the children. But that is what we do with the electoral roll!

So we need to create a new measure of church – one that is not an increasingly unreliable 'attendance' proxy for a Christian community in a fast-changing world, but one which actually measures 'church' as community as its organizational and cultural forms evolve. This measure is simply a list of all the effective participants in the worshipping community of the local church. The size or circumference of the church is the length of the list. This list should be compiled by the leadership of each local church and kept up to date.

So from 2012 the Church of England's 'Statistics for Mission' form asks every church for the number of its worshipping community split by age group. This should in time become the principle measure of the size and growth of the Church.

Naturally, there are issues. The Church of England has traditionally had porous boundaries. We do not like to sit in judgement on who is 'in' and who is 'out'. The criteria need to be clear and consistent – the national Church has to fix them. How much time and effort does it take a church to compile and update its list?

But many churches already have such a list for pastoral reasons or as a contact list. It must be good practice for every church to know their own participants to enable pastoral care without people slipping through nets. If a church is caring for its people by name in this way there will be little extra effort required to tot up the total for a diocesan return. Lists do not need to be published. Simply having a list of currently active participants passes no judgement on people's standing before God or the church – it is simply attempting to reflect current reality.

Joiners and leavers

When Luke describes the growth of the early Church in the book of Acts, he emphasizes not only the total number but also the additions to it. For example, the original group prior to Pentecost was 120 strong (1.15). But at Pentecost 3,000 were baptized and added to their number (2.41). In the period after Pentecost, 'the Lord added to their number daily those who were being saved' (2.47). Following Peter's speech in chapter 3, 'many who heard the message believed, and the number of men grew to about five thousand' (4.4). As the apostles kept performing healing miracles and testifying to the resurrection, 'more and more men and women believed in the Lord and were added to their number' (5.14).

Only two out of ten church-growth references in the first half of Acts quote the actual size of the church (120 and 5,000). The other eight all refer to the numbers of new people joining the church. Luke starts by quoting an actual number (3,000) but thereafter the sheer volume precludes an exact number so he falls back on a stock phrase such as 'a great number' of joiners.

Charting progress by counting the joiners has some advantages. Counting the size of the community is never an exact science, so estimates of the change between two inexact counts may be even more inexact. It is easier to make an accurate count of the joiners. And the number of joiners is a guide to the evangelistic success of the church. Average attendance can go up not because new people come to faith but existing members attend more frequently or there is a spate of baptisms. A church's membership can rise simply through transfer from other churches but a count of joiners places them into categories – for example those who have transferred from another church and those who are new to church. The contribution each individual church is making to overall growth can then be estimated. And information on the composition of the joiners (for example, by age or gender) can help reveal what sort of people the church is attracting, what direction the church is moving in and what the future may hold.

Simply trying to increase the number of joiners gives a one-sided picture and encourages rapid throughput rather than genuine growth. Half the business of growing the church is keeping the people we already have. So a measurement method focusing on joiners should also focus on leavers.

Following experiments in the Dioceses of Leicester and Lichfield, the 2012 Statistics for Mission form also asked for numbers of joiners and leavers in different categories. These measures chart not only the overall trend in the size of the church but also the flows in and out that have generated that trend.

Counting the Church of England in these ways is still new and it will take several years for people to get used to completing their returns in a consistent way. But to date the clear excess of joiners over leavers suggests the Church may now be growing overall numerically, primarily among families and children, and mainly through attracting people with no previous churchgoing background. These initial figures are so startling, and run so counter to the 'ageing and declining' narrative so beloved of the media, that they demand the detailed examination found in Chapter 5.

2

Measuring growth in depth and vitality

> Stephen, a man full of God's grace and power, did great wonders and miraculous signs among the people. (Acts 6.8)

The relationship between numbers, depth and vitality

In Chapter 1 we saw that healthy churches grow in three dimensions at once – numbers, spiritual depth and the vitality of their ministry. Numbers growth is about enlarging the whole worshipping community. There is no net gain from transfer growth from one church to another. Numbers growth happens when more new people start worshipping Jesus in the Christian Church than existing members lapse or die. Numbers is about how many there are of us, depth is about who we are and vitality about what we do. Growing in depth is about allowing the Holy Spirit to change us as individuals and a church community. Vitality growth is about how we work together with the Holy Spirit to change the world around us.

The New Testament suggests that all three elements matter. The description of the first church in Acts 2.42–47 intertwines descriptions of growing depth (they devoted themselves to teaching, prayer and the breaking of bread), growing vitality (they sold possessions and gave to anyone who had need) and growing numbers (the Lord added daily to their number those who were being saved). In Ephesians chapter 4 Paul says that church leaders have a responsibility to provoke the ministry-vitality of the people so that they can grow in unity and depth: Christ 'gave some to be apostles, some to be prophets, some to be evangelists, and some to be pastors and teachers, to prepare God's people for works of service, so that the body of Christ may be built up until we all reach unity in the faith and in the knowledge of the Son of God and become mature' (4.11–13).

The importance of measurement

I used to be an economic adviser to the Government. We tried to improve the real world (honest!) but we only measured it through statistical indicators we invented and compiled. So the policy aim became to impact the statistical indicators, hoping these reflected the real world. We aimed at the things we could measure. The Government can measure national income so increasing it is a policy aim. The Government cannot measure national happiness, so that is not a policy aim. Personally I would rather be happy than rich. So when the Government's aim is to make me richer but not happier the priorities get skewed, and we can end up with an unbalanced, unhealthy society – money-rich, time-poor, stressed, acquisitive, consumerist, and socially dysfunctional. Church communities exist to worship God, be foretastes of heaven and agents of the kingdom of heaven. Aiming to grow the bits of that agenda we can measure shouldn't stop us growing the kingdom holistically, but there is a danger that it will.

Measuring the size of the church is tricky, but Chapter 1 showed we can make the attempt. However, we have no indicators measuring either the depth or vitality of churches. It is all too easy to pay lip service to the three-dimensional nature of growth while focusing most effort on the one dimension we can measure – numbers of people. So perhaps we should look for indicators of depth and vitality to help churches aim at all three at once.

Should we measure depth and vitality?

The education and national health services have become target-driven cultures. To drive up standards a target is set. But then people running schools and hospitals might start aiming at the narrow target rather than increasing quality overall. They serve the target rather than human beings. This skewing of effort can actually reduce overall quality rather than increase it. The same danger lurks for anyone wishing to chart or measure progress in the spiritual depth and vitality of churches. How can you measure the depth of the faith of a Christian or the spirituality of a human being or the quality of a human community? We can produce a list of quantifiable ingredients for a spirituality or vitality index. But if churches are asked to judge their own progress by this index they will be encouraged to ignore other, less easily quantifiable, aspects, having a narrow and mechanical view of what constitutes depth and vitality. If a diocese or denomination gets its hands on such data they could easily start judging churches and church leaders on the basis of it. Ofchurch here we come.

Yet washing our hands of measurement means we can never really know whether churches are moving forwards or backwards. Neither can we identify ways of improving the quality and effectiveness of churches. We will be left with numerical size measures being the only success criteria, and so with the imbalance that will probably bring. Diocesan and denominational leaders always take a view of individual churches and clergy. All too often it is based on a half-remembered anecdote from five years ago. Trust me on this – I've spent far too many hours sat in bishops' staff meetings! So perhaps it is better to base this judgement on better evidence.

Attempts to measure quality, vitality, health and depth

Most researchers have not attempted a neat separation between measures of depth (or health) and measures of ministry-vitality. So here I summarize five approaches to the business of getting a handle on the quality, depth, spiritual maturity, health or vitality of the life of a church.

The National Church Life Survey (NCLS)

This long-established Australian research institute conducts a national survey for Australian denominations every five years. Church members spend 20 minutes during a church service filling in a detailed questionnaire asking their view of the state and quality of aspects of church life and their own role in it. Groups of answers are condensed into scores for a range of qualities of church life that can be compared with those from five years ago and other churches. Individual churches in other countries can access the process through the NCLS website.

The indicators are a summary not of some apparently objective measures set by experts, but of the views and experience of church members themselves. This has the strength that churches make their own judgement on how they are doing. The almost impossible difficulties of agreeing common criteria among diverse churches are avoided. However, the weakness is that the standards by which people judge themselves may shift. For example, as a Christian develops, their standards might change. Someone could score something lower than last time simply because they are more aware and less naive. Nevertheless, this internal assessment gives churches a helpful self-assessment themselves and dioceses or denomination a helpful snapshot of their health and vitality.

The questionnaire is designed to yield information on nine core qualities of church life (Figure 2.1).

Figure 2.1 The nine core qualities of church life

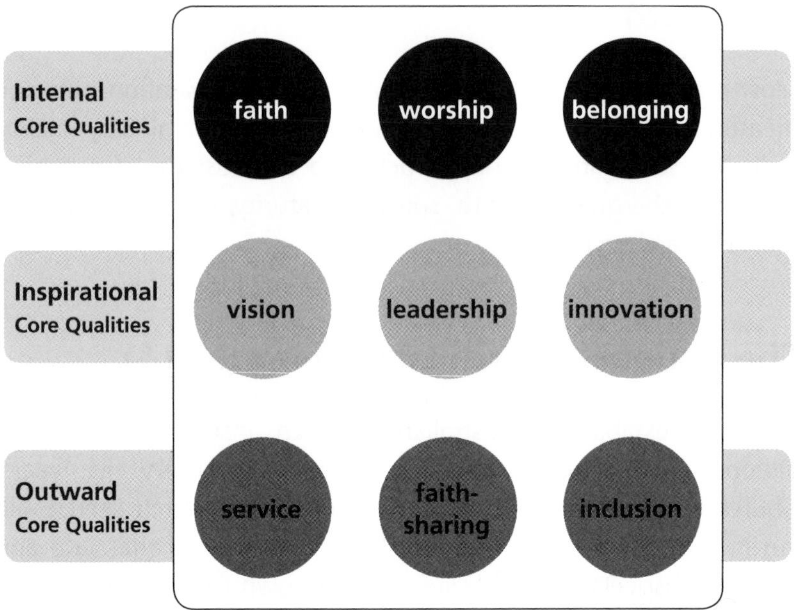

The Internal Core Qualities focus on the inner life of the community of faith, being foundational to church life and providing shape and energy to the other qualities. The score for each quality reflects the extent to which church members believe they have an alive and growing faith, experience vital and nourishing worship and enjoy strong and growing belonging to the church community.

The Inspirational Core Qualities relate to leadership and direction. Having a clear and owned vision, inspiring and empowering leadership, and imaginative and flexible innovation are seen as the hallmarks of growing churches.

The Outward Core Qualities concern the vitality of its outward-focused ministry, the way the church proclaims and lives out the Christian gospel. The scoring depends on an assessment of practical and diverse service, willing and effective faith-sharing, and intentional and welcoming inclusion.

The attendance measures used are the degree of young adult retention, the numbers of newcomers, and attendance change.

So NCLS is designed to yield numeric values for all three of our growth dimensions – depth, vitality and numbers. Some years ago an attempt was made by a UK ecumenical group (including the Church of England) to begin an every-five-years NCLS survey of a large sample of churches. However, problems arose at the data-analysis stage and funding ran out. The project was abandoned. In view of the currently renewed determination of the Church of England to attend to its own growth holistically understood, it is perhaps high time that some sort of renewed attempt is made either using NCLS or something inspired by it.

In the meantime there is nothing to stop individual churches, deaneries or dioceses picking up on the process for themselves.

Natural church development

The *Natural Church Development Handbook* (Schwarz, 1996)[1] offers eight quality characteristics of churches:

1. Empowering leadership.
2. Gift-orientated ministry.
3. Passionate spirituality.
4. Functional structures.
5. Inspiring worship services.
6. Holistic small groups.
7. Need-orientated evangelism.
8. Loving relationships.

Church members are invited to use a large questionnaire scoring their church on each characteristic. Churches with high scores should expect to grow naturally, organically. It is the church's job to attend to its quality characteristics and then God will be enabled to grow the church naturally. Churches should attend to the qualities they have scored lowest; their limiting factors. Once they have improved the quality of their weakest link they can then grow up to the capacity constraint provided by the next lowest score, the next weakest link, which then becomes the new priority for attention.

This process is backed by international research linking numerical growth to each of these eight significant characteristics.

So this process identifies depth and vitality qualities, measures them and identifies priorities for improvement that result in further numerical growth. Healthy churches grow in all three dimensions at once.

The Diocese of Coventry has adopted NCD as a strategy to commend to each church and to help them through. This is in contrast to the large number of dioceses that (as shown in Chapter 6) have adopted Mission Action Planning as their core intervention strategy. It will be important to compare the results in Coventry over the next few years with those in other dioceses and so to see what each approach can learn from the others.

The process is only as good as the chosen characteristics are appropriate. NCD focuses on activities such as good worship services and small groups. But activities are not the stuff of spiritual or vitality growth. That was the mistake Willow Creek had been making before their 'Reveal' survey (see below). Just because someone is participating in an activity does not mean that they are growing through it.

Healthy churches

Robert Warren (*The Healthy Churches' Handbook*, 2012[2] and *Developing Healthy Churches*, 2012[3]) identifies seven marks of a healthy church that are not activities but values, goals and characteristics found in the numerically growing churches investigated as the basis of the analysis. The seven marks of a healthy church identified in this analysis of growing English churches are:

A healthy church

- is energized by faith
- has an outward-looking focus
- seeks to find out what God wants
- faces the cost of change and growth
- operates as a community
- makes room for all
- does a few things well.

As with NCD, it is clear that these 'healthy churches insights' cohere well with the research findings in Part 2 of this book.

'Reveal' from Willow Creek

Willow Creek is a large church in Chicago that sponsored some research between 2004 and 2007 into how its congregation was growing spiritually. This church had been assuming that 'The more a person far from God participates in church activities, the more likely it is that those activities will produce a person who loves God and loves others.' The study found this assumption to be invalid. 'Does increased attendance in ministry programmes automatically equate to spiritual growth? To be brutally honest it does not.'

The study divided church attendees into four groups according to their stage of spiritual formation, that is those who are

- exploring Christianity
- growing in Christ
- close to Christ
- Christ-centred.

The only groups who seemed to benefit from the church's programmes were the first two – the more mature Christians tended to be stalled in their spiritual growth or dissatisfied with what the church was doing to help them grow. The stalled and dissatisfied totalled over a quarter of the congregation and many were considering leaving. Those 'close to Christ' tended to be stalled and the 'Christ-centred' to be dissatisfied. The church and its ministries were helping people in the earlier stages of their Christian lives but the programme of the church increasingly disappointed people as their Christian faith developed. It looked like the church was able to nurture adolescent Christians but its programmatic approach was inappropriate for mature Christians. Yet these were the best equipped and most motivated Christian examples and advocates, so failing them was likely to lead to the whole church stalling.

Subsequently the researchers surveyed 200 other churches and found the same result. The researchers discovered that what the more mature Christians wanted, instead of a church trying to act as a spiritual parent, was a spiritual director, mentor or coach, someone with whom they could be honest and to whom they could be accountable. So the 'Reveal' focus now includes a 'Christian coaching centre'. Those familiar in this country with the culture of spiritual directors will here be nodding their heads sagely. Clergy who value meeting a spiritual counsellor or support group from time to time might consider whether their lay people might benefit similarly.

The Reveal survey is made available, at a price, to any church through its website. The survey delivers a snapshot of the spiritual life of the congregation from which indications will be given of the next steps to help the congregation deepen their relationship with Jesus. A subsequent survey will deliver another snapshot and so an indication of progress made.

Once again, the results are composed of the assessments of the church members themselves, but the research also points out why this is the least problematic route to use. Suppose, instead, that a picture of the spiritual state of the congregation was built up from a list of activity factors such as:

- Average giving per head.
- Proportion of congregation in small groups.
- Proportion of congregation with a role or ministry in the church.
- Numbers attending prayer meetings or daily mass.
- Average attendance frequency at weekly services.

The Reveal finding is that those most engaged in these activities are exactly the people who tend to be stalled, dissatisfied and thinking of leaving. Rather than assuming that participating in programmes equates to spiritual progress, it seems better to ask the people themselves directly. The answers given may not make comfortable reading for clergy but they are more likely to point the way to genuine future spiritual growth.

The Reveal research also demonstrates that attending to spiritual and numerical growth are not two different or rival agendas. They are the same agenda. Unless the most mature and Jesus-focused people in the church feel that they themselves are growing and being fulfilled in the life of the church they will not be at their best in bringing new people into the church and nurturing them in the faith.

John Truscott's Church Health Review

John Truscott is a UK church consultant and trainer who makes available on his website (www.john-truscott.co.uk/Resources/Health-checks) many helpful tools for church leaders, including 'The Church Health Review'. This is a means of assessing any church's general state of health. Instead of picking on a number of 'marks' of good health, it investigates every area of church life through five themes:

1. Godward.
2. Usward.
3. Outward.
4. Leadership.
5. Support.

A survey form asks nine questions in relation to each theme, making 45 questions in total. The method is partly derived from Christian Schwarz and Robert Warren but also from the 'Excellence Model' developed by the European Foundation for Quality Management for the 'not for profit' sector. The first three themes reflect the purposes of the church in relation to God, itself and others. The other two are enabling themes. Amalgamating the answers of all participants gives general measures of church health and indications of areas of strength and weakness.

So, should we measure or not?

It is impossible to measure the spiritual maturity of a Christian human being. We are not mass-produced types. I am not a 'Type 3b' human being and you are not a 'Type 2a'. We are all unique, hand-crafted, unfathomable masterpieces of creation. We are not mechanical beings or biological machines but organic, integrated, indivisible spiritual beings with body, mind, spirit and soul all wrapped up marvellously together in one skin. To be human is to be sacred. We are hard-wired for spirituality. To presume to measure us, to mark us on some common scale, would demean the immeasurable God who created us each uniquely in his own image. To quote Queen Elizabeth I, we cannot make windows into men's souls – and we should not presume to try. It is for God alone to be our judge and all will be revealed by him one day.

However, Christian leaders need to understand how to encourage the spiritual and vitality growth of Christians gathered together as churches. We make Jesus' concern that his disciples grow to be like him our concern also. This inevitably means looking for some measure by which progress can be judged, but we are not going to be able to measure the spiritual progress of individuals on some common scale. That is why every resource available relies on assessment by individual church members of the corporate state of play.

How can we get better at assessing progress?

These five programmes can be accessed by all, but probably none of them is the last word. The Church of England at national level has heeded the reasoning embodied in Chapter 1 and introduced new ways of measuring the numerical growth of the church. Perhaps it is now time to commission work on assessing progress in the other two dimensions of its threefold primary strategic goal – to grow spiritually and in service to the world.

It may be that a church's vitality in serving its community is more amenable to measurement than is its spiritual depth. Perhaps vitality can be captured by activity – for example a church with a play-group and a lunch club is serving its community in ways that a church without them is not. The Church Life Survey is probably more successful at capturing vitality than spirituality. The Church of England is already trying to measure, for example, how many of its people are involved in voluntary work. So perhaps the first step in building a new way of capturing broader progress in church growth would be to develop a vitality index based on the Church Life Survey experience. This could be done ecumenically, but it may be simpler and quicker as a single denomination project.

How can we stimulate – not just measure – spiritual and vitality growth?

The answer to this question may involve mysteries beyond my competence. Fortunately for me it is also beyond the confines of a book primarily about numerical growth. However, these are all parts of the same agenda so it is important at least to work out some principles.

Identify the weaknesses and attend to them

When a church has discerned its areas of ill-health and attends to them it stands a better chance of growing numerically. A church using Robert Warren's material might find that its weak spot is it fails to do a few things well. Activities have multiplied over the years as people have had ideas but nothing has been stopped. People are overstretched maintaining stuff from the past and do nothing well.

Nobody is satisfied or flourishing in their ministry. So the church decides what its priorities are and focuses on them. Non-priorities are dropped. Christians each have one ministry and do it well. They have more time and energy to develop themselves.

Nurture the mature as well as the new Christians

Another church might use the Reveal materials and conclude that it is failing its more spiritually mature or able members. Its worship and its programmes work at growing people only so far, as though adults are still repeating the A-level course but never progressing to university. Some may worry that they are losing their faith, but all that is happening is that they are leaving behind a simpler form of faith.

So church leaders will work at how whole-of-life spiritual growth can be stimulated. This may be through the provision of spiritual directors for those who would value them. It may be through encouraging Christians to read some deeper, more demanding theology. My wife is currently reading a stimulating theological book in the hour before I get up each morning. The trouble is she gets so energized by it she then wants to talk to me about it before I've really woken up. St George's in Leeds has 'Way In' groups for seekers and new believers but also 'Way Out' groups for the more mature, focused on expressing their faith in family, church, work and community contexts.

It may be the adoption of a new ministry will stretch experienced Christians so they can grow afresh. I was vicar of an Urban Priority Area church which also included middle-class worshippers who motored in. A lot of personal growth was stimulated when we set up a Social Action Centre to meet the needs of local residents, including the homeless.

Church services tend to be attempts at 'mixed ability' learning. The preacher is trying to speak to a first-timer as well as the deepest saint on the planet. One of the most satisfying church services I have ever been involved in planting was a Tuesday evening event that started with food, followed by 20–30 minutes classic worship together, including a Bible reading that introduced the theme. For the next half hour or so everyone was free to choose a different activity – private prayer in a corner of the church building, an Alpha course, a directed small-group study of the passage, a more challenging discussion group for people who wanted to address the difficult issues, and so on. Many of our most able people are bored by church services. How can intelligent Christians be stimulated and excited by them? One answer must be to help them interact with each other, to contribute, to articulate, not just to sit and listen to a dog collar.

Shape church around the people, not the people around the church

Enabling the able or experienced to keep on growing and flourishing in church life will clearly involve more than bolting on a few specialist provisions to the existing programme. It may require church life to be turned on its head. In many churches there is a list of jobs and office holders required to maintain the status quo. It somehow becomes the job of the vicar and wardens to keep on finding people to fill the current job vacancies to keep the show on the road. Square pegs are continually being asked to fill round holes. Shaping the people to fit the church, using them to maintain a pre-existing structure, is not a good way to help them flourish. And it becomes less practical with each generation. I grew up in the 1950s working out how to fit into the given, stable world around me. If someone asks me to fill a role in the church that is not really 'me' I may agree because I see the need. Postmoderns, however, have grown up in a consumer culture expecting the surrounding world to fit with them. They are likely to steer clear of a church brandishing lists of jobs, office holders, committees, job vacancies and weekly commitments constructed in my generation's image. And they may be right – perhaps human beings flourish best when they are free to express and be themselves, to relate to each other and to God without becoming trapped as minor functionaries in some antiquated ecclesiastical machinery.

Turning church on its head involves finding out what are people's gifts, abilities, passions and energies. Their roles and the life of the church are then constructed afresh using these ingredients. Shaping the church's life to fit the church's people may be a better way of enabling them to flourish and deepen. Instead of using the people to serve the church we use the church to serve the people. Someone now enabled to use the gifts and passions God has given them is likely to grow, mature and contribute more effectively. One church had a system of house groups. The vicar prepared Bible studies for them all to follow. One summer the vicar asked for volunteers to lead groups for the next year based on their own passion or interest. One person led a group focused on environmental issues, one convened a support group of schoolteachers, and so on. The energy and satisfaction levels soared because the groups were shaped around the people rather than the people around the groups.

Yet the church will still need a treasurer. Real churches probably have to be constructed both ways round at the same time. But what would your church look like if it was reconstructed for, by and with its current members rather than being mainly shaped by a past structure and tradition?

For the sake of others – keep growing yourself

Church leaders have little hope of stimulating spiritual growth in others if it is not happening in them. If the vicar is tired, jaded and stuck they are of little help to the others. Leaders owe it to the whole church to keep on refreshing their own spiritual journey, to have a spiritual director, to read demanding books, to talk at depth with each other, to find new ministries, to recharge their own physical and emotional batteries, so that they can lead and inspire rather than simply go through the motions.

Don't just copy – find out what works where you are

Pre-packaged programmes are not nearly as good at deepening disciples as church leaders like to think they are. The further on in the Christian life someone is, and perhaps the more able they are, the harder it is to find satisfying spiritual food in the everyday life of the church. Yet a major job of church leaders is to enable all the people of the church to become all that Christ made them to be. As every individual, and so every group of Christians, is unique then the answer to the question 'How do I enable spiritual growth?' needs to be individually crafted in each situation.

Helpful resources

Here are three books that can help stimulate spiritual and vitality growth. Doubtless there are others.

Mark Yaconelli, *Contemplative Youth Ministry.*[4]
Though the focus is on youth ministry, this striking book is essentially about the nurture and development of a contemplative ministry that can bear rich fruit in the lives of those involved, and through them also bears fruit in its wider setting. The final three chapters, 'Noticing', 'Naming', 'Nurturing', provide a clear and achievable framework for developing awareness of God at the heart of personal discipleship and at the heart of church life. It will take creative adaptation, but it is well worth leadership groups working through together – with the focus on application, testing and adaptation to the local setting.

Mike Starkey, *Ministry Rediscovered: Shaping a unique and creative church.*[5]
Mike Starkey sets out a series of steps to make the most of the unique setting of each church, the unique gifting of church members and the unique contribution that each church leader brings to the life of the church. Essentially it is a call to look to God first and foremost and to make the most of what we have. Leadership is a call to be

creative and unique in the outworking of the faith in and through the life of the local church. God has a 'top copy' for each church, leader and church member so we do not need to restrict ourselves to the constraints of a 'carbon copy' of another person, church or leader.

Robert Warren, *Developing Healthy Churches.*[6]
Arising out of the response to his *Healthy Churches Handbook,* Robert Warren draws on his more recent experience of working as a consultant to many churches. He addresses issues churches need to face if they are to *be* what they *preach,* including being clear about what church and the faith are all about – *knowing and showing the love of God.* He faces obstacles in the way of stimulating spiritual and vitality growth – including *the tyranny of the urgent, blurred vision, confusing means and goals* and *losing sights of God's agenda, gifting and timing.* In a crucial chapter he explores how church life can itself be evangelized through the focused development (one at a time) of a range of distinctive marks of the life of Christ. He then moves on to explore some new practical approaches to *nurturing spirituality* and *reworking pastoral care, home groups, evangelism* and *mission.* There is much here to aid the stimulus of spiritual and vitality growth.

3

Growth initiatives

> See, the former things have taken place, and new things I declare; before they spring into being I announce them to you. (Isaiah 42.9)

The journey we are on

The way we do mission, evangelism and church growth has transformed over the last thirty years. Evangelism has mutated from an event outside the normal life of the churches to a process within it. A new range of tools and initiatives has emerged to replace those that used to work. Remembering the journey we are on helps us understand where we are today ...

The way it was

It was the last and greatest night. I climbed to the top of the stand behind Billy Graham for a bird's-eye view of the packed stadium, bathed in the glorious evening light of Sheffield's summer sun. Billy was cranking up towards the invitation to come forward and receive Christ. The greatest pitch invasion in the history of English football was about to begin. The first man on the pitch was my own churchwarden. 'About time, Arthur,' I thought. He was followed, so it seemed, by half the crowd. I glanced down at the thin line of counsellors I was responsible for. They were utterly overwhelmed, like cashiers facing a run on the bank. I dashed down the steps and moved among the remaining crowd looking for any Christian I knew, appointing them emergency counsellors.

It seemed like the queues and the counselling went on for ever, but finally, in the dying light of the June evening, we made it back to our double decker for the ride home to my parish. Both our children had gone forward, as had many others on the bus. Our daughter was six. Eighteen years and one day later she would be ordained. What a night!

As a local vicar, I received over a hundred referrals of locals who had gone forward, and tried to visit every one. About 25 became regular church members. A year later I spent a day in the Sheffield Diocesan Office going through the statistical returns every church sent in annually, counting attendance before and after Billy's visit. It was clearly the first time anyone had ever done such a thing but the result was clear – after years of decline, diocesan church attendance following those eight nights at Bramhall Lane in June 1985 had risen 10 per cent.

The search for new ways

Since those heady days the era of mass evangelism ended and the long-term decline of the church reasserted itself. Postmodernism, multiculturalism and secularism waxed while Christendom waned. But the Church has not been inactive. Many initiatives in evangelism and church growth have had an impact over the last 25 years and some in the list below will be revisited in Part 2. Our story starts in 1990.

The Decade of Evangelism

Evangelism in the days of Billy Graham was about evangelists speaking at organized events to people with a good background knowledge of the faith, many of whom were lapsed churchgoers. When George Carey became Archbishop of Canterbury in 1990 he appointed two evangelists (Michael Green and Bishop Michael Marshall) to head up 'Springboard', his flagship vehicle designed to make a reality of the 1990s Decade of Evangelism. They were to speak at weekend 'missions' up and down the country.

The Church declaring a Decade of Evangelism was like the Bakers' Federation declaring a 'Decade of making bread'. But the main problem was the method. The times were changing. People were more reluctant to be dragged along to evangelistic meetings. Respect for evangelists had plummeted. Secularism was beginning to bite. Churches all over the country were shrinking and a few missions here and there were no more likely to turn the tide than some sandcastles on the beach. Newer generations had less background knowledge, they started from further back. Even if they awakened an interest in Jesus they were increasingly less likely to join a church as a result.

And coming to faith was becoming a lengthy process not a one-off event. Through the 1990s it became apparent that only the local church could accompany people on their faith journeys. The emphasis of Springboard began to shift. The focus of the last two Springboard Missioners, Robert Warren and myself, was to equip local churches to grow organically, incorporating evangelism into the regular rhythms of their daily lives. We were moving from the era of evangelism as event outside church structures to that of evangelism as process within them.

In one sense the Decade of Evangelism was a failure. Church attendance in the Church of England went down 17 per cent between 1990 and 2000, double the decline rate in the 1980s. Evangelism became overshadowed by the controversies over the ordination of women. But the Decade was also a deeper, long-term success as it helped change the Church's own culture. The Church of England had traditionally seen itself as a pastoral church caring for a Christian nation. The not quite respectable business of evangelism was franchised out to people like Billy Graham. But, by the start of the new century, evangelism was increasingly being accepted as an integral part of the Church's core business. Unless the Church of England was able to morph into being a missionary church for the new post-Christian secular society then its days may be numbered.

Somewhere deep in the womb of the Decade of Evangelism that long, rocky and unfinished journey from pastoral to missionary church was conceived.

The ordination of women

The ordination of women, with all its short-term costs in the 1990s, was also key to helping the churches survive and thrive. It gave the church greater credibility in the new age of gender equality and also attracted large numbers of women clergy. Fears that churches led by women would struggle have been unfounded. Attendance trends in churches with women clergy appear to have been at least as good as in those led by men. And now about a quarter of all stipendiary clergy are women. Without them the problem of declining clergy numbers would have become an overwhelming crisis.

A new paid workforce

Although fewer clergy are now employed, overall, there may be more people employed by the churches than ever before. To the traditional ranks of vergers, organists and secretaries have been added youth ministers, families ministers, children's ministers, administrators, operations managers, outreach workers, church planters, worship leaders, and many others. For some roles professional training is now available along clergy lines. The Centre for Youth Ministry began in the early 1990s and now operates out of five theological colleges across the country. The employment of specialists has been greatly facilitated in some dioceses since around 2002 by grants made available out of the Church Commissioners' 'Mission Development Funding' stream. A body of knowledge is growing about the sort of appointment that appears to lead to numerical growth.

Discipleship courses

Christian basics and nurture courses such as Alpha became widely used during the 1990s. They had been around for a long time – Alpha itself was written in 1977. But in 1990 Nicky Gumbel took over the running of the course, a marketing revolution began, and Alpha's rise to prominence accelerated. Somewhere around 20 million people around the world have now been through an Alpha course. But there are also many other courses on the market, suiting the whole range of traditions and situations.

Taken together, discipleship courses form a major route by which people journey into Christian faith in contemporary Britain.

Spiritual renewal

When I was an undergraduate at Cambridge in the 1960s I began to hear rumours of Anglicans who had started speaking in tongues even though the Christian Union knew that Holy Spirit phenomena had died out after the Bible had been written. No need for them any more, you see. We could all relax with our nice safe Trinity of Father, Son and Holy Scripture. However, the Holy Spirit seemed to have other ideas as churches went through successive waves of spiritual renewals from tongues in the 1960s to prophecy in the 70s, to healing and power evangelism in the 80s to Toronto Blessings in the 90s. The charismatic element of the Church of England grew at first in a number of specific churches, then spread and diffused through many others, particularly through the influence of its new style of church music.

With each wave came the hope that the Holy Spirit was going to bring about revival as well as renewal. But mass conversions never happened. Some became exhausted or disillusioned by the successive waves, which, since the mid-1990s, appear to have died away.

Yet it is still true today that major church growth requires the power of the Holy Spirit as well as human changes in the organization, culture and life of the churches. There can be no major numerical growth in the twenty-first-century Church without its inner spiritual renewal. But equally there can be no growth of the Church without major change in its outward form. Revival of numbers requires both reform of the Church and renewal of its faith. Renewal, however, is to be measured not in manifestations but in deeper spirituality, changed lives and revitalized communities.

Healthy churches and quality practices

My wife's vicar when she was a girl was 'Old Mr Naggington'. He was a widower in his seventies or eighties who could not afford to retire, a faithful parish priest who no longer had the capacity to do much more than mumble through the Prayer Book on Sunday mornings. Church services were duller than a dull day in a dull mortuary in Dulltown. Yet the church was packed every week. This was the 1950s and the people of respectable suburbs went to church out of habit, duty, loyalty and convention. What else was there to do on a Sunday?

Today, of course, poor old Mr Naggington would be mumbling to an empty church. People (or, as we are now known, 'consumers') look for quality, relevance, authenticity, helpfulness and community in church life and services. Churches that deliver grow and those that don't shrink. And so there has been a new emphasis on quality, health and good practices. Christian Schwarz emphasized the need to attend to key quality characteristics to enable churches to grow. My own books (*Hope for the Church*, 2002[1] and *The Road to Growth*, 2005[2]) showed how good practices were growing the churches. Many clergy have now attended the residential 'Leading your Church into Growth' course. Church leaders are being increasingly well equipped to lead the fightback against a century of decline through attending to the quality, health and relevance of church life.

Intentionality and mission-planning

When David Hope was Bishop of London in the early 1990s he made the diocese intentional about mission. Job descriptions for clergy described their main role not as parish pastors or congregational chaplains but as leaders in mission and enablers of lay people's ministries. Each church was asked to draw up a 'Mission Action Plan' (MAP). In some churches it is said that all three of those concepts were novelties – mission, action and plan. Membership and attendance in the Diocese of London turned round in dramatic fashion. The electoral roll almost halved between the early 1970s and 1990 and has nearly doubled since. Although there are many factors involved, the new intentionality and mission-planning regime were key. (See *Another Capital Idea*, Jackson and Piggot, 2010.)[3]

Gradually other dioceses began to encourage all their churches to write and implement MAPs. By 2014 MAP has become the primary vehicle for the growth effort of around half the dioceses and churches in the Church of England. MAP is a process rather than a programme and it has to be handled well to be effective, but it is both agent and symptom of a fundamental culture change.

Fresh expressions

From the 1990s onwards new congregations and churches were being set up to reach the postmodern generations and people-groups traditional churches were missing. Instead of attractional-church ('come and join us in what we already do') this was incarnational-church ('let's see what sort of Christian community emerges from this group of people'). As Archbishop George's personal initiative was 'Springboard', so Archbishop Rowan's was 'Fresh Expressions'. The Fresh Expressions organization was set up in 2004 jointly with the Methodists. Its definition of a fresh expression is: 'A fresh expression is a form of church for our changing culture, established primarily for the benefit of people who are not yet members of any church.'

The idea was that the Church of the future would fly with two wings – the traditional wing and the fresh expressions wing. The two are not in opposition to each other, they need each other. When I was Archdeacon of Walsall I noticed that there were very few young adults attending any church in Wolverhampton, our largest population centre. So I worked for a year or two with our Methodist colleagues to put together the money and organization to start a new 'incarnational' church in the city centre for young adults. Traditional church provided the money and the initial leaders, but over the years 'Vitalize' has nurtured a number of next-generation leaders, including several ordinands. The future of the whole Church appears just as dependent on the success of fresh expressions as the fresh expressions are on traditional church to resource them.

Invitation, welcome and integration

In 2004 some people in the Diocese of Manchester had a bright idea – to ask church members to invite someone to come to church with them one Sunday in September. They called the day 'Back to Church Sunday'. The idea seemed to work and caught on. A large-scale telephone survey suggested that about 5 per cent of the UK population (3 million people) would consider going to church if someone invited them. But the traditional denominations in the UK do not by and large have a strong culture of invitation, so Back to Church Sunday was designed to change that.

In 2007 the Diocese of Lichfield decided to make the most of Back to Church Sunday. The majority of churches took part and a diocesan enquiry ascertained that 6,000 guests came on the day, almost all by personal invitation. A repeat enquiry six months later found that just under 800 had become at least monthly attenders. A further 3,000 retained some sort of link six months later and had perhaps attended at Christmas. There are not many Sundays when 800 people join the worshipping communities of a diocese, but nevertheless 88 per cent of those who came by invitation failed to translate this into any sort of regular attendance. The Church Life

Survey in Australia found it was 92 per cent there. Many individual churches confirm this experience – they regularly have newcomers attending their services but few of them actually join the church community.

So it seemed that the Christian Church could grow simply by increasing the retention rate of those who try the churches out. The training course *Everybody Welcome* (Jackson and Fisher, 2009)[4] is designed to help churches get better at welcoming and integrating new people into their communities.

Families, children and young people

As the Church of England's worshipping numbers declined, the average age of its people rose. An ever smaller proportion of each new generation attended church. The numbers of children shrank much faster than the numbers of adults. There have been many responses to reverse this trend – smartening up Sunday schools, introducing monthly Family Services, trying All-age Worship, offering children's teaching groups at other times of the week, varying the times of family-friendly services to include teatimes, taking church activities into schools, and a range of fresh expressions aimed at families.

St Wilfrid's Cowplain, Portsmouth, had lovely buildings and facilities and some creative people but they were reaching hardly any children. In 2004, frustrated by this, a group led by Lucy Moore, the vicar's wife, invented a new way of doing church for families and called it 'Messy Church'. The idea worked and soon began to spread. Messy Church has quickly become the most widespread and well-known new church format for families. Today there are over 2,500 Messy Churches registered on the Messy Church website and it is thought that there may be, perhaps, two unregistered churches for every one registered. Average attendance at a Messy Church is around 55. A pure guess at monthly attendance is therefore 2,500 x 3 x 55 = c. 400,000.

Finding ways such as Messy Church of re-engaging with parents and their children has become a major part of the Church's agenda to start growing in new ways.

Missionary congregations

Until recently the life and mission of the churches seemed largely dependent on the clergy. Lay people 'attended' churches run by clergy. Active clergy pastored passive congregations. Ministry was done by 'ministers' not by lay members of congregations. Since 1990 a sea-change has been underway from passive congregations pastored by pastoral clergy to missionary communities led by missional clergy.

This move has been driven by declining numbers of stipendiary clergy, by a reawakened ecclesiology replacing the old 'pastor and flock' model of church with a 'whole people of God' model, and by a new understanding of the role of the clergy. Increasingly today the paid clergy are not there to do the ministry on behalf of the people but to equip the people to do the ministry themselves.

And so 'Natural Church Development' and 'Healthy Churches' exercises invite the whole people of God to take counsel together to identify strengths and weaknesses in the body of Christ and to put right the weaknesses. Mission Action Plans are best written and implemented by the whole church. A MAP that is actually the vicar's private plan is unlikely to get ownership and buy-in. Back to Church Sunday only works through lay people inviting their friends. The 'Everybody Welcome' course needs to be done by a large proportion of the community together if new people are to feel generally welcomed. Research by the Church Army (see Chapter 11) has found that 40 per cent of fresh expressions have as their main leader someone who is lay, unpaid, untrained, and possessing no official or diocesan authorization or recognition whatsoever. The *Leading your Church into Growth* course began in the 1990s as a course for clergy only. Then small numbers of lay leaders were allowed on to the residential courses. Then in 2014 the LyCiG team published the new *LyCiG – Local* course[5] for whole church communities to work through locally.

The underlying logic is that the whole community must be released, encouraged and equipped to grow the church of the future. The battle for the future of the church must be conducted not just by an officer class of clergy and other selected leaders but by every member of the body of Christ.

The Spirit and strategy

Not many of the initiatives listed have been initiated by the central or official bodies and leaders of the Church. The Evangelism Task Force and the Pilgrim Course may be two recent examples of centrally directed initiatives. But there has been no coordinated master plan for the new growth of the Church of England. Most initiatives have come from the grass roots and inspired individuals. Official leaders have sometimes seen what is happening and encouraged it along the way, as in the case of Fresh Expressions. But more usually it is private entrepreneurship that has both developed and shaped the new growth toolkit. Whether it is discipleship course authors, the LyCiG team, training course authors, Back to Church Sunday, Messy Church or Mission Action Planning the energy has come from diffuse sources. The strategy, if it exists, can only be that of the Holy Spirit.

This is no criticism of the Church of England for it is not set up as a command and control organization. Anyone wishing to compare central planning and private enterprise as rival ways of generating growth should compare the economies of North and South Korea. However, the official diocesan and national institutions have a vital role in providing a helpful framework in which entrepreneurs can lead growing churches, and in encouraging and resourcing specific initiatives showing promise. There is abundant evidence that the Spirit is at work in the churches for their future flourishing. Growth is entering the bloodstream of the Church, becoming part of its DNA.

It is up to us all not to quench this work of the Holy Spirit but to join in wherever we see the Spirit at work. In Chapter 18 we will take a fuller look at the relationship between the work of the Holy Spirit and the growth of the Church.

4

Growth in patterns

'He must become greater; I must become less.' (John 3.30)

There are always growth-spots

The new vicar had five rural churches. One made it plain they thought a mistake had been made in the appointment process and would prefer him to leave. He was too keen – not their type. Three made it plain they were not prepared to consider changes, or even to adapt to give newcomers a chance. The fifth congregation was tiny and elderly with an unsafe building – an obvious closure candidate. But English Heritage surprisingly offered a large grant to restore the church building and develop it for multi-use. While the work was underway both the key church members died so there was no congregation to occupy the restored building. Other villagers started coming to services and the congregation quickly grew from zero to 30 or 40, many of whom were soon wanting to go on Christian basics courses and get confirmed.

In a sea of defiance and decline, the God of resurrection had created an island of life and growth. Often in the Christian Church in the midst of death we are in life. This mosaic of growth and decline will always be true in relation to individual churches whether overall numbers are going up or down.

John the Baptist had his day, his ministry flourished, the crowds flocked to him but were about to switch to Jesus. John's individual role would decline even though the kingdom of heaven was growing. Some individual churches will always be expanding while others contract, but are there discernible overall patterns in the current decline and growth story of our churches?

The decline narrative

The normal characterization of academic sociology and the media is that the whole Christian Church in Britain is in serious and possibly terminal decline. A smaller proportion of each new generation become churchgoers, congregations are ageing and so future decline is already built in. But the patterns and trends are far more complex than this lazy analysis suggests. Some segments are growing numerically while others are shrinking. Where the overall balance lies is surprisingly hard to estimate. It is likely that the Messy Church phenomenon has already reversed the decline in children attending church. All this is made clear in the book *Church Growth in Britain* (ed. Goodhew, 2012)[1] and also in other, detailed, statistical studies such as Peter Brierley's report on the 2012 London Church Census (*London's Churches are Growing*, 2013).[2]

Seeing some patterns

1. Some traditional denominations are shrinking but newer groupings are growing

This is shown, for example, in the 2005 and 2010 UK Church Census undertaken by Peter Brierley (Table 4.1).

Among the traditional denominations, the Anglicans were in comparatively slow decline, but that was offset by growth in Pentecostal, new and ethnically based churches. Immigration has greatly enriched the mix of churches and has set up a new growth-dynamic. For example, the London Church Census of 2012 found that 8 per cent of the white population of London was in church on an average Sunday but 16 per cent of the Chinese, Korean and Japanese population, and 19 per cent of the black population.

Table 4.1 UK church membership by denomination (thousands)

Denomination	2005	2010	% change
Presbyterian	918	741	–19
Methodist	295	238	–19
Catholic	1,667	1,473	–12
Baptist	208	198	–5
Anglican	1,537	1,458	–5
Independent	215	215	0
Orthodox	316	331	+5
New Churches	188	211	+12
Pentecostal	342	435	+27
Smaller Denoms	158	215	+36

2. The Church is growing in London

The London Church Census found that attendance in October 2012 was 720,000 compared with 620,000 in 2005, an increase of 16 per cent. This was not because individual churches had got bigger – they hadn't. It was because there were 17 per cent more churches overall. This is not unusual – overall church growth more commonly results from church planting than from existing churches growing larger.

The London Church Census found slightly fewer Anglicans in church in London on their Sunday in October than in 2005. The 'Statistics for Mission' four-week count in October, however, suggests a slight rise in average all-age weekly attendance between October 2005 and 2012 in the Dioceses of London and Southwark, which between them cover about 90 per cent of London (Table 4.2).

It looks as though in the same period the average London Anglican was coming to church less often so the implied increase in the worshipping community is greater than this.

Table 4.2 Average all-age weekly attendance in October

	2005	2012	
Diocese of London	79,300	81,600	
Diocese of Southwark	43,900	43,700	
Total	123,200	125,300	+1.7%

Electoral rolls also increased between the two years of 2006 and 2012 that were at the same stage of the six-year electoral roll cycle (Table 4.3).

Table 4.3 Electoral roll increases

	2006	2012	
Diocese of London	63,800	68,600	
Diocese of Southwark	46,200	48,500	
Total	110,000	117,100	+6.5%

In 2012 the Diocese of London reported 8,160 joiners and 4,818 leavers, a net gain of 3,342, or 4 per cent of the worshipping community in that year alone. Unfortunately Southwark was the one diocese in the Church of England not to send in joiners and leavers numbers. But, overall, the Church's own statistics suggest that numerical growth continues in the capital city. This is in the context of rising churchgoing across the capital fuelled by the planting of many new churches.

3. Small churches are more likely to be growing

Within the Anglican Church the smallest churches have been conspicuous for their numerical growth, especially when they are not part of a larger benefice. The table below shows that 230 churches on the national database with an adult usual Sunday attendance of under 25 in 2001 averaged 23 per cent attendance growth between 2001 and 2011. Over most of the size range of churches the larger the church the poorer the attendance trend. There is just a slightly better attendance trend for the largest groups of churches than for the most vulnerable group to decline – those with an adult usual Sunday attendance of between 150 and 200.

Table 4.4 Adult uSa change in Church of England single church benefices

Single church benefices size group	no. churches	2001 total	2011 total	change	% change
0–24	230	3,498	4,309	811	23%
25–39	309	9,953	10,035	72	1%
40–49	260	11,509	11,165	–344	–3%
50–74	715	43,934	39,870	–4,064	–9%
75–99	553	47,175	41,671	–5,504	–12%
100–149	555	66,851	57,737	–9,114	–14%
150–199	191	32,125	26,606	–5,519	–17%
200–299	110	25,893	22,226	–3,667	–14%
300 plus	51	22,925	21,722	–1,203	–5%
	2974	263,863	235,341	–28,532	–11%

Figure 4.1 Percentage change in adult uSa in 3,000 single church benefices in the Church of England, 2001–11

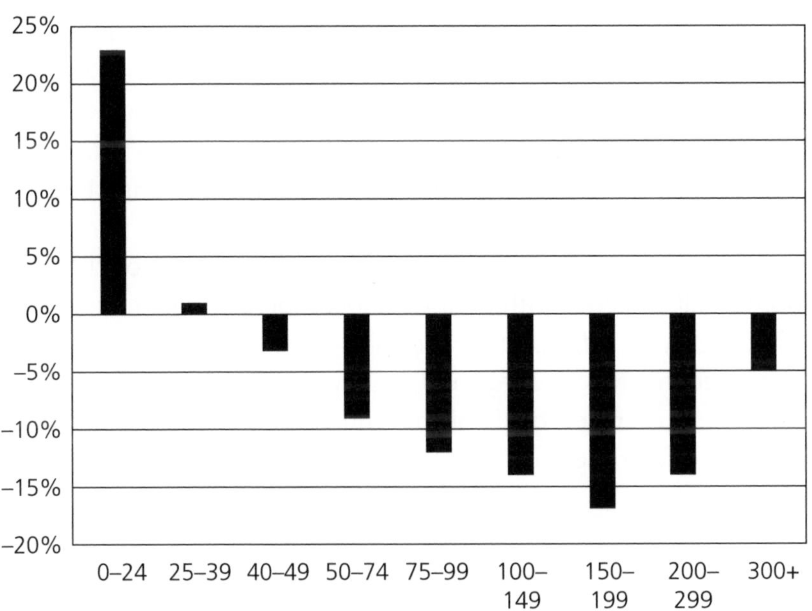

Most of the smallest churches are in the villages, often in apparently isolated and vulnerable situations with elderly congregations. Yet they have the best attendance trends. In a congregation of ten if you bring a friend the church experiences 10 per cent growth. Some small churches keep gaining newly retired people who move out into villages looking for community. There may be a warmth of community and belonging in a small church it is hard to replicate in a large one. Also, loyalty levels tend to be higher in small churches so there is great commitment to keeping them going. Very few small Anglican churches have closed in recent years.

The growth dynamic in the above graph and table relates to churches with their own incumbent. It is perhaps no surprise that when a vicar only has one congregation of up to 25 people that it tends to grow. In multi-church benefices Chapter 7 shows that the pattern whereby the best trend is in the smallest churches remains, but the significant growth disappears.

4. Cathedrals are growing

At the other end of the scale, as shown in Chapter 14, cathedrals have also been a growth element recently. Most of the attendance growth has been at an expanding number of smaller weekday services rather than main Sunday services. Average all-week all-age attendance grew 43 per cent from 2002 to 2013 (26,500 to 37,800) compared with a drop of 6 per cent in parish churches. The composition and causes of this are analysed in Chapter 14. Perhaps the clearest link between cathedral and tiny-church growth is that both small churches with their own incumbent and cathedrals with three clergy paid for by the Commissioners are comparatively well resourced in terms of clergy and money. It would be a surprise if the better resourced segments of the Church of England did not show superior growth performance.

5. Plants and fresh expressions

London churches, small churches and cathedrals are three examples of growing streams identified by their profile. We now turn to growing streams identified by their strategies. First, churches grow when they plant a new congregation or fresh expression. Typical evidence comes from the Diocese of St Davids. A survey of all diocesan churches undertaken for their 2013 Diocesan Clergy Conference found that average attendance in churches that did not start a new service between 2010 and 2013 had shrunk 6 per cent. But in those that had started a new service adult attendance grew 16 per cent and child attendance 176 per cent. As many new services and fresh expressions are focused on families, children and young people it is normal for the impact of planting on child attendance to be proportionately greater.

There is some evidence to suggest that much of the growth in the profile-streams comes from transfer – Christians moving into London for work, transferring from parish churches to cathedrals, and towns to villages on retirement.

However, the research by the Church Army reported in Chapter 11 shows that on average only some 25 per cent of the members of fresh expressions of church are previously churchgoing Christians. This includes the planting team. About 35 per cent are lapsed church attenders, perhaps who went as children or young people but not since (de-churched), and 40 per cent had never been churchgoers before (un-churched). Evidence from the first ten dioceses surveyed by the Church Army team found that fresh expressions of church were on average by 2013 adding about 10 per cent to diocesan church attendance and most of the fresh expressions had been started in very recent years.

6. Churches that change are growing

Survey results overwhelmingly show that churches that have been making changes to their church life or services tend to grow and those that have not been changing tend to shrink. Data showing this correlation in five different dioceses was reported in *The Road to Growth* (Jackson, 2005, p. 58).[3]

Surveys since that time have found the same correlation. For example, the St Davids survey in 2013 asked: 'What significant changes have been made to church life in the last three years?' Ninety-two churches replied 'none' and their adult church attendance went down 9 per cent and child attendance went down 17 per cent. Sixty-seven churches reported a credible change to church life and their adult church attendance went up 11 per cent and child attendance went up 64 per cent. No differentiation is made here between types of change, simply that some intentional change of some sort has taken place.

This relationship between change and growth is examined in more detail in Chapter 12.

7. Churches with missional intention tend to grow

The evidence laid out in Chapter 6 shows that churches with a Mission Action Plan are more likely to grow than those without one. And churches having a 'good' plan are more likely to grow than others with a less well-formed plan. Chapter 15 shows that dioceses with an intentional growth strategy are more likely to be growing numerically.

Doubtless there are more patterns and growth segments than listed here. But at least it is clear that there is some net growth among London churches, tiny churches, cathedrals, planting churches, changing churches and churches with a plan. Put together, the growing segments of the Church of England are balancing the shrinking segments. Were more churches to learn the lessons from those with a growth profile and to emulate those with a growth strategy then overall growth would be inevitable.

5

Growth in total?

The word of God continued to increase and spread. (Acts 12.24)

The late twentieth century

The first chapter of my book *Hope for the Church* (Jackson, 2002) was entitled 'Facing the truth'. The first table, summarizing the stark data of decline over the previous two decades, is reproduced below. Everything apart from PCC income was going down, some indicators, such as child attendance, rather fast (Table 5.1).

The truth we had to face was clear and obvious. I spent no time at all agonizing over whether the Church of England really was shrinking – of course it was! Some indicators were going down more slowly than others but they were all going down. So I moved swiftly on from this reality-check to argue that decline mattered deeply but there were things we could do to turn the trends around. We had spent a century largely ignoring our own decline, perhaps it was not premature to tackle it now.

Since the publication of *Hope for the Church* the Church of England has embraced a 'change and grow' agenda with more energy and imagination than I had ever envisaged in 2001. From fresh expressions to mission action planning to diocesan growth strategies to *Leading your Church into Growth* courses to Back to Church Sunday we've been pouring our time and effort into this project to arrest decline and start growing. And, frankly, I've been rather surprised at my own transition from prophet of doom to respectable growth guru.

Table 5.1 Decline in church numbers, 1980–90 and 1990–2000

	% change 1980–90	% change 1990–2000
Baptisms	–13	–24
Confirmations	–39	–43
Marriages	–11	–46
Stipendiary clergy	0	–15
Churches open	–3	–1
PCC voluntary income*	+42	+30
Electoral rolls**	–10	–13
Easter communicants	–11	–16
Christmas communicants	–14	–24
Adult attendance	–5	–14
Child attendance***	–17	–28
Total attendance	–8	–17

*At constant 1999 prices
** Adjusted for position in the six-year cycle
*** Children are defined as under 16 years of age
Source: *Church Statistics and Statistics of Licensed Ministers* (Church House Publishing)

It takes a long time to turn a big ship around and the growth project is still in its early days. But has the Church of England stopped shrinking yet or are we still declining despite all our best efforts? Could we even say that it has started to grow?

As I write, in 2014, finding a clear answer to this question is much harder than it was in 2001. We now have more indicators to look at, the rise of fresh expressions and weekday congregations has made church life more complex and harder to measure, and the indicators are no longer all moving in the same direction. So we'll look at each one then assess overall progress. Most statistics on the various indicators both in this chapter and throughout the book come from the 'Statistics for Mission' and 'Ministry Statistics' sections of the Church of England's website.

Error margins

The *Statistics for Mission* annual reports now include error margins caused by estimation procedures of non-returns. The error margin suggested for the October count all-week all-age total, for example, is plus or minus 5 per cent. This implies a range in 2012, for example, of 995 to 1,100 thousand and in 2008 of 1,040 to 1,148 thousand. The ranges overlap. So it is possible that in the real world there was no decline at all in that period. It is equally possible the decline was faster than estimated here. In truth we cannot be sure.

The number of churches

If someone asks you how big the solar system is, providing you have got your head around the Pluto problem, you will probably tell them how many planets there are. Only a geek would tell you their combined mass. The most obvious way of measuring the size of a denomination is by the number of its churches. This indicator went down slowly in the 1980s and 1990s, and that snail's pace has continued this century (Table 5.2).

Table 5.2 Number of churches in the Church of England

2003	16,196
2009	16,011
2010	15,976
2011	15,924
2012	15,861
2013	15,799

In the ten years 2003–13 the number of churches fell by 397, 2 per cent. In the same period a modest number of new free-standing fresh expressions of church have been planted, by no means all of which have been assigned church code numbers and included in the totals in the table. Most of these do not have their own buildings.

Including these additions, the net decline would be significantly less than 397.

At the same time there has also been a large increase in the number of fresh expressions congregations of existing churches. The Diocese of Lichfield in 2012 had 570 traditional 'churches' (15 less than in 2002) but also almost 100 new 'Messy Churches'. Nationally, 1,400 Messy Churches were reported on the Statistics for Mission forms in 2012, all new in the previous handful of years. It looks like the Church of England has added at least 300 new Messy Churches per annum in the last few years. Many other fresh expressions in other styles have also been planted in the period.

There will have been unreported changes in the numbers of traditional services put on by the churches. Some churches have tried to grow by putting on more services, others have closed a service due to small numbers or leadership stretch. We don't know the net difference, though my own hunch is that it will be pretty small.

On balance, therefore, it seems likely that the overall number of worshipping congregations in the Church of England has been rising in the twenty-first century. If the evidence of Chapter 11 is anything to go by it is set to rise further in the next few years.

The proportion of churches growing and shrinking

The Church of England's 2013 Statistics for Mission report contained estimates of the proportion of churches shrinking and growing. Only slightly more churches showed decline in the number of adults (23%) than those showing growth (18%). However, 23 per cent of churches showed growth in the number of children compared with only 17 per cent showing decline. This is despite the fact that in 2013 school services were stripped out of the totals for the first time. The 2012 totals were 24 per cent showing growth and 14 per cent decline. Taking 2012 and 2013 adults and children together, the proportion of churches showing growth and decline are almost in balance (Figure 5.1).

Figure 5.1 The proportion of Church of England churches showing growth and decline in child weekly attendance, 2013

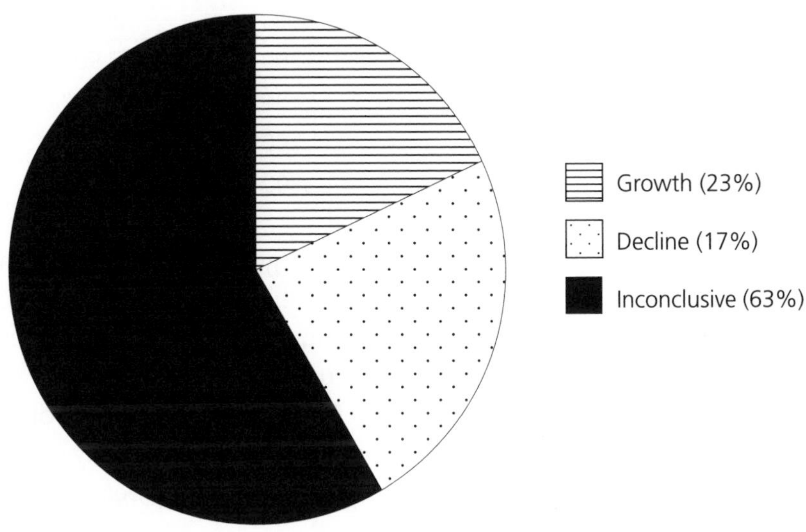

The number of clergy

The number of full-time-equivalent stipendiary clergy fell by 14 per cent between 2002 and 2012, almost the same rate as in the 1990s. It is forecast to fall a further 5.5 per cent by 2017, a slightly slower rate. However, the numbers of self-supporting and active retired clergy both rose substantially. Overall, the number of clergy officiating at services actually rose by about 1,000 (6 per cent) over the decade. 'Active retired clergy' are those with appointments, licences or permission to officiate Table 5.3). The total number of retired clergy in 2011 was 8,800 – a figure now significantly in excess of the number of stipendiaries. Since I took the archdeacon's pension a few years' back I have become more conscious of this great auxiliary army of clergy of which I am now a part. I'm pleased to say I led the service at our church this morning and was not too doddery, though I did learn that the teenagers were taking bets on whether I'd trip down the chancel steps when dashing off after the blessing to get to the back door before the rush for coffee.

Table 5.3 Numbers of active clergy

	2002	2012
FT equivalent stipendiaries	9,200	7,900
Self-supporting clergy	2,100	3,200
Active retired clergy	4,500	5,700
Total	15,800	16,800

So whether you say that the number of clergy has gone up or down in the decade depends on who you include. The stipendiaries were 14 per cent fewer in number and having to cover more churches each, but there were 35 per cent more unpaid and retired clergy to help them. In Chapter 7 I will be suggesting that, as part of a radical shake up of ministry-responsibility, some of this growing army could be better used leading churches themselves rather than being assistants to overworked stipendiaries.

Statistics are not available of the numbers of other paid church staff, such as administrators or youth ministers. Judging from the growth of the Centre for Youth Ministry and the numbers of posts created in many dioceses with the help of the Church Commissioners' mission development funding stream it seems likely that their number has risen significantly.

Baptisms

The numbers of baptisms, weddings and funerals undertaken by the Church of England are indicators of the degree to which the people of the country call upon it at the great moments of their lives. If the country as a whole continues to move away from the Church and become more secular then we would expect these indicators to keep declining as they did in the late twentieth century.

The number of infant and child baptisms performed by the Church of England continued to fall at the start of the century but stabilized after 2008, at least until 2013 (Table 5.4).

Table 5.4 Infant and child baptisms (thousands)

2003	136
2008	126
2009	126
2010	125
2011	128
2012	127
2013	122

Adult baptisms are less a 'Christendom' indicator and more of people coming to faith later in life. The number of adult baptisms is still small (less than one per church per annum) but it has continued rising during the period (Table 5.5).

Table 5.5 Adult baptisms

2003	8,300
2008	9,600
2009	10,100
2010	10,100
2011	10,500
2012	11,000
2013	10,900

This rise may partly be because a higher proportion of adults who come to faith today were not baptized as children. However, it is encouraging that there were 31 per cent more baptisms in 2013 than 2003.

Marriages

The number of marriages performed by the Church of England in 2012 saw the biggest rise for many years but there was a subsequent fall in 2013. This may be a reflection of reality, but it may also reflect the wide error margins placed on these statistical series. The 2013 figure for marriages carries an error margin of plus or minus 10 per cent due mainly to low response rates in some dioceses. So the 2012 number could simply be a statistical blip. Similar health warnings apply to most of the statistical series reported here. Overall it does not look like there has been much change in the number of marriages conducted since 2008 (Table 5.6).

Table 5.6 Marriages (thousands)

2003	56
2008	53
2009	52
2010	54
2011	52
2012	56
2013	50

Funerals

The number of Church of England funerals reported has continued to decline, though the rate of decline has been slowing and numbers stayed the same in 2013 (Table 5.7).

Table 5.7 Funerals (thousands)

2003	227
2008	186
2009	173
2010	169
2011	161
2012	159
2013	159

Part of the long-term decline is due to lower death rates, but the rise of secular funerals and undertakers' 'in house' funeral takers have also contributed.

Confirmations

Confirmation has long had a social, coming of age, dimension for teenagers, and the number has been declining for over a century. Numbers continued to fall in the twenty-first century, but appear to have stabilized in 2011 and 2012 followed by a large drop in 2013 (Table 5.8).

Table 5.8 Confirmations

2003	31,800
2008	27,000
2009	25,000
2010	22,300
2011	22,200
2012	22,500
2013	19,500

PCC income

Total PCC income continued to rise up to 2007 but then fell back in real terms during the recession (Table 5.9).

Table 5.9 PCC total income

	PCC total income (£ million at constant 2012 purchasing power)
2002	930
2003	958
2004	987
2005	1,002
2006	1,013
2007	1,055
2008	1,045
2009	1,009
2010	973
2011	945
2012	929

Given the time-lags involved in data collection it is too soon to say whether real PCC income will recover along with the economic recovery.

Electoral roll

Electoral rolls grow slightly most years then shrink a lot when a new roll is compiled. New rolls were compiled in 2002, 2007 and 2013. From 2002 to 2007 the roll fell from 1.211 million to 1.173 million, 4 per cent over five years. From 2006 to 2012 it fell 5 per cent over six years. From 2007 to 2013 (re-signing years) it fell 7 per cent. So it continues to go down slowly, at a rate of around 1 per cent per year.

It is likely that a large proportion of the adults who have started attending fresh expressions have not been joining church electoral rolls. Chapter 11 suggests that members of fresh expressions started this century now constitute around 10 per cent of the Church of England. This growth might well largely offset the drop in electoral roll members.

Easter attendance

An increasing proportion of Easter and Christmas services are non-eucharistic, so we will here look at the attendance figures rather than the communicant numbers used in *Hope for the Church* (Table 5.10).

Table 5.10 Easter attendance (thousands)

2002	1,504
2008	1,429
2009	1,429
2010	1,411
2011	1,382
2012	1,395
2013	1,272

Easter attendance fluctuates with the weather and time of year but it is clear there has been an overall drop in numbers in the decade, although 2012 showed an increase followed by a fall in 2013.

Christmas attendance

This varies more than Easter attendance because numbers are higher when Christmas Eve or Christmas Day falls on a Sunday. This means the series below is hard to interpret. Overall, numbers appear to have held up quite well, though perhaps there has been a small overall drop when comparing similar years. However, we do not know the trend in attendance at Christmas services held prior to Christmas Eve. There was also a definitional change in 2012 whereby, instead of asking 'how many people attended on Christmas Eve *and* Christmas Day?' the form asked 'how many people attended on Christmas Eve *or* Christmas Day?' There is some evidence of churches misunderstanding the word 'or' – sending in the total for just one of the two days. So it is not entirely clear whether or not numbers have gone down slightly over the decade (Table 5.11).

Table 5.11 Christmas attendance on Christmas Eve and Christmas Day (thousands)

2002	2,607
2003	2,653
2004	2,629
2005	2,786
2006	2,984
2007	2,657
2008	2,639
2009	2,446
2010	2,329
2011	2,642
2012	2,521
2013	2,368

Usual Sunday attendance

Until 2000 this was the only measure of regular attendance available. A 'usual' Sunday is deemed to be one with nothing special happening and churches are asked to estimate the average of these. Weekday attendance is not included and sometimes neither is attendance at fresh expressions, either because churches are unsure about including them, or because they are reluctant to do so for fear of parish share rising as a result (Table 5.12).

Table 5.12 Usual Sunday attendance (thousands)

	Adults	Children	Total	Per annum
2003	757	145	902	
2008	714	126	840	−1.4%
2009	704	120	824	−1.9%
2010	693	118	810	−1.7%
2011	689	116	805	−0.6%
2012	674	114	788	−2.1%
2013	672	113	785	−0.4%

Overall usual Sunday attendance was down 12 per cent in the decade, rather slower than the 17 per cent decline in the 1990s because child attendance decline has slowed.

This decline is probably caused by a mix of several factors – fewer people attending, people coming less often, people switching to weekday attendance, the switch from traditional to fresh expression church lowering reporting rates, and parish share fears in a recession tempting churches to mark down their reported numbers. There are signs that the rate of fall slowed further in the most recent years but there is no escaping the fact that the usual Sunday attendance figures have not turned around.

October count

Since 2001 each church has been asked to count the number of people attending services during four weeks in October. Fresh expressions are specifically included. The average of the four weeks is taken as the best guide available to total average attendance throughout the year. These figures are more volatile than usual Sunday attendance because they are affected by special events, weather, the timing of harvest and of half term. Churches have been unsure whether or not to include certain services, especially those put on for schools. This makes the weekday figures (especially for children) hard to interpret.

A recent definitional change worked back to 2008 changes the allowance made for churches not having a service every week and also the estimation procedures for non-returns. Here an adjustment is made to the previously published 2003 total to make it comparable. Most of the adjustment relates to adult attendance on Sundays (Table 5.13).

Table 5.13 Average attendance in October

	Adults Sunday	Children Sunday	Adults Weekday	Children Weekday	Total all age all week
2003	853	164	104	66	1,187
2003*					1,126
2008	768	139	109	76	1,092
2009	758	134	109	77	1,078
2010	741	130	110	78	1,059
2011	728	127	112	80	1,047
2012	732	128	112	74	1,046
2013	722	124	119	(41)	?

*adjusted for definitional change (estimate)

October attendance in 2012 was 6.5 per cent lower than 2002 and 4 per cent lower than 2008. There was a slight increase in weekday attendance offsetting the drop in Sunday attendance. In contrast to the 1990s, the fall in child attendance was no faster than that of adults. The equivalent child and all-age figures for 2013 are not known due to the definitional change whereby attendance at school services was counted separately and excluded from these totals for the first time. However, it may be that as there was a significant further rise in adult weekday attendance, there may also have been with children. In this case the weekly all-age total will have been little different from 2012.

So the October count suggests attendance decline continuing at only half the rate of usual Sunday attendance, and possibly drawing to a halt in the most recent couple of years.

Attendance frequency

Church attendance numbers can go down either because fewer people are going to church or because they attend less often. Average attendance numbers have probably gone down for both these reasons, but can we get any handle on the mix between them?

Many clergy are convinced that the average frequency of church attendance has been falling. As the pace of life has increased, people have travelled more, the range of available Sunday activities has increased, and a higher proportion of churchgoers have had to work on some Sundays, churchgoers have become less regular. Also, new churchgoers are much more likely to come monthly or fortnightly than older generations. This trend has accelerated in the most recent years due to the growth of fresh expression congregations meeting monthly or fortnightly.

However, it has been remarkably difficult to find objective numerical evidence to back this up. Perhaps clergy have drawn the wrong conclusion from surveys showing infrequent attendance patterns. Perhaps the reality is not that frequency has dropped but that people always came infrequently. British Social Attitudes surveys seem to suggest that attendance frequency has not declined at all between the mid-1980s and the most recent years. However, such data is rather too far removed from the realities of church attendance numbers to be accorded much authority. Much more relevant are actual attendance and membership numbers in real churches.

So what evidence can we assemble to help us get a better statistical handle on frequency changes? Over the long term we can compare electoral rolls ('membership') with usual Sunday attendance. If membership is going down slower than attendance then it looks like people are indeed coming less often. There are, of course, problems with relying on electoral rolls as a measure of membership, but at least it gives us one handle on the issue. Expressing usual Sunday attendance as a percentage of electoral rolls in the first year after everyone has to re-sign enables comparable years to be used (Table 5.14).

Table 5.14 Usual Sunday attendance as percentage of electoral rolls

1990	82%
1996	79%
2002	76%
2007	74%
2013	72%

Between 1990 and 2013 usual Sunday attendance fell 31 per cent. If it had continued to be 82 per cent of the electoral rolls, as in 1990, then it would only have fallen 22 per cent. So the suggestion from this data is that about one-third of the adult attendance decline is because members are coming less often and two-thirds because there are fewer members.

Christmas attendance may be one guide to the total size of the worshipping community because 'everyone' goes at Christmas. Comparing recent years on which Christmas Day has fallen on the same day of the week gives an average drop in attendance of about 4 per cent. Over the same period average attendance numbers have gone down by around 6 per cent. So this straw in the wind also suggests that two-thirds of the drop in average attendance may be because the total community has shrunk and the remaining third because they come less often.

Surveys of Roman Catholics also show a long-term decline in attendance frequency. For example, the European Values Survey in 1990 found 59 per cent of Catholics saying they attended mass frequently, 23 per cent infrequently and 18 per cent never. By 2008 only 40 per cent attended frequently, 33 per cent infrequently and 27 per cent never.

With the very rapid recent rise in the number of fresh expression and family congregations meeting monthly it seems highly probable that average attendance frequencies have been going down rapidly recently. Much of the recent rather modest drop in average attendance is probably due to the average Anglican coming to church services less often.

One large church conducted a census of its three main Sunday morning services in October 2014. The results illustrate clearly the trend towards less frequent attendance (Figure 5.2).

Figure 5.2 Attendance frequency census, October 2014 (% attending)

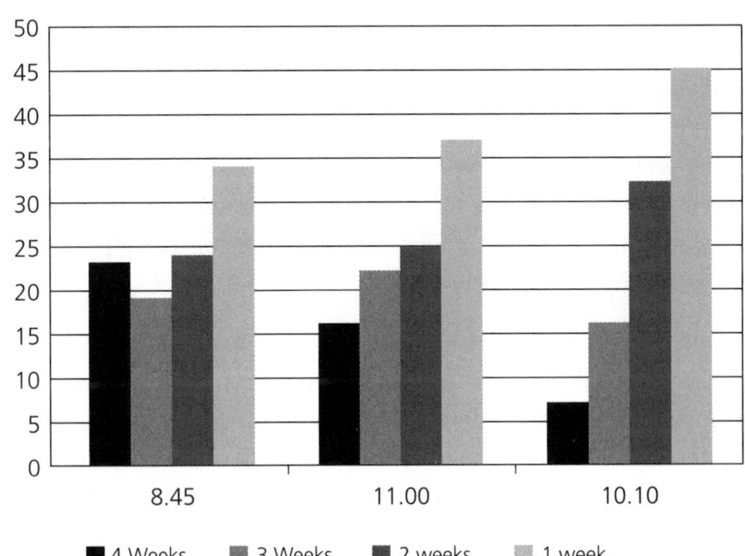

The 8.45 service was a fairly traditional communion with 106 people attending over the four weeks, the 11a.m. service a well-established family service with children's groups and 318 people, and the 10.10 a fairly new 30-minute all-age fresh expression with 202 people. All the services had a majority of people coming only once or twice in four weeks, even at the traditional service with a mainly sixties and seventies age profile. Even these people are leading busy lives

today. The overall size of the church community was almost double average attendance. But the newer, more contemporary the service the less frequently people were coming. On average people came 2.3 times out of 4 to the traditional service, 2.2 times to the family service and 1.8 times to the fresh expression. Only 7 per cent of the people came all four weeks at 10.10 and 45 per cent came only once.

Joiners and leavers

As mentioned in Chapter 1, churches were asked for the first time in 2012 to estimate the total size of their worshipping community and the numbers of joiners and leavers during the year. It will take several years for all churches to learn a good consistent estimation method for their worshipping community but eventually it is hoped that this will take over from the attendance measures as the main indicator of the size of the Church of England. Already it is possible to estimate a trend by expressing joiners and leavers as a percentage of the worshipping community.

The main question with joiners and leavers is whether churches find it is easier to recall who joined last year than who left. However, the two dioceses that have been asking these questions for some years (Leicester and Lichfield) have found the answers highly consistent from year to year. Slightly fewer people are recorded as moving out of the area as moving in, which, in a national survey, suggests that a few of those moving away are being missed. But the numbers are not great. So it is possible to have some modest confidence that the answers being given are meaningful (Table 5.15).

The number of joiners exceeded the number of leavers in almost all dioceses. The net excess of joiners over leavers suggests a growth rate of 3 per cent of the worshipping community in 2012. The join rate was 7 per cent and the leave rate 4.5 per cent. The joiners contained a large proportion of children – probably many of them plus their parents were joining monthly events such as Messy Church. So

Table 5.15 Joiners and leavers 2013 (thousands)

	Joiners	Leavers	Net
Died or became too ill to attend	0	17	–17
Moved into or out of the area	19	14	+5
Left churchgoing or returned to it	9	7	+2
Moved to/from another local church	8	6	+2
First-time churchgoers	31	0	+31
Could not categorize	8	3	+5
Total joiners and leavers	75	47	+28

the 3 per cent rise in the worshipping community could be entirely consistent with steady average attendance. A loss of weekly churchgoers equivalent to 1 per cent of the worshipping community combined with a gain of 4 per cent of monthly churchgoers would achieve that twin result. Attendance falls but membership rises.

Worshipping community

Although one day it is hoped that this measure will become the main indicator of the size of the worshipping community of the Church of England it is not yet well enough established to be very meaningful. However, for what it is worth, the reported worshipping community was 1.010 million in 2012 and 1.056 million in 2013, a rise of 5 per cent. Although this is quite consistent with the reported excess of joiners over leavers we will need a higher response rate and more consistent estimation methods before beginning to rely on this indicator. But it is well worth every church taking the trouble to discover the size of its community and the flows in and out of it to inform their own ministry not just in order to fill in a form.

Large-scale surveys

Several times I have surveyed all the churches of a diocese in England or Wales, asking them their average attendance 'today' and 'three years ago'. Each time the overall trend has been significantly better than that in the official attendance returns. My form was no threat to their parish share bill, so I wondered whether churches were telling me a fuller version of the truth than they were telling their dioceses. On the other hand, perhaps churches give me an optimistic estimate to make them look good in my research. Talking to many of the people actually filling in both sets of forms suggests to me that the truth probably lies somewhere in between.

A large-scale survey of 4,500 committed Anglican churchgoers for the *Church Times* conducted by Professor Leslie Francis, reported in the paper in February 2014, found that 40 per cent of church members believed their church would grow in the next twelve months and only 18 per cent believed it would not. The rest were uncertain. Fully 50 per cent of the clergy expected their churches to grow in the next year. Are the clergy and their lay church members simply naive optimists for ever assuming next year will be different from the past? Or do they have solid ground for their optimism, based, perhaps, on their perception of the last year or so? This possibility should not be dismissed. The joiners and leavers data for 2012 and 2013 suggests that church membership is growing, especially among younger people.

In 2012 the Church Commissioners commissioned various pieces of research into church growth under the general heading 'From anecdote to evidence'. The results were published in early 2014 and are available on the Church Growth Research Programme website (www.churchgrowthresearch.org.uk). A major element of this research was a survey of 1,700 Anglican churches conducted by David Voas of the University of Essex. Each church was asked: During the past five years (i.e. 2008–2013), has the number of people who attend for worship at least monthly ...

- Declined substantially?
- Declined a little?
- Stayed about the same?
- Grown a little?
- Grown substantially?

A clear majority of church leaders believed their church had grown over the past five years:

- Declined substantially 6 per cent
- Declined a little 20 per cent
- Stayed about the same 19 per cent
- Grown a little 39 per cent
- Grown substantially 17 per cent

Some 56 per cent of churches reported growth and only 26 per cent decline. David Voas wonders whether this self-reported growth is exaggerated because the *Statistics for Mission* numbers for these churches on the national database tell a different story (Table 5.16).

Table 5.16 Statistics for Mission figures on church growth and decline

	Self-reported	Database
Declined substantially	6%	16%
Declined a little	20%	20%
Stayed about the same	19%	37%
Grown a little	39%	10%
Grown substantially	17%	16%

However, it may be possible to reconcile the two:

1. The database attendance changes covered the period 2001–11, the self-reporting related to 2008–13. This is a very different time period in which attendance trends generally were rather better than 2001–08.
2. The database relates to average attendance whereas the self-reported changes relate to membership of the worshipping community ('the number of people who attend for worship

at least monthly'). The new joiners and leavers data now also suggests an increase in this measure and so seems to support the self-reported growth.

3. The database attendance numbers have such wide error margins around them that it is hard to use them to dismiss survey findings.

It is always wise to be cautious about survey bias and overall numbers might not be rising if growing small churches are being offset by a few shrinking large ones. But the headline finding of this survey that the Church of England, at its grass roots, believes it is growing might just be true.

A balanced judgement

How big is the solar system? To answer that question you don't just have to get your head around the Pluto problem. There is the question of how to treat the whole Kuiper Belt of which Pluto is a part. Then there are those fresh expressions of planets recently discovered even further out – Sedna and the excitingly named 2012VP113, probably plus others the radar has not yet spotted. The solar system, like the Church, is more complicated, and may be bigger, than you first imagined.

So has the Church of England stopped shrinking? Is it even growing? The answer depends on which indicators and time period you use, and on whether you take any notice of expressions of church currently off the statistical radar. Because there have clearly been recent changes and improvements to the trends, we'll here compile the results for 2008–13, 2011–12 and 2012–13. The period 2002–08 is no guide to the trend today. The frustratingly slow process of compiling national data means that in a book that most people will read in 2015 and 2016 the latest year we can talk about is 2013 (Table 5.17).

Table 5.17 Indicators in church growth

Indicator	Trend 08–13	Change 11–12	Change 12–13
Number of churches	steady	steady	steady
Number of congregations	growth	growth	growth
Proportion of churches – adults	–	decline	decline
Proportion of churches – children	–	growth	growth
Number of stipendiary clergy	decline	decline	decline
Number of active clergy	growth	growth	growth
Infant and child baptisms	steady	steady	decline
Adult baptisms	growth	growth	steady
Marriages	growth	growth	decline
Funerals	decline	steady	steady
Confirmations	decline	growth	decline
PCC income	decline	?	?
Electoral rolls	decline	decline	decline
Easter attendance	decline	growth	decline
Christmas attendance	decline	?	?
Usual Sunday attendance adult	decline	decline	steady
Usual Sunday attendance child	decline	steady	steady
October count adults Sunday	decline	steady	decline
October count child Sunday	decline	steady	decline
October count weekday adult	steady	steady	growth
October count weekday child	steady	decline	?
Joiners – leavers	–	growth	growth
Worshipping community	–	–	growth
Surveys (mainly membership)	growth	growth	growth

A summary of indicators looks like Table 5.18.

Table 5.18 Summary of indicators in church growth

	Growth	Steady	Decline	Decline %
1990–2000	1	1	10	83%
2008–12	5	4	11	55%
2011–12	9	7	5	24%
2012–13	6	5	8	42%

It would certainly seem as though the trends are continuing to improve. The 'Christendom' measures have mainly stopped going down, the attendance measures continue to go down but more slowly than in the past, and membership measures look like they are going up.

Someone still wedded to attendance measures could argue that the Church of England is still shrinking. Taking all the indicators together, a prudent commentator might say that it is neither clearly growing nor shrinking. Chapter 1 argued that the best measure of the size of the Christian Church was the number of its active members rather than average attendance at particular events. If that argument is accepted then the Church of England is probably now growing.

What the future holds, of course, is not predetermined. But it does look as though the collective project to turn things round is bearing fruit and the prospects for future growth are brighter than they have been for some years. It would be equally as wrong to think either that the growth-project is not working so we should forget it, or that the decline problem has been solved so we can forget it. The prospects are brighter, but only if every diocese and church maintains a growth agenda.

The second part of this book will look in some detail at exactly how the churches have started growing and can continue to do so in the future.

Part 2

What is working on the ground today?

6

Intending to grow

> It is my judgment, therefore, that we should not make it difficult for the Gentiles who are turning to God. (Acts 15.19)

Intentionality

James, summing up the Council of Jerusalem, acknowledged the danger that the Church, with its strange, demanding rituals and culture, can make it difficult for people to meet with God. Instead, we should make it straightforward for newcomers to find God in the church.

It has always been true that churches are likely to grow only if they try to. An Indian friend of mine grew up in the Mar Thomas Church in Kerala. He complained vehemently because they spent all those centuries since Thomas keeping the gospel to themselves when they had the whole of India as a mission field. They didn't try to grow so they stayed small. It was left to Western missionaries in the nineteenth century to share the good news with the rest of India. It may be my friend left a few historical details out of this narrative, but there was some force to it.

It is those who intend to grow the church who tend to grow the church.

Is your church a magic roundabout or a gospel train?

Older readers will remember the *Magic Roundabout* characters from the daily teatime TV programme. A magic roundabout church is one that trundles thoughtlessly around the church's year. If it is Christmas the church will 'do' Christmas, by which is meant repeating as exactly as possible what was done last year. The Bethlehem Carol Sheets will be located in the usual place, the same team will decorate the church building with holly, and the same carols will occur in the same order as usual in the various traditional services. When it is Mothering Sunday the daffodils will be provided as normal, there will be three hours at the cross on Good Friday because that is what you are supposed to do, everyone will look after their customary stall for the Spring Fayre, and the Harvest Supper will be the usual pea and pie.

There is nothing wrong with marking the church's year – I've done it myself for decades. The problem lies in the unthinking repetitions. The church's life is not planned with the future in mind, it is composed of endlessly replicating the past. There is no need to make any decisions. Without strategy, intentionality or debate, the magic roundabout church goes through the motions, its strength gradually waning and its relevance gradually disappearing.

In a gospel-train church, however, the members take stock of where they are, assessing what the church is like and what it does. Then they catch a vision of where they want to be – of what God is calling them to be and do. Once the gospel-train church knows where it is and where it wants to get to, it will develop a travel plan. It will lay railway lines, get up a head of steam and move along intentionally to the destination. The magic roundabout church goes round in ever decreasing circles but the gospel-train church is travelling the line it is constructing into the future.

Many churches betray elements of magic roundabout and gospel train at the same time. Which is your church most like? Would someone else in your church have a different perspective from your own?

One of the key findings of the research programme 'From anecdote to evidence' is that churches with a plan for change tend to grow better than those without a plan. In his detailed survey of 1,700 churches, David Voas found that 64 per cent of churches with a clear mission and purpose were growing but only 26 per cent of churches without one.

This is hardly surprising because to grow accidentally you need to get lucky. An isolated initiative in an otherwise aimless church may have an impact, but a strategy that pulls together the various elements and identifies priorities is much more likely to inspire the whole church and generate solid long-term growth.

Plans and gimmicks

But there is a subtlety about planning to grow, sometimes called the principle of obliquity. You don't aim directly at the outcome you want – growth. Rather you aim to produce the conditions in which God is able to grow the church – quality and relevance. Churches in which quality and relevance have been improved seem able to grow naturally up to the new higher ceiling level the improvements have created. Then further improvements are required to get to the next stage, and so on.

So the way to grow is not through an endless series of gimmicks to attract people to one-off events but through a steady focus on the range and quality of church life. A growth plan may seek to improve the quality of worship services and the range of styles, the quality of the church's community and the range of people who will fit into it and the quality of the church hall and the range of users of it.

A balanced plan will involve an intention to grow in all three aspects outlined in Chapter 1 – depth, numbers and service to the community. Churches that grow in one aspect only become deformed, unbalanced and dysfunctional.

Mission Action Planning – a brief history

Some churches have always made plans for the future. The church where I was curate in the early 1980s wrote five-year plans to guide its development – and it grew enormously under their influence. Planning mission strategy goes back to the church of Antioch, Barnabas and Paul. However, a particular way of doing this has recently spread through much of the Church of England – Mission Action Planning is becoming the main lever for change and growth in many of our dioceses and churches.

The story of the invention of Mission Action Plans (MAPs) in the Diocese of London in the early 1990s was told in my book *The Road to Growth* (2005).[1] Previously, the diocese had shown an unhealthy acceptance of decline coupled with a focus on fighting internal ecclesiastical battles rather than doing mission. The new bishop, David Hope, asked every church to produce a written plan of mission action to change this culture. In many churches all three concepts appeared to be novelties – mission, action and plan. He provided advisers to accompany churches as they devised and implemented their plans. Clergy vacancies were advertised with job descriptions looking for a leader in mission rather than a parish pastor. And the parish share system was reformed to incentivize growth rather than tax it. These early changes to encourage a culture of mission-intentionality triggered a reversal of trend in the diocese from decline to growth that has continued to this day. Twenty years on, MAPs are still integral to how churches in the Diocese of London operate. They have become part of the normal culture.

Around the turn of the century some individual churches and one or two other dioceses adopted MAP themselves. More recently many dioceses have adopted MAP as their main lever for encouraging change and growth in the parishes. The degree to which each diocese requires or simply encourages MAPs does vary, as does the degree of help and accompaniment on offer. A few dioceses have adopted a similar strategy but under a different name – the Dioceses of Chester and Peterborough, for example, ask their churches for 'Growth Action Plans'.

Does MAP work?

There are dangers in copying the latest fashion. Mechanical imitation of a system that worked elsewhere might lack the individuals and culture that made it a success in the other place. There can be a big difference between the prototype designer outfit strutting its stuff on the catwalk and the mass-produced version ordinary people end up wearing. A MAP does not provide the substance of change for growth, merely the framework within which it can happen. Can you really change the culture of a church simply by asking the leaders to write some aspirations down on a piece of paper and send them to the bishop? Some churches may be incapable of producing a good MAP without a lot of help. Even if they manage to write a good MAP document, unless it is implemented it is a waste of time. Until now the evidence-base on which MAP enthusiasm is predicated has been thin. Could MAP become just another in a long line of Anglican enthusiasms, like the creation of team ministries, that have hit the sands of reality once they went into mass production and the cracks appeared?

MAP and numerical growth

It is not easy to provide good statistical evidence for the success of MAPs in stimulating numerical growth. No one piece of evidence will conclusively demonstrate cause and effect between the adoption of MAPs and the growth of churches. However, if data from a range of dioceses all points in the same direction then the evidence-base becomes convincing.

1. London

The graph below shows the scale of turnaround in London following the adoption of MAPs. It would be wrong to ascribe the whole turnaround to MAP. All we can say is that MAP was an integral part of the culture-shift that reversed the trend and continues to be so up to the present (Figure 6.1).

Figure 6.1 The effects of MAP on the electoral roll in London, 1972–2013

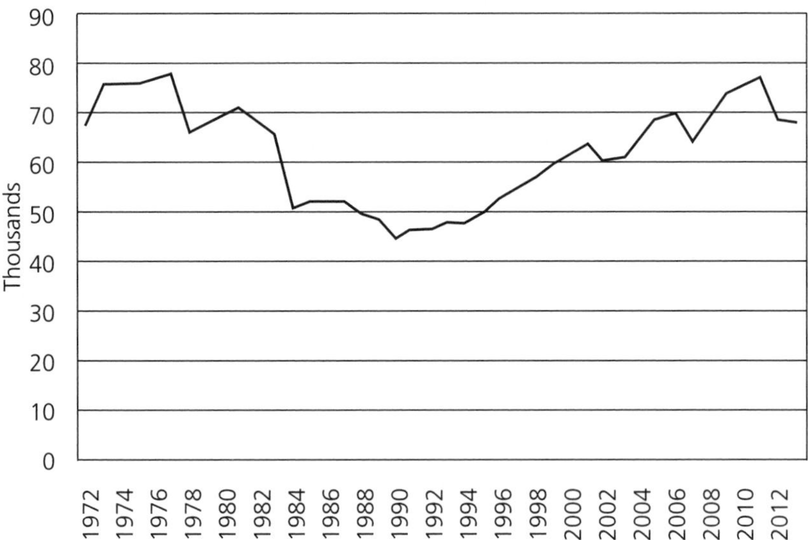

2. Blackburn

Advised by Mike Chew, one of the authors of the MAP guidebook (*Mission Action Planning*, Chew and Ireland, 2009),[2] the Diocese of Blackburn was an early adopter of MAP as a lever for change in parishes. Figure 6.2 shows that in the years during which MAPs were introduced to the parishes the previous decline trend in attendance was more or less halted.

Figure 6.2 MAP and the halted decline in Blackburn, 2004–11

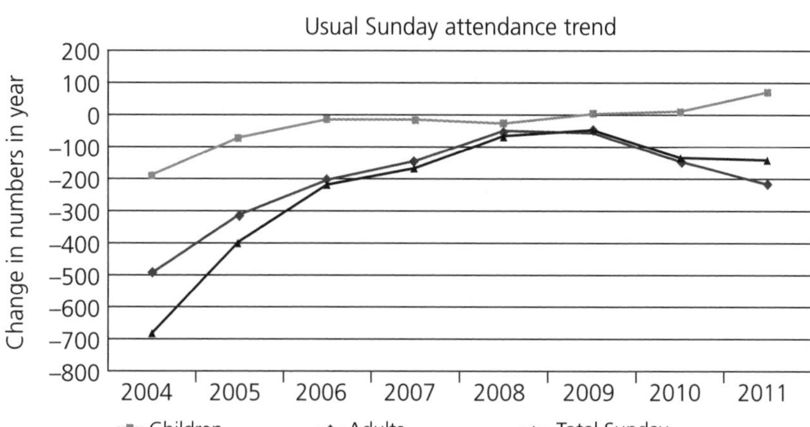

Moreover, the Blackburn team graded the MAP documents according to a list of quality characteristics. Figure 6.3 shows that the higher the quality of the MAP the better the growth trend of the church.

Figure 6.3 Higher quality of MAP: better growth trend of the church

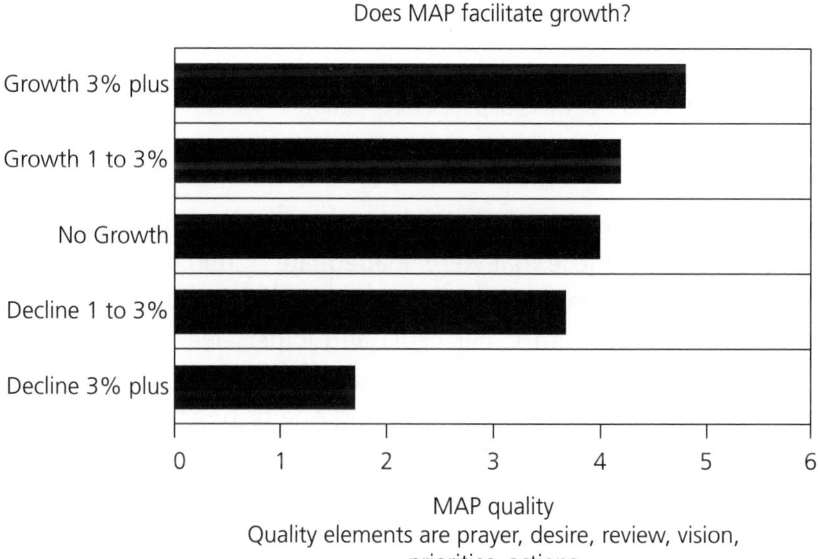

3. Lichfield

In the Diocese of Lichfield there was no universal compulsion to introduce MAPs so there is a good-sized control group of non-MAP churches to compare with. The graph shows that churches with a MAP were growing better than those without a MAP in relation to all three main indicators – usual Sunday attendance, October attendance and the balance between joiners and leavers. Prior to the adoption of MAP these two groups of churches had similar trends – the trend divergence coincides with the adoption of a MAP culture.

Figure 6.4 Growth with MAP higher than growth without MAP

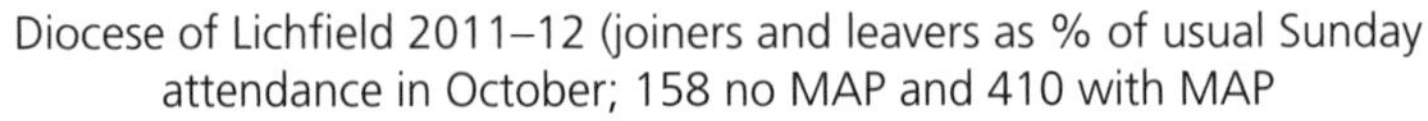

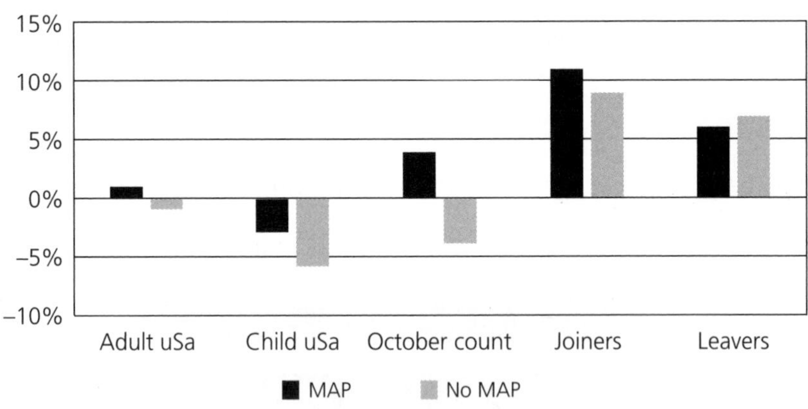

The Lichfield team also divided up the church MAPs into those that were 'good' and those that were 'inadequate'. Churches with good MAPs grew better on the evidence of the October count (6 per cent growth compared with 0 per cent) and joiners–leavers. However, the uSa results were the other way around (Figure 6.5). Possibly this was for other specific reasons, including one or two large churches with good MAPs going through a vacancy. But this result does show that good MAPs do not automatically result in church growth. There may be a clearer pay-off for the diocese in persuading the remaining 158 churches to adopt MAP than in working with the 114 churches with poor MAPs to improve them.

Figure 6.5 Relative growth between a good MAP and an inadequate MAP

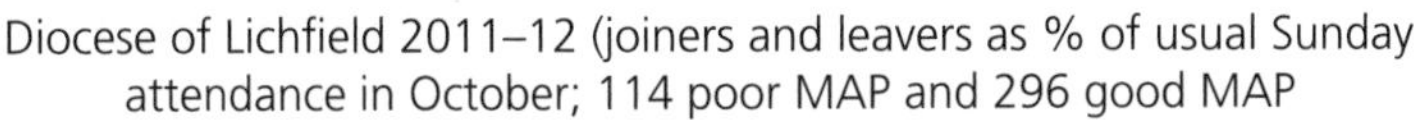

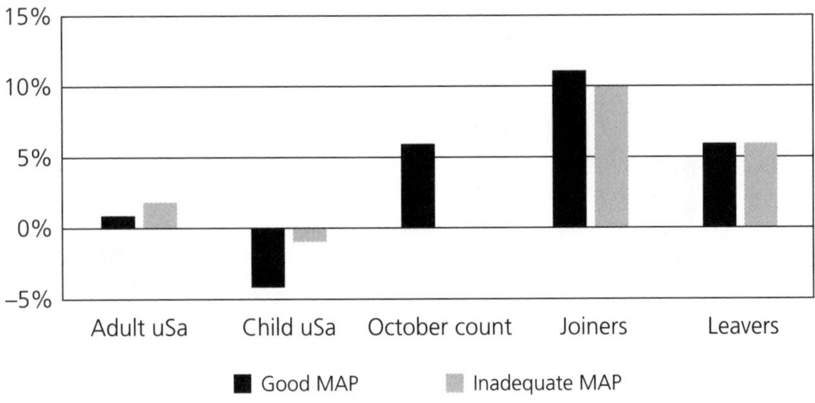

4. Derby

The Diocese of Derby began with a group of 38 churches willing to pilot MAP on behalf of the rest of the diocese. Many of these churches were in steep decline, being in particularly difficult situations for growth, but willing to try something new because desperation was setting in.

MAPs were drawn up during 2010 and came into force on 1 January 2011. Figure 6.6 shows the change in attendance and joiners/leavers over the first two years of their MAPs – 2011 and 2012. The turnaround from the past expressed in all three measures was quite dramatic but especially in relation to usual Sunday attendance. However, the change in October count numbers (0 per cent) was still not as good as the average for the diocese. But overall there is no doubt that a large improvement in trend has accompanied the adoption of MAP by these 38 churches.

Figure 6.6 MAP and change in attendance and joiners/leavers in Derby, 2010–12

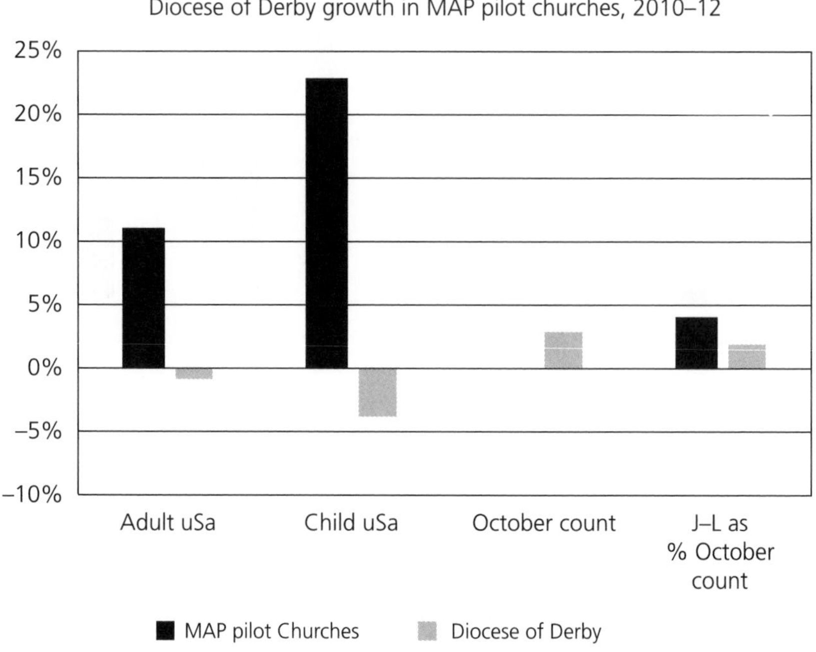

5. St Davids – Church in Wales

St Davids does not have a diocesan strategy for encouraging MAP in every church. However, in common with most other dioceses without a centralized MAP system, some individual churches do have their own written mission plans. Figure 6.7 shows that the 20 churches with a written strategy had on average a much better attendance trend than the rest of the diocese without one. It could be argued that these are likely to be the best-led churches so they would grow anyway whether or not they had a written plan. Local knowledge, however, suggests that this is not always the case – having a strategy is their main distinctive.

Figure 6.7 MAP, or a written mission statement, and church growth

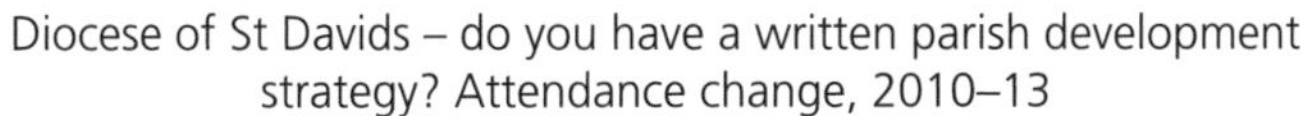

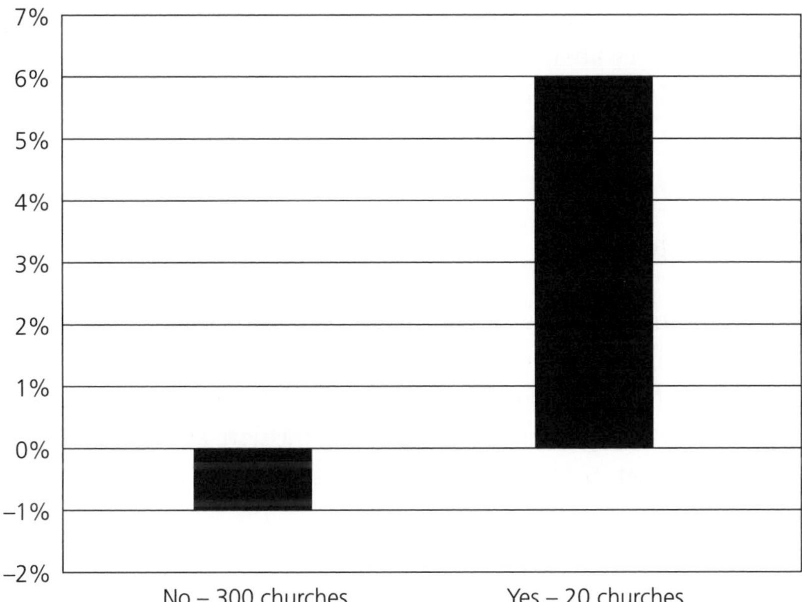

How well is the MAP tool being understood and applied?

It is no surprise to learn that having a thought-out plan for mission grows the church. But there may be further potential because many churches still lack a sense of urgency to get better at what they do. It is this sense of urgency that drives business progress in a world where the competition will swallow you up if you don't keep learning and improving. Most churches spend too little time seeking new vision, and researching new possibilities. In many manufacturing companies, research and development is the main activity not a peripheral one. Few churches invest significantly in training even though their members are their main asset. Successful businesses recognize it is their people who create success and will invest in them to produce it. Finally, not many churches are good at reviewing progress and thereby completing the learning loop by using the lessons learned from review to inform future vision and strategy.

Churches, of course, are not businesses. But they are not less than businesses, they are more than businesses, with more dimensions to their life. MAP will realize its full potential when it is the driver not just of what we do but also of the desire to do it better.

Conclusion

The accumulation of evidence strongly suggests that MAP is associated with improving numerical growth trends. Adopting MAP is no magic bullet and there may well be disappointments, but persuading churches into intentional planning for mission and growth does seem to pay off. MAP is a genuine lever for change and growth and there is more potential to be unlocked.

Wisdom about mission planning for a diocese

1. Persuade rather than demand

Churches that feel the bishop has ordered them to produce a piece of paper against their will, will just produce a piece of paper. Better to spend time persuading churches that MAP is a good idea. Explain that MAP is about process not content. Content is up to each church and could simply be a systemization of what they are already planning. In small churches the MAP does not need to be sophisticated. Invite people from dioceses where MAP is part of the culture to commend the process. Convince people this is not the latest diocesan gimmick, but a long-term culture-shift. Ask some parishes to pilot MAP for a year or two and get them to commend it to others. Work with the willing and monitor their progress against the unwilling. Make willingness to use MAP a condition of clergy appointments.

2. Offer initial training

Offer a range of good-practice MAPs as templates, together with wisdom about creating a MAP. Buy each church a copy of *Mission Action Planning* (Chew and Ireland, 2009).[3] Offer clergy training days.

3. Provide mentoring and accompaniment

Experience shows that the impact of MAP is weakened when churches send off their initial plan to the bishop then hear nothing back in return. It is important that the diocese provides people to visit, mentor and encourage churches as they construct and implement their MAPs. A church should be able to call on an expert friend two to three times a year. Knowing that someone will be visiting keeps MAPs on church agendas. Otherwise they can soon get forgotten. This process has a budgetary cost, but if the diocese is not willing to budget for MAP then MAP is not a priority. One or two dioceses have found a large group of volunteers, done some training with them, and set each to accompany one or two churches, unpaid, part time. However, such a system needs considerable paid time to set up and maintain, and results seem patchy. With so many individuals involved it is very hard for the centre to know what is going on. It is probably better to have a handful of paid posts to represent the diocese and build up experience and expertise. One per archdeaconry is a good guide. The overall coordinator could be the diocesan missioner.

4. Facilitate sharing of good practice

It is usually better not to try to impose ideas of good practice but to facilitate sharing between clergy and lay leaders through conferences and partnership or twinning links.

5. Coordinate

Don't have alternative or rival programmes to stimulate mission and growth – everything should be channelled through the MAP process. The bishop and all diocesan staff should routinely read its MAP before any involvement with a parish. Diocesan people should work as a coordinated team to help and support churches in their MAP processes.

6. Offer grants

Every diocese should have a mission or growth fund to which churches can apply for funding to enable them to achieve the aspirations in their MAPs. The grant system can be coordinated with the MAP system by asking applicants to show how the grant will help them achieve their MAP goals.

7. Make it about quality and culture as well as activities

Often a better question than 'What more can we do?' is 'How can we get better at what we do?' Use MAP to help churches be learning organizations.

8. Monitor and learn

Dioceses should keep on learning good practice in terms of process, content and delivery. It is not enough that individuals gain their own experience and expertise – this should be diffused through the diocese so that good practice gets into the long-term culture of the organization.

9. Stay honest!

A MAP process is about a diocese helping local churches flourish. It is a means of holding churches to action in mission but it should not be used as an instrument of control.

Wisdom about mission planning for churches

1. Make a corporate decision

Rather than reluctantly acceding to a diocesan request, it is best if the PCC positively decides it wants to make or revise its MAP.

2. Involve everyone

The MAP should not simply be written by the vicar or a small group. If it is to be implemented by the church it has to be owned by the church. It will be owned by the whole church if produced by the whole church. Use open meetings, ask a range of groups to look at different aspects, invite written suggestions and comments from all. Leaders will have to write a draft to send round for comments. When these have been incorporated the PCC should vote on adopting the MAP. When a MAP is a corporate document, rather than being the vicar's plan the others go along with, it offers continuity across vacancies and incumbencies. A good MAP forms the basis of a parish profile and job description when looking for a new vicar. It enables change and growth to continue in a vacancy because the church is simply implementing its MAP. The new vicar should be expected to help shape future mission but should also be happy at first to work with the current MAP.

3. Pray

Mission is God's business. It is not the Church of God that has a mission in the world, it is the God of mission who has a Church in the world. God's mission is universe-wide. The redemption of fallen humanity and the growth of the Church are set within the context of God's concern to reverse the cosmic consequences of the Fall, renew creation and establish his kingdom. A church does mission when it finds out what God is doing and joins in. What God is doing always has a general dimension common to every church but also specific aspects unique to every church. So every church needs both to work at its understanding of God's mission in general and also to pray that God will show it how to join in its own specific situation – what mission is God calling us to in our unique time and place? Churches should pray for guidance in developing a MAP and success in implementing it. Otherwise they are probably wasting their time.

4. Do vision first, then strategy

Vision is where you want to get to, who you want to be and what you want to be doing by the end of the period of the MAP. Vision is best summarized in a clear, pithy, compelling phrase that people can remember and get excited by. Once it is clear where you want to go then you can develop strategy for getting there. The strategy is the interlocking set of changes and initiatives that will enable the church to realize its vision.

5. Have a broad understanding of mission

Be guided by the five marks of mission adopted by the 1998 Lambeth Conference. Under the overall heading 'The Mission of the Church is the Mission of Christ' they are listed as

a to proclaim the good news of the kingdom
b to teach, baptize and nurture new believers
c to respond to human need by loving service
d to seek to transform unjust structures of society, to challenge violence of every kind and to pursue peace and reconciliation
e to strive to safeguard the integrity of creation and sustain and renew the life of the earth.

All five marks are about the growth of the church – (a) is primarily about numerical growth; (b) about spiritual growth and (c), (d) and (e) about growth in the vitality of the church's ministry. A church MAP should normally include all three elements.

6. *Have a few mission priorities*

Mission is a limitless project for every church. It is impossible to try everything. A church with lots of mission priorities ends up with none. So a good MAP will include just a few priority aims and actions clearly expressed.

7. *Make sure the MAP is about mission and action*

I helped a church through the process of developing their first MAP. As the warden and I wrote up what the people had said we realized there was very little about mission! When my area bishop and I asked our churches to write MAPs the clergy said, 'Okay but can we please drop the "action" word, it frightens the natives.' So for years we talked about 'Mission Plans' and only gradually introduced the 'A' word. A Mission Action Plan needs to be a plan for action in mission!

8. *Do the plan as well as write it*

There are still some churches who think they have made enough progress simply by writing a plan. What a waste of time!

9. *Make it SMART*

A good plan is *specific, measurable, achievable, realistic* and *timed.* It should be possible to monitor the degree to which every aspect of the plan is achieved. A MAP composed of pious platitudes, holy generalities and unrealistic expectations might say: 'The Lord has placed a burden for families on our hearts. Children are the church of tomorrow. We want to reach out to young people, teach them to love God and bring them in to our worship of the Lord and Saviour Jesus Christ.' A SMART MAP might say:

- 'We intend to start Messy Church in the hall, inviting families from the local school and our playgroup.' (Specific)

- 'We aim to attract at least 25 adults and 25 children who currently do not go to church.' (Measurable)
- 'We will drop Tuesday Fun Night to free up some leadership time to get Messy Church up and running.' (Achievable)
- 'We will offer Messy Church once a month because that is all we can manage at the moment.' (Realistic)
- 'We aim to start on the first Saturday in February next year.' (Timed)

10. Allocate tasks and responsibilities

The plan should name individuals and groups responsible for the delivery of each aspect. That way something might actually get done. Not allocating responsibility means nobody taking it. So the SMART plan for Messy Church will end up saying: 'The Families Action Team will take responsibility for setting up Messy Church but they will expect the rest of the church to help.'

11. Subtract as well as add

A MAP can be a marvellous opportunity for already overstretched churches to add yet more things to do. Churches become places of frantic activity because they find it easier to start activities than stop them. So a MAP should review what happens already and prune those things not bearing fruit. Healthy churches are focused not frantic so what should we focus on? A church may even decide through its MAP process to be less activity-centred, less defined by what it does, and more relationship-centred, more defined by what it is.

12. Write every 3–5 years and review annually

Writing a good MAP is a time-consuming exercise for the whole church. It should only be done periodically when the previous MAP is starting to look out of date. During intervening years it is usually best for the PCC to review progress and decide on amendments to the MAP.

13. Think long term – don't revert

The area bishop made it his personal business to ensure that every church in his area had a MAP. Then he moved on to another diocese. His successor devolved responsibility for accompanying churches to others, who proved ineffectual. Within a few years a third of the churches no longer had a MAP at all and many had forgotten about the whole thing. It is very easy to revert to type once there is nobody to remind you otherwise. So remember that MAP is not a momentary aberration but a permanent change of culture.

7

Leading to grow

Remember the former things, those of long ago. (Isaiah 46.9)

Good old days?

There used to be a word for the practice of being the incumbent of more than one church at once – pluralism. For hundreds of years pluralism was considered a national evil to be restrained by Parliament. The Act Concerning Peter's Pence and Dispensations of 1534 vested dispensation to hold more than one living in the Archbishop of Canterbury alone. In 1604 new canons forbad a minister to hold benefices in plurality if they were more than 30 miles apart. Yet the problems on the ground persisted into Victorian times: an 1830 survey of the South Lindsey area of Lincolnshire found that 140 out of 221 parishes had no resident clergyman (Obelkevich, 1976, p. 120).[1] So the Pluralities Act 1838 made it illegal to hold more than two benefices at once and these must be within ten miles of each other. The Pluralities Act 1850 narrowed this down to three miles and one of the benefices must be worth less than £100 per annum.

Mr Gladstone, speaking in the debate on the 1850 Bill, made his view plain: 'The existence of pluralities in the Church of England has been a great blot upon its recent history. The House ought to travel towards their extinction as fast as possible.'

By 1875 only 57 of the 221 parishes of South Lindsey lacked a resident clergyman. Pluralism was being cured.

The problem was absentee clergy obtaining multiple livings, appointing ill-educated assistant curates to serve them, and living off the difference between the value of the livings and the stipends paid to the curates. Pluralism thereby deprived the inhabitants of many parishes of the ministry of their own dedicated, educated clergyman.

The greater wealth of the nineteenth-century Church and the copious supply of Victorian clergy made the Pluralities Acts practical propositions. One church one vicar became almost universal. We now look back on this as 'the good old days', when every parish had its publican, postmaster and parson. Spinsters cycled to evensong. Afterwards, the church choir sank warm beer in the sepia glow of a golden sunset, while the vicar settled down with his cocoa to follow *A book at bedtime* on the old steam radio. All was well with the steady, slow rhythms of parish life in England's green and pleasant land, our garden of Eden gifted by God, granted by Gladstone.

Every vicar with a church, every church with a vicar

Handling the fall in numbers

Whether or not this idyll actually existed between the Pluralities Acts and the 1960s, the drop in clergy numbers over the last 25 years has rendered it a distant dream today. The number of full-time stipendiary clergy in the Church of England has fallen from over 11,100 in 1990 to under 7,800 today. Yet the number of churches – around 16,000 – has hardly changed. The arithmetic is inevitable. In 1990 there were 1.4 churches per full-time clergy, today there are 2.1. Pluralism is back with a vengeance, though today's clergy receive only one stipend and their band of helpers tends to be unpaid. But the problem of ministry leadership in plural parishes has returned.

Also, the average age of the stipendiary clergy has risen to 52, of the self-supporting clergy to 60. Adding increasing numbers of active retired clergy means that, though the total number of clergy available to lead services has not decreased, a far higher proportion are unpaid and elderly.

Because of their age structure, we know the decline in the number of stipendiary clergy will continue into the foreseeable future. When my daughter was ordained at the age of 24 I said to her, 'Congratulations, you do realize that, given the age range of the rest of us, one day you will be vicar of Yorkshire?'

This new reality has been accommodated partly by rising vacancy lengths. Fewer clergy go round the same number of posts because they are vacant for longer. The average vacancy length today is probably around 11 months, perhaps twice that of 25 years ago. If this is true then around 10 per cent of churches are in vacancy at any one time today, compared with 5 per cent, enabling the same number of benefices to survive with 5 per cent fewer clergy. But the number of paid clergy has fallen by about 35 per cent – so longer vacancies have only accommodated a small proportion of the drop.

Most of the reduction in clergy numbers has been enabled by amalgamations into multi-church benefices. Rarely has this been done through a grand reorganization plan based on objective criteria. Usually a diocese undergoes periodic rounds of cuts in which every deanery is asked to reduce its clergy by a certain amount. Often, therefore, the next posts that happen to become vacant have been the ones reorganized on a piecemeal basis. Attempts to create sensible new units are hampered by the lack of freedom to impose change on clergy currently in post. Some multi-church benefices are amalgams of several parishes, others have created one parish with several churches.

Many clergy asked to take on increasing numbers of churches testify to increasing stress and workload and reduced overall effectiveness. One vicar took on the incumbency of three churches with a combined average attendance of around 200. After two years he was exhausted and had to conclude it was not possible to attempt evangelism, mission and growth in more than one of his churches at once. He asked his bishop to show him just one multi-church benefice in the diocese where more than one of the churches was growing numerically, but the bishop could not. As Adam and Eve discovered, life is definitely more complicated and restricting after the Fall.

After the Fall ... in numbers

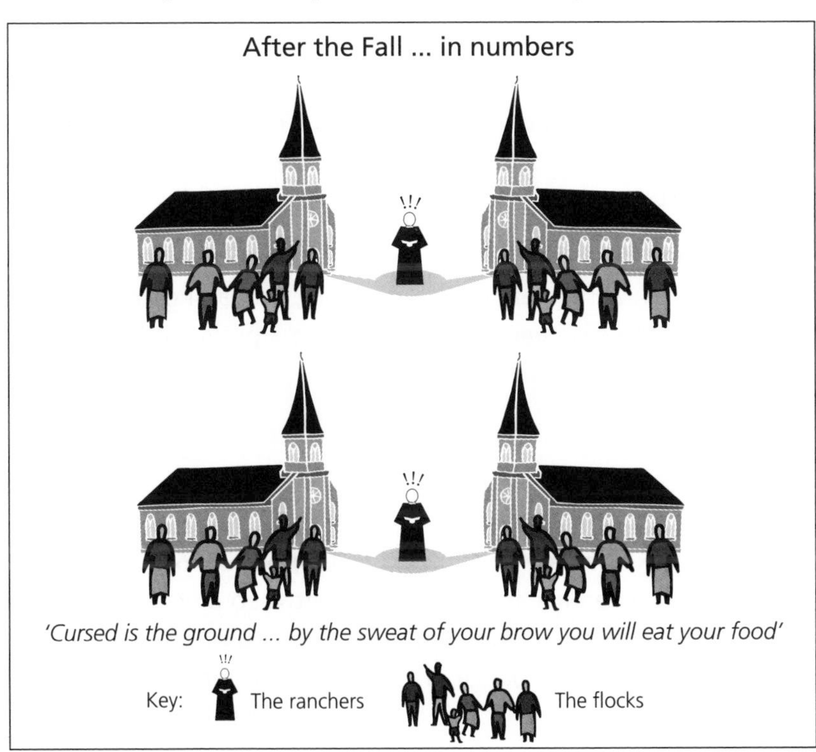

'Cursed is the ground ... by the sweat of your brow you will eat your food'

The 16,000 churches of the Church of England are currently divided roughly as in Table 7.1.

Table 7.1 The range of benefices

In single church benefices	3,700	23%
In two church benefices	3,200	20%
In three church benefices	2,600	16%
In four–six church benefices	4,400	27%
In seven plus church benefices	1,900	12%
Not designated/uncertain	200	1%

If clergy try to sustain the same model of ministry as they take on increasing numbers of churches, and if congregational expectations remain, there will be tears before bedtime. One shepherd may look after one flock, but not several all at once. And if the vicar and team are all elderly then the congregation will tend to be the same. It has long been observed that clergy tend to attract people ten years either side of them in age.

On the other hand, if the clergy find new models of ministry, and churches without their own vicar develop a ministry of all believers, including young ones, then spreading the clergy thinner might actually help churches flourish as healthy communities.

So what has been the impact of amalgamations on numerical growth? Is pluralism part of the problem, spreading malaise and decline as in the eighteenth century, or is it a providential response to falling stipendiary numbers?

Comparing the dioceses

My 2005 book *The Road to Growth* (2005, pp. 125–6)[2] reported no growth trend difference for 1997–2002 between dioceses shedding clergy at different rates. Those cutting clergy numbers quickly were not seeing faster attendance decline. This suggested that amalgamations did not seem to be creating decline. However, when I was an archdeacon from 2004 onwards we began to suspect that the clergy cuts of those years were the easy ones doing little real harm. Recent cuts have been more painful. The one diocese that has not cut clergy numbers, but kept the traditional pattern of almost universal single church benefices, is London – the best growing diocese in the Church of England.

Repeating the earlier exercise for the period 2008 to 2012 does indeed reverse the conclusion – in more recent years the bigger the reduction in clergy numbers in a diocese the bigger the attendance loss. This is shown in the graph below. Dioceses where the number of stipendiary clergy changed between +4 per cent and –3 per cent saw an average 3 per cent fall in attendance; those with a 4 per cent to 7 per cent drop in clergy saw a 4.5 per cent fall in attendance; those with an 8 per cent to 11 per cent drop saw a 6 per cent fall in attendance; and those with a 12 per cent or greater drop in clergy saw an 8 per cent fall in attendance (Figure 7.1).

Figure 7.1 Change in all-age uSa in 2008–12 in groups of dioceses with different falls in clergy numbers

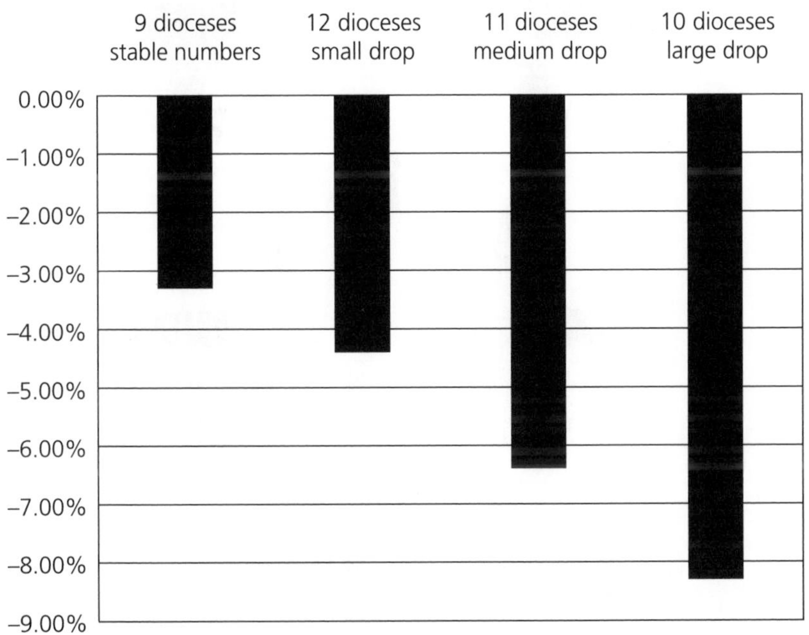

This is no more than common sense and common experience would suggest. There is a decline-cycle that runs 'financial problems – fewer clergy – more amalgamations – smaller congregations – new financial problems – yet fewer clergy – yet more amalgamations – yet smaller congregations', and so on. This cycle is strengthening as the cuts hit larger churches as well as small ones. Amalgamations began as a small rural church issue, then spread to some smaller urban churches but now churches of any size and situation may be involved. Leading five congregations of ten is one thing, leading three of eighty is quite another. Unless this cycle is broken then the project to grow the churches will be hampered by an ever more damaging process of amalgamations until my daughter becomes the stuff of Gladstone's nightmare, the ultimate pluralist, vicar of Yorkshire.

The nightmare vision

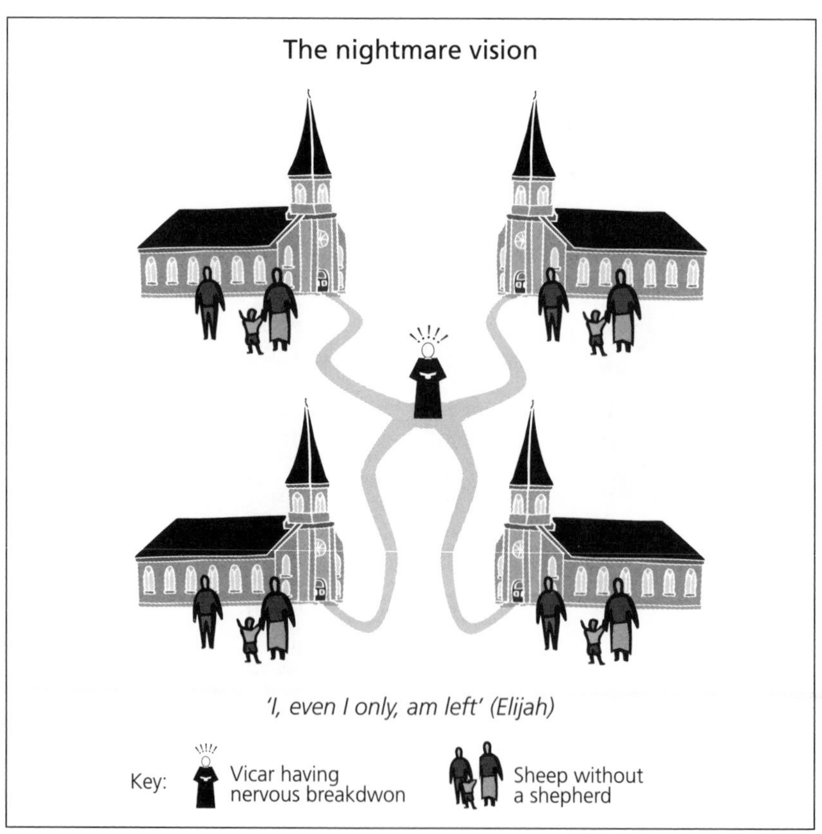

'I, even I only, am left' (Elijah)

Comparing single and multi-church benefices statistically

Although this analysis seems compelling, it is still important to look carefully for evidence to test it out. Clarifying the actual impact of amalgamations on numerical church growth and decline should be a continued preoccupation for statistical research. The evidence so far is that there seems to be no significant attendance-trend difference between single church benefices and multi-church arrangements overall. This was found in a study of 332 benefices in Lichfield Diocese between 2007 and 2012 and in two studies commissioned by the Church Commissioners for their 'Anecdote to Evidence' programme – one from a team (including myself) based at Cranmer Hall, part of St John's College, University of Durham, and one from Fiona Tweedie entitled 'Stronger as one?' These are currently available on Church Growth Research Programme website: www.churchgrowthresearch.org.uk. However, the Lichfield study and Durham team both found that as soon as similarly sized churches were compared with each other then the bigger the amalgamation the worse the attendance trend. Smaller churches are both more likely to be growing than large ones and also more likely to be amalgamated – so the link is masked by the size effect when all churches are simply lumped together. It looks as though clear evidence has been found to link amalgamations with decline within each size category of church but there is still a need for further research to address the key questions:

- *What exactly is the relationship between church size, amalgamation size and attendance trend?* Churches in multi-church benefices are, on average, smaller than those in single church benefices and smaller churches have had a better attendance trend overall in recent years. In the Lichfield study, for example, churches with under 50 adults on Sunday grew 2 per cent between 2007 and 2012 in single church benefices and shrank 7 per cent in multi-church benefices. Are such differences between single and multi-church benefices caused by amalgamations or by something else?

- *Is finding a correlation between amalgamations and decline also evidence of causation?* If the more difficult and demanding churches have been amalgamated then correlation does not demonstrate causation. But if amalgamations happened rather randomly depending on when vacancies came up, and if churches shrink and grow in cycles, then correlation may well be evidence of causation.
- *What is the impact of the often difficult and lengthy vacancy at the time of an amalgamation?* It would be good to disentangle any impact-effect of the amalgamating process from any ongoing effect of living in an amalgamation. But this is tricky because often the legal date of an amalgamation is very different from the actual change on the ground, of which there is usually no record.

In the end, of course, it will not be research findings that dictate the response of dioceses and benefices on the ground but hard-won experience of the joys and problems of different amalgamations and leadership models.

Leadership wisdom

Leadership is key to the growth of churches. Distracted, unfocused, absentee leaders are rarely the best option. If someone is the head teacher of seven schools we would not expect every school to thrive. If you are on a cruise and learn that the captain is actually skipper of seven ships and he is on a different one today, your confidence might begin to wobble as you round Cape Horn. And if you were the captain in question you might feel queasy about being pulled in so many directions at once. This is not criticism of multi-church leaders, who are usually performing heroically in difficult circumstances. But it is criticism of a system that imposes impossible job descriptions with little or no training or support.

Not all amalgamated benefices are shrinking and single ones growing. There are many growing multi-church benefices – the gap is simply in the average growth trend taking several thousand churches together. From a church-growth point of view, there is nothing wrong with a model of church without paid leadership.

The volunteer and lay leaders get on with the business of being leaders and can do very well. Forty years ago I was a deacon at a Baptist church with no minister. The church grew hugely. Forty per cent of the Church of England's fresh expressions of church are being led by unpaid lay people (see Chapter 11) and they are growing well. And there is nothing wrong with a 'paid leadership' model of church either. The problem arises when you stick with the paid-leader model but don't provide one, either because there is a lengthy vacancy or because the paid leader is unable to fulfil the role in any one church because they have too many.

Positives and negatives for growth in multi-church benefices

The Durham team brought together 80 clergy and lay leaders from a range of settings across the country in amalgamated benefices and rector-led teams to discuss their issues. The factors these leaders commonly and persistently cited as leading to numerical growth in their complex multi-church situations are similar to those cited in any situation and that keep cropping up in this book (see the list in relation to cathedrals in Chapter 14). The principles appear to be pretty universal. There is a full list of these factors in the research report but they include a focus on children, young people, families, schools, Messy Church, fresh expressions, congregation-planting, discipleship courses, lay leadership, prayer, clergy presence in the local community, and an outward-facing mindset.

All of these factors are about the strategy, culture and health of the church community itself. Any church in any situation can work towards them. They also cohere with the findings of previous studies of growth factors such as the 'healthy churches' approach of Robert Warren in *The Healthy Churches Handbook* (2012)[3] and the 'change for growth' approach in *The Road to Growth* (Jackson, 2005).[4]

The burden of administration and the difficulty of communication are frequently cited as major encumbrances to church growth in these complex situations with multiple churches to administer. Small, elderly congregations with little remaining energy or leadership are also seen as difficult to grow, with the key being raising up and empowering lay leaders, perhaps to act as a 'focal minister' embodying and encouraging ministry in that locality.

It was widely felt by the clergy and leaders consulted that the more churches in a grouping the less mission the grouping is able to do. One multi-church vicar commented: 'You seem to be spending all your time thinking about PCC agendas or buildings or sorting out arguments – the more churches you've got the more arguments you've got. The focus somehow moves ... it's very easy for the focus to move off helping people grow in their faith and just become about keeping the show on the road.' Many commented on being pulled in too many directions at once – leadership becoming 'like juggling jelly'. Clergy leave services early and arrive late so they are unable to build relationships and meet new people at the key periods before a service starts and after it ends. Managing lots of buildings was found to be particularly draining. Immediate practicalities take precedence over long-term strategy. One incumbent commented: 'Spreading clergy ever more thinly means they focus more on maintenance, conducting communions, baptisms, weddings and funerals, and less time on training and equipping others.'

In my consultancy work with dioceses I increasingly find that lay leaders, clergy and diocesan leaders all believe they are reaching the end of the line with the amalgamations response to falling stipendiary numbers. The Diocese of Lincoln has over 600 churches and in recent years has been reducing its stipendiary numbers from around 200 to 150, with a plan for 100. Seeing the result of this on the ground in terms of stress, decline and abandonment, the new bishop has reversed this and set the diocese an aspiration to grow stipendiary numbers back to 200. There are issues about where these clergy are to come from and how they will be paid, but there has been an immediate effect on morale and expectations as the diocese appears to be moving from managing decline to fighting it.

Turning a problem into an opportunity

The Diocese of St Davids in south-west Wales has about 330 churches and used to have 200 clergy to serve them. It now has just under 100 and that number is likely to fall significantly in the next few years because of the usual four factors. Stipends funding from the central body of the Church in Wales is being reduced and many churches have been shrinking, making it impossible to compensate with higher parish share. These two factors make it likely that the diocese will only be able to afford to pay a reduced number of clergy in the future, perhaps 80, perhaps 60. The age structure of the clergy means that there will be many retirements over the next few years and the number of ordinations is insufficient to keep up with them. These two factors mean that the supply of available clergy will be going down as well. Within a few years there will be one parish clergyperson for about every five churches.

The bishop consulted on the future at deanery meetings with large numbers of church members. The consensus he found was that amalgamating ever more churches into ever larger benefices had reached the end of the road. Far from being the solution, amalgamations were a major part of the problem, rendering the clergy overworked and less effective at the business of mission and growth. Longer vacancies, another symptom of the clergy and money-supply crisis, were also sapping the strength and vitality of the churches. Although there were ever fewer clergy, the church culture was still clergy-centric so the lay leaders felt disempowered in the face of the obvious need, and there were no clear processes for change.

So the bishop began to look for a different strategy involving re-imagining the structure of ministry and leadership in the diocese. The need for such radical rethinking may increasingly become apparent in many dioceses. St Davids is an extreme example of the ratio of churches to clergy but other dioceses are following in its wake. So St Davids may be in the vanguard of change and it will be important to monitor how well it goes. The new strategy now being rolled out will be outlined below. But before we get to that it is important to consider the other possible alternatives to ever expanding benefices served by ever more stretched clergy.

Alternative responses to shrinking clergy numbers

Some responses – such as teams – are only partial answers. Others – such as longer vacancies – only make things worse.

The team

The main solution adopted so far has been for ministry teams (composed of retired clergy, self-supporting clergy, readers and other authorized ministers and team members) to form around multi-church incumbents. Service rotas are prepared and service times adjusted to enable the team to cover the patch. Without such teams

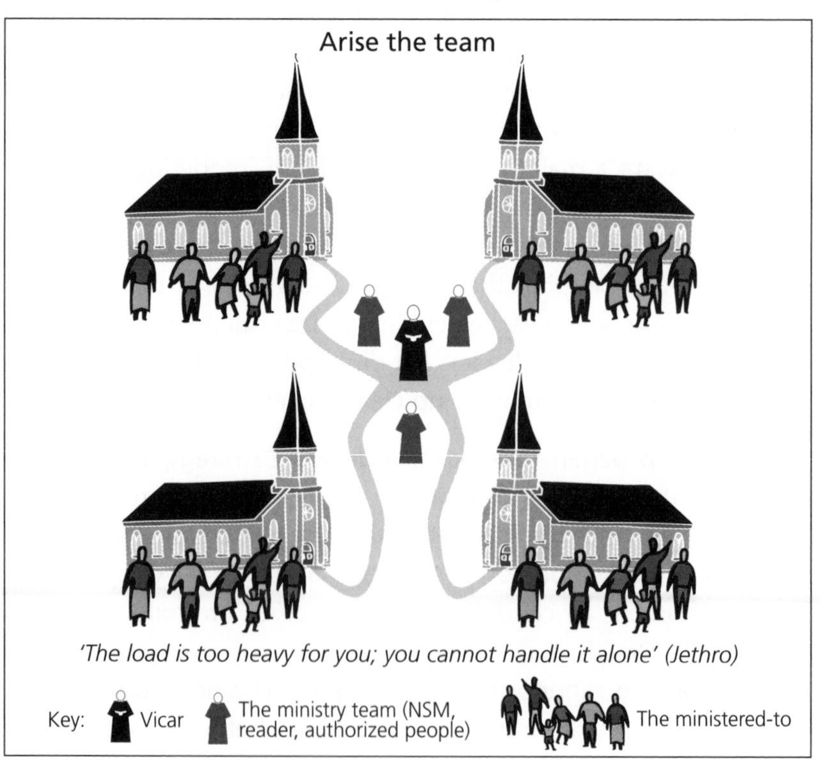

'The load is too heavy for you; you cannot handle it alone' (Jethro)

multi-church benefices would become unworkable. This has long been true in the countryside and is now becoming true in many urban situations as well. But teams also bring their own problems.

The very title 'Ministry Team' divides the churches up between the 'ministers' and the 'ministered-to'. One full-time minister in every place has been replaced by one full-time and several spare-time ministers across the benefice. This is no move to 'every member ministry'. The team can be slaves to 'the rota'. The incumbent tries to get around each church as often as possible while the other team members fill in, plugging the gaps. The result is that no church has continuity of ministry or their own leader around whom they can unite. Pastoral care for those drifting away from church is hard enough when people come to church on average one week in two, but when the leader is also only present one week in two or three it becomes impossible. It is similarly difficult for the leader to spot and get to know newcomers. The team is better than the lone wolf, but it is not the final solution.

Longer vacancies

These have been a part of the response to reduced clergy numbers but all the research suggests that vacancies over six months are associated with rapid loss of congregations (see Chapter 8 and also *Growing through a Vacancy* (Jackson, 2013)).[5] It looks like the average vacancy length is already around eleven months. What is needed is shorter vacancies, not ever longer ones.

Fewer churches

The Roman Catholic Church in Britain has a policy of establishing a small number of large churches, each serving a substantial area. Could that work in the Church of England? It would mean the remaining clergy could each focus on doing a quality job in fewer churches. The parish system of the Church of England means that there are 16,000 churches spread throughout the country. But when churches close, on average rather more than half their remaining members simply cease churchgoing. Their community has gone and they may not have the inclination or ability to go looking for another. The best growing size-group of church in the Church of England is the very smallest, the ones that would be the prime candidates for a closure programme. Why close the growing churches in pursuit of a growth policy? Dioceses would not save money from a closure programme as they don't pay for the upkeep of churches and parish life, only for the stipendiary clergy. Fewer churches and fewer people paying parish share would reduce the number of clergy who could be paid. The process of forcing through closures against unwilling villages and communities would be draining of diocesan time, energy, money and goodwill and would probably fail anyway. So a Beeching Plan for branch-line churches looks like a loser. A few should doubtless close, saving repair bills, maybe removing a burden from those struggling to maintain it, and possibly realizing income from a sale. But, in general, if we want the Church to grow overall, the best way of doing that is to plant new churches and congregations (see Chapter 11). We should be trying to increase the ratio of churches to clergy, not reduce it.

More clergy

If there are too few clergy to go round then it should be possible to find some more. Only around one-third of benefices (and a much smaller proportion of churches) have been sources of ordinands over the last ten years. Most churches are vocationally inert. Surely more could follow the example of those few churches that produce multiple ordinands. Many younger Christians are becoming youth or children's ministers or worship leaders. Around 40 per cent of all the fresh expressions in the Church of England are being led by unpaid lay people. A policy of active recruitment might increase ordinations compared with the traditional policy of waiting for potential volunteers to contact the Church authorities and then screening out the unsuitable. A large influx of young clergy would surely turn a lot of churches around.

This is all true and the Church is now starting to be more proactive in recruiting young clergy. But there are three big limitations: 1. The Church might not be able to pay for a big influx of paid clergy. Not every diocese has as much historic wealth as Lincoln. Budgets are stretched even with projected falls in numbers. More clergy might result in bigger churches, and therefore the capacity to pay for them, but would only happen after a lengthy time lag. It takes months to empty a church when something goes wrong and years to fill it when things go right. 2. It would take a large influx of new clergy even to halt the projected decline in numbers. There were 256 stipendiary ordinations in 2012 and the total number of stipendiary clergy is forecast to go down by about 100 a year. So ordinations would need to rise to about 350 to bring that decline to a halt. 3. It takes about eight years for someone enquiring about ordination to become an incumbent. Moves to increase stipendiary ordinations cannot bear fruit for years to come. However hard the Church tries to reverse the trend, stipendiary numbers will keep going down for the foreseeable future.

However, there are already more clergy than in the past. It is only stipendiary numbers that are going down (Table 7.2).

Table 7.2 Numbers of active clergy

	2002	2012
FT equivalent stipendiaries	9,200	7,900
Self-supporting clergy	2,100	3,200
Active retired clergy	4,500	5,700
Total	15,800	16,800

There are now, perhaps for the first time ever, more active clergy in the Church of England (16,800) than there are churches (15,800). Rather than lament the fall in the number of one type of clergy perhaps we should rejoice in the overall increase and consider how best to deploy such abundance. Of course there are issues with the advanced age of many self-supporting and active retired clergy, but many are probably well able to take responsibility for a church rather than simply fill in the gaps for a hard-pressed incumbent. It is surely time for dioceses to become more organized and strategic in welcoming and deploying the volunteer ministry of the now 53 per cent of the active clergy who are unpaid.

Focal ministers

It may feel as though the Church is trapped between a rock and a hard place. It needs more clergy to lead growing churches but it can't have them. It is forced into the increasingly counterproductive response of amalgamations because the alternatives are limited and worse.

So the future needs re-imagining. The key element is that a diocese with too few paid leaders needs more unpaid ones. The key assumption crying out for reworking is that every church needs a 'paid, ordained incumbent' to be responsible both for the church and the 'cure of souls' in its parish. Other denominations in Britain, and many Anglicans overseas, operate perfectly well without such people. Many of the people setting up and running Church of England fresh expression congregations are not paid, ordained or authorized by a diocese – and they are doing rather well. This is the key element in the 're-imagining' ministry element of the new diocesan strategy in St Davids. The truth is that, for its own health and growth, every church community needs its own designated leader, a focal point for the worshipping, community and ministry life of the church. Such a focal leader should be an ever present integral part of the church community, not an occasional visitor to it. The job of church leadership in the twenty-first century is hard enough. It is much better for the health and growth of leaders, whether paid or unpaid, ordained or not, to ask them to attempt to lead one church at once.

So the new strategy of the Diocese of St Davids is to find and train a 'focal minister' for almost every church in the diocese (a few churches are so small they are best kept together at least in pairs). The focal minister might be ordained or not, paid or not, but they will form the natural core of their own church life and community. The paid clergy will each become the focal minister for one – or at most two – churches and be tasked to lead the mission and growth of that church. Some stipendiary clergy will also become the coordinators of a Ministry Area composed of perhaps ten to twenty churches and focal ministers. These Ministry Areas will replace deaneries. The area coordinator has no incumbency responsibility for the other churches but rather a 'mini-episcope' oversight, caring pastorally for the focal ministers, and coordinating the churches to do the things they can do better together. It is envisaged that new Ministry Areas will have the resources to employ an administrator or premises manager to take on board a lot of practicalities, such as responsibility for the church buildings. This would allow the designated 'ministers' to get on with the job of ministry.

This re-imagining is pictured below.

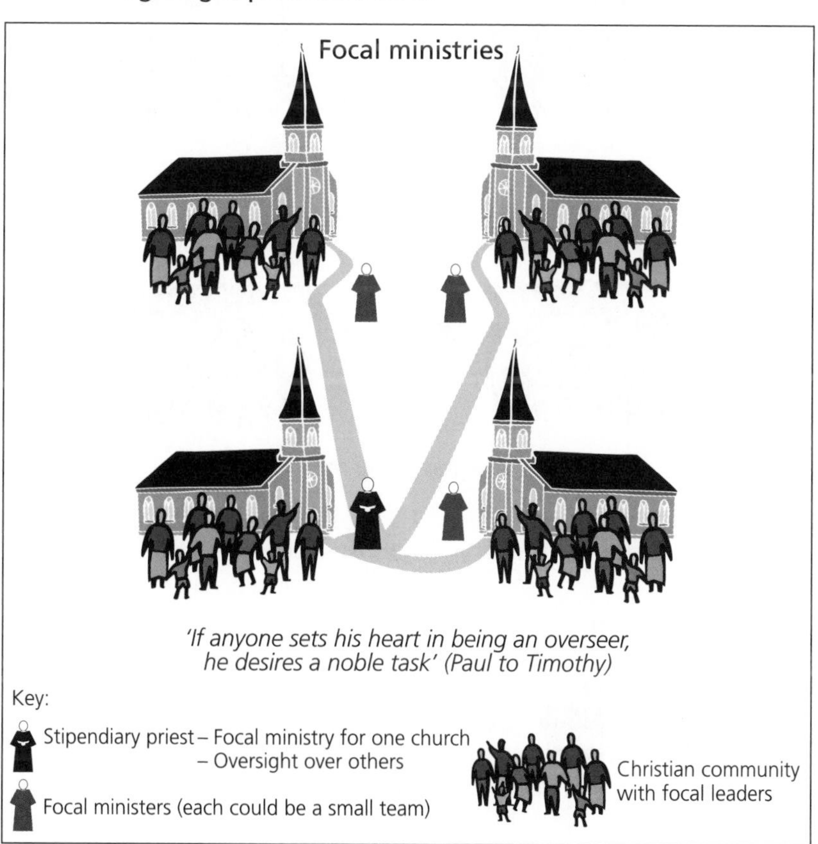

It is not the job of the focal minister to imitate an old-fashioned vicar, doing the ministry to and on behalf of the congregation. The cure of souls is not to be vested in the focal minister but in the whole local church community. The role of the focal minister is to lead the mission of the church and galvanize the ministry of all. Unless the final stage in this process – re-imagining congregations to become missionary communities – becomes a reality then the potential of this restructuring will never be realized.

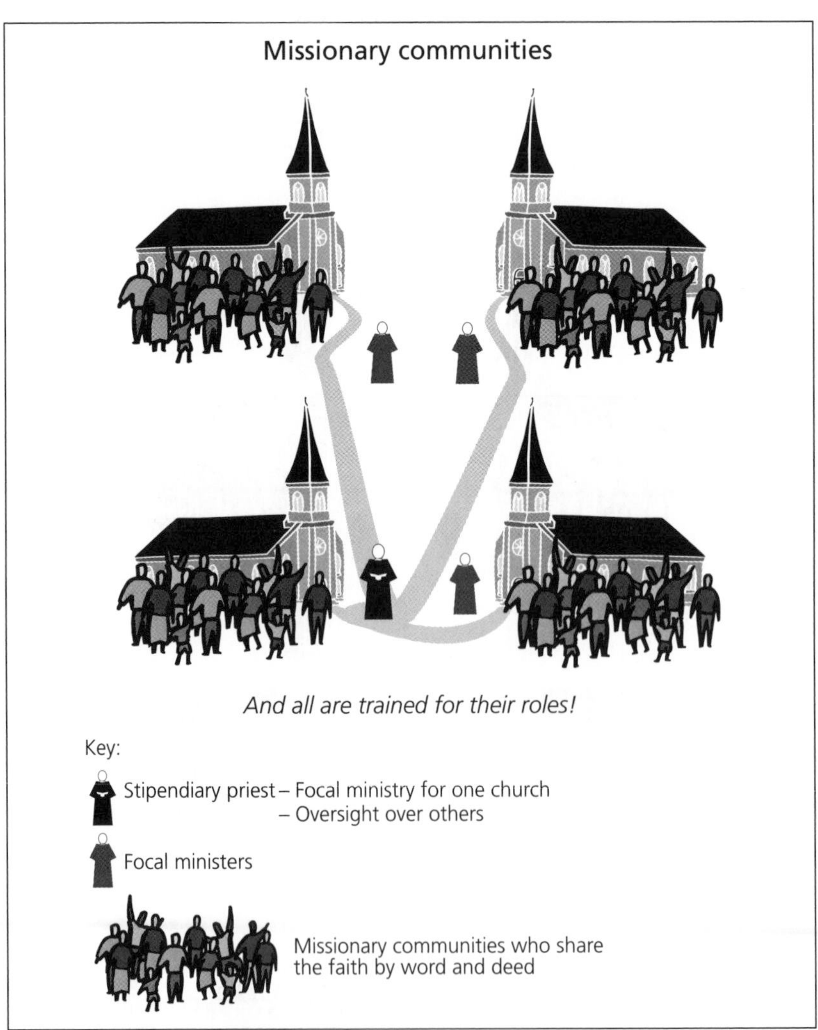

Focal ministers will need training, not to attain a certain ecclesial status, but for the task, whatever their status. Area leaders will also need training for their new role. It is likely that, if this new way of structuring church leadership spreads, the need for this sort of training will become very widespread. But whole church communities also need training for their new self-understanding as missional communities. In St Davids Diocese this is being partly done through focal ministers attending a residential *Leading your Church into Growth* course[6] and then leading their local churches through the companion *Leading your Church into Growth – Local* course.[7]

Threefold ministry training

- **Stipendiary clergy** (and others?) for oversight and focal ministry.
- **Focal ministers** for church community leadership, whatever the hat or title.
- **Everybody** as part of a missionary community sharing the faith by word and deed.
- Much of the training should be *in the parish*.
- Focused on *outward mission* not interior maintenance.

St Davids Diocese is rolling out the new structure one area at a time and monitoring how things go to learn the lessons and make the adjustments over a period of time. But it is also important to look for evidence for the effectiveness of focal ministry arrangements in places where something similar is already happening on the ground. The key elements to look for in a 'focal ministry' church are a single designated leader who only has one church but is part time or spare time in that leadership role, while the official 'incumbent' in practice leaves the designated leader to get on with it without interfering, perhaps because they have their hands full with other churches. House for Duty posts may fulfil these criteria, as might part-time stipendiary clergy. But so too might a 'Reader in Charge' situation and other informal arrangements. These are not exactly focal minister situations as envisaged in St Davids, but they are the closest thing to them.

A trawl through the nearly 600 churches in the Diocese of Lichfield revealed 18 churches in this sort of situation, mostly quite small. Their aggregate adult usual Sunday attendance was 468 in 2007 and 560 in 2011, a growth of 20 per cent in just four years. Thirteen of the 18 shared in the growth. A further enquiry across six dioceses uncovered 24 similar churches. Their combined adult usual Sunday attendance grew from 703 to 811 between 2006 and 2011, a rise of 21 per cent. Eighteen of the churches shared in the growth.

Since 2010 the nine parishes of the Bridgnorth Team Ministry have operated their ministry on a focal minster basis as the best common sense arrangement. Examples include the following.

Case study 1

In 2010 the Revd John Ward was invited to take charge of the small village parishes of Aston Eyre and Monkhopton. The parish of Aston Eyre had a twice-monthly congregation of approximately five people, and the parish of Monkhopton a monthly congregation of two, and a serious problem with the fabric. John insisted he would only take on the latter if regular Sunday services ceased in their present format, and that a new ministry based around festivals and appropriate village events was set up.

Initially in Monkhopton there was concern about whether it was worthwhile keeping the church open. Fabric repairs would cost £127,000 which even with an English Heritage grant of £80,000 represented a major task for a community of 60 people in 10 months. In conjunction with the team rector a series of meetings was arranged, and village events staged to draw the community together, and inspire them with hope in what they could achieve together. The required £47,000 was raised well within the ten months and the works completed. Services now often attract 35–60 people. At the same time the village of Aston Eyre has seen a growth in the regular twice-monthly congregation from five to ten.

Case study 2

In 2009 retired clergyman John Webb was invited to take charge of two parishes, Tasley and Astley Abbotts. Both have a pattern centred around the Prayer Book but, following the retirement of a churchwarden and organist, the PCC of Tasley resolved to try out a monthly family service led by a congregation member. This involves crafts for use during the service, for the half hour before the service time, and refreshments afterwards. On this Sunday the usual number has increased from an average of 20 people to 30, including all ages and supported by the regular members.

We are beginning to see that de facto focal ministry leadership arrangements can transform small churches. Small to medium churches led by part-time focal ministers may be getting the best of both worlds – their own dedicated leader around whom they can coalesce and develop, but not a full-time fully professionalized leader expected to do most of the ministry. So they are getting an ever-present leader plus the ministry of all believers. Amalgamations may be a way of organizing decline and focal ministers of generating growth.

The introduction of focal ministers will not lesson the need for professional full-time clergy. The paid clergy will doubtless continue to be the best leaders for larger churches, some of the best pioneers of new situations, and the best people to offer oversight, coordination and care to groups of churches and focal ministers. The paid clergy will be as important as ever and the skill set needed broader than ever. But the paid clergy will be sharing local community ministry and congregation-planting with a great many other leaders to enable the Church to grow into the future.

8

Training to grow

To the church of God in Corinth, together with all the saints throughout Achaia. (2 Corinthians 1.1)

To Timothy my true son in the faith. (1 Timothy 1.2)

Who is Paul trying to train?

It is true that Paul's training and instruction letters to the individual leaders Timothy and Titus have made their way into the New Testament. However, Paul mostly addresses whole churches, in Rome, Corinth or Ephesus, guiding the development of whole Christian communities. In our own day, leadership training is still important to the growth of the church, but training support for the whole community should still be the main event.

Does training work?

But is it a truth universally acknowledged that Christians in possession of a gospel fortune must be in want of a training course? The survey conducted by David Voas for the 'From anecdote to evidence' research found that churches where the vicar had been on a leadership training course were no more likely to grow than other churches. This, together with a correlation found between personality typing and church growth, may suggest that clergy selection impacts growth prospects more than clergy training does. Chapter 11 will show that many of the fresh expressions now powering new growth are led by lay people who have had no training for the role. Perhaps leaders in mission are born not made.

Although David Voas did not find clear evidence for the effectiveness of training, other research has done so. For example, a detailed examination of the most used national leadership development course, *Leading your Church into Growth,* towards the end of this chapter, does indeed show growth following attendance at the course. Chapter 11 reports that fresh expressions whose leaders had been on a relevant training course are more likely to be growing. We need both to get the right people into leadership positions and to train them well.

Lay vs clergy training

The Church of England has traditionally focused its training on the paid clergy. Clergy selection, ordination training and in-service ministerial training are significant budget items employing highly qualified full-time staff. Training and equipping lay church members has appeared to be a lower priority, with fewer staff and smaller budgets. This imbalance may be less than in the past but it still probably exists.

Underlying this spending and employment pattern is the professional model of Christian ministry. Church ministry and leadership is largely exercised by paid professionals called by God to be priests and ministers. The priest is the primary person in the church who mediates God to the people and the people to God. Indeed, that intermediary function is a definition of priesthood. Along with the bishop, it is the priest who possesses the cure of souls of the parish. 'The minister' conducts the ministry of the church while the congregation and the local population are the largely passive recipients of that ministry. So the work, life, mission, ministry and growth of the churches is largely in the hands of the professional clergy. It is, therefore, logical to resource their selection and training. Just as hospitals spend large amounts of money training doctors and nurses, but very little training patients, so the Church trains its clergy but not its laity.

Simply describing the training policy emanating from clergy-centric ecclesiology is almost enough to bury it. But it may be worth knocking a few extra nails into the coffin lid.

First, lay people are not the patients of spiritual doctors. They are not the clients of the Church, they are the Church. The New Testament knows nothing of a priestly caste doing the work of the church on its behalf, only a church that is a kingdom of priests. Peter says to the Christian community, 'you are a chosen people, a royal priesthood, a holy nation, a people belonging to God, that you may declare the praises of him who called you out of darkness into his wonderful light' (1 Peter 2.9). In Revelation the elders and living creatures sing to Jesus: 'with your blood you purchased men for God from every tribe and language and people and nation. You have made them to be a kingdom and priests to serve our God, and they will reign on the earth' (Revelation 5.9,10). To serve, praise and witness to Christ, standing like priests between God and humanity, is meant to be the role and status of the entire holy nation of Christians not just an ordained few.

Those with an ontological view of the priestly ministry of the ordained hold this largely in connection with eucharistic presidency rather than ministry monopoly. The Roman Catholic Church has gone further than many denominations in developing lay ministry as the number of priests has continued to decline. In the Anglican Church, large numbers of self-supporting clergy are not ordained to conduct its ministry on behalf of others, but to sustain its eucharistic life so that the church can continue to minister.

The number of paid clergy in the Church of England continues to go down. Any denomination trusting in the personal ministries of the paid clergy for the growth of the churches is bound to be disappointed in the face of declining numbers. But the number of lay church members and employees may now be rising. Churches are not suffering a new shortage of human resources. It is the category-mix that is changing so that all the eggs can no longer be put in the clergy basket. We need to focus on training and supporting, not just the diminishing numbers of paid clergy, but the whole people of God.

Appointing full-time paid clergy as church planters is always a high-cost option and often an ineffective one. At most a diocese can only afford a few posts of this nature. Many new congregations and fresh expressions are being planted by teams of lay people from local churches, usually unpaid and often untrained. Without trying to control people or quench the Holy Spirit, dioceses should focus on support and training for these lay teams already delivering the church growth goods.

Training to equip for mission rather than ecclesiastical promotion

It was reported in *The Road to Growth* (Jackson, 2005, pp. 141ff.)[1] that schemes for training and authorizing lay people in 'ministry teams' to take on some of the work of ministry from ever more thinly spread clergy were failing to deliver the church-growth goods. A few individuals are selected, taken out of their current ministries, trained under a diocesan scheme for several years, then reinserted into parish life in new roles with impressive labels. The work of ministry has been moved from the minister to the ministry team. The rest of the church members, instead of being helped to take responsibility collectively, remain the passive recipients of the ministrations of the trained elite. Such a training model may be needed for some functions but it too easily disempowers rather than equips the whole church for its work of mission and ministry.

A common complaint about diocesan training programmes is that they are sledgehammers to crack nuts. Local church members primarily want some low-key help to be more effective in the ministries and roles they already have as Christians in the world and as members of their local churches. Instead, what is offered is a bells and whistles semi-academic course leading to a qualification or status. The outcome is not enhanced ability to pursue their own calling, but a higher ecclesial status and a different role.

The training most likely to equip churches to flourish and grow is not primarily about moving individuals up the ecclesiastical pecking order. It is about equipping the whole people of God to be more effective missional communities. This truth is increasingly being acknowledged and reflected in the processes and courses being made available to churches today for their growth and flourishing.

Training to help churches make the most of MAPs

Chapter 6 describes how dioceses are asking churches to develop, implement and update MAPs. MAPs should be written by the whole community through an open process rather than behind closed doors by a vicar or a couple of wardens. Then they will be owned and implemented on the ground, not just treated as a piece of paper to keep the bishop quiet. The MAP is corporate rather than personally identified with a vicar or other leader and so will survive their moving on. If the production of the MAP involves the whole community then so will its implementation. So here is a lever for growing the church as a missional community and Chapter 6 shows there is evidence that it is effective.

In many dioceses there are, however, two major restrictions on the effectiveness of MAPs. Initial and ongoing training and support for developing good MAPs tends to be thin and patchy and there are few people and resources on the ground to accompany churches on their MAP journey. Experience suggests that an external partner monitoring progress and acting as a catalyst for new ideas is an important part of the process. Many dioceses have not prioritized the financial resources needed to make this happen so initial plans stall, enthusiasm evaporates, other priorities take over and MAPs get forgotten or categorized as yet another diocesan initiative that didn't work.

A diocese working to stimulate growth through MAPs should make all its interventions in parish life through the MAP process. Churches can do without a multiplicity of confusing diocesan initiatives. A diocese should offer or advertise a range of whole-church training programmes covering the range of things parish MAPs want to accomplish. So far such joined-up thinking is not exactly universal.

The usual problem is that, although the public strategy matches the new priority to provoke the flourishing of missional communities, the diocesan budget does not. The budget is still largely being spent, without significant debate, on clergy stipends and support so that little can be spared to be spent on the flourishing of missional church communities through the MAP process. The diocese through its budget still looks like an organization for employing clergy rather than supporting churches. Churches are indeed supported through employing clergy, but that is not the only way. We need to disentangle the means from the end – employing clergy is one of a range of means, not the end in itself. The ultimate end has to do with raising up Christian disciples, sharing the good news of Jesus Christ and growing the kingdom of heaven. Budgets should serve these ends and not be trapped by one delivery mechanism however honourable and effective.

Training for the new sorts of leaders

The new growth in both lay-led fresh expressions (Chapter 11) and local churches led by focal ministers (Chapter 7) is creating a large new group of people who are the main leader of a church or congregation but who are not being paid, may not be ordained, and may have received little or no training for the role. The research in ten dioceses reported in Chapter 11 found over 200 unpaid lay leaders of fresh expressions with numbers rising all the time. Nationally in the Church of England, in 2014, it is reasonable to suppose there are at least 1,000. The Diocese of Leicester is aiming to plant one new lay-led fresh expression for every parish church over the next few years.

The Diocese of St Davids is looking to a future of 300 churches with perhaps two-thirds led by an unpaid or part-time focal minister – that is up to 200 in one small diocese in the Church in Wales. The Church of England has around 16,000 churches and 7,800 paid parish clergy. If, in the extreme case, each of the clergy were in future to lead only one church then there would need to be 9,000 new-style focal ministers covering the rest. Any training institution spotting this future trend would do well to develop training programmes to help and support these two new armies of church leaders. The training should not be geared at raising ecclesial status but at equipping people for the role they already have or are about to take on. Such training should not be hijacked as an instrument of control ('Nobody can be a church or congregation-leader in this diocese unless they have got the relevant diocesan certificate'), but should be an instrument to support growing leaders of growing churches. Rather than every diocese developing its own course it would be better if a small range of national courses were developed which every diocese or individual church could buy into.

Training whole communities

This chapter is not a plea for shifting resources away from clergy training into lay training but for treating church communities holistically, encouraging lay and ordained, leaders and pew fillers to train together. The most effective evangelist is probably not an individual but a Christian community. The commonest route into faith today is that first people belong to the Christian community, then they start to believe its message, then they start to behave as Christians in their daily lives. The key to evangelistic success, therefore, is having Christian communities that are relevant, attractive and easy to join, which are then found to live and breathe their shared faith.

The first question people have about the Christian faith is rarely 'Is it true?' ('Did the resurrection actually happen?') It is more likely to be 'Does it work?' ('Does it transform people's lives?') or 'How does it feel?' ('Does it feel good to be part of this?' 'Is it authentic?' 'Life-enriching?') The truth question is answered by the arguments of the experts, the work question by the testimonies of the people, the feel question by the quality of the church community. The ministry of the vicar may help unlock that quality but the vicar may be helpless without it.

That is why church training should be a single function, with programmes integrated with each other. There will always be some training elements just for clergy but the most effective training for the future flourishing of the church is likely to be offered in situ to the whole church community. There is a growing body of whole-church courses and processes beginning to prove their worth for growing the churches. This is where I focus my own effort with courses such as *Everybody Welcome,*[2] *Growing through a Vacancy*[3] and *Leading your Church into Growth – Local.*[4]

Growing through a vacancy

Church growth is 50 per cent about helping new people join and 50 per cent about stopping existing members leaving. The main point at which Anglican churches have been losing people in recent decades has been during lengthy vacancies of six months or more between vicars. The handbook *Growing through a Vacancy* (Jackson, 2013)[5] reports the same finding as previous research – the longer the vacancy the more the church shrinks. The graph below shows attendance change up to a point at least a year after the end of the vacancy – so this is not just a temporary blip, much of the average loss during a vacancy is permanent. In fact the size of the average vacancy loss is such that it would seem that vacancies are the occasion of most of the Church of England's recent attendance loss. Churches with vicars in place have on average been steady or even growing – the damage is being done in vacancies.

Figure 8.1 Attendance change from the year before a vacancy to a year after it ends by length of vacancy

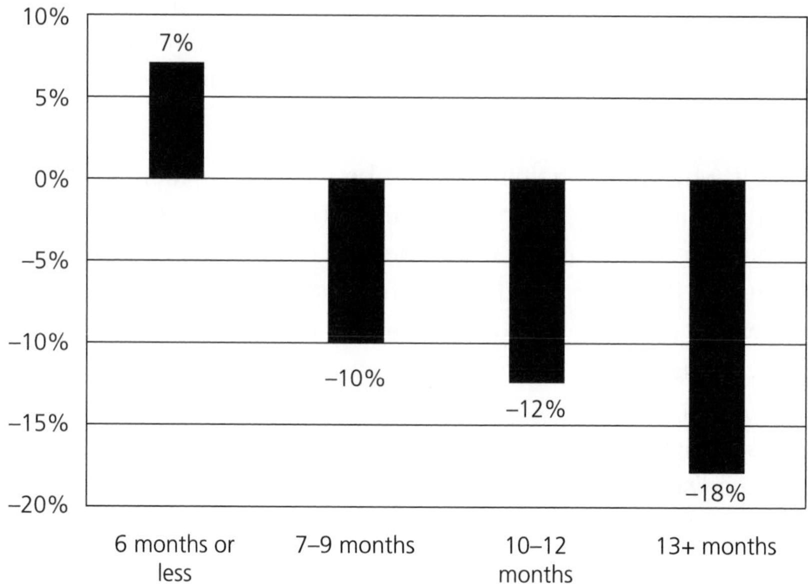

Through extended interviews with people who had recently led 40 different churches through a vacancy, the research team uncovered both the reasons why churches shrink in lengthy vacancies and the measures that can be taken to combat this.

The handbook is designed to be used by PCC members as a way of training churches in how to have a good vacancy missionally, however long it lasts. Some of the training lessons apply to clergy, especially in relation to the preparation they should make prior to their own departure. But mostly the training is for lay leaders and the whole church community as they are the ones who are left when the vicar leaves.

Leading your Church into Growth (LyCiG)

This residential training course was developed around 1994 by a group of clergy concerned at the lack of church-growth training available to clergy, and their consequent lack of expertise. A four-day residential training course was offered about twice a year for individual clergy to sign up to. After a few years, dioceses began to ask for extra courses just for their own clergy. Then the courses began to be opened up to lay leaders along with their clergy. They covered key areas for the growth of the churches, with sessions on vision in a secular society, being a positive leader, developing a missional culture, balanced strategies for mission, developing a culture of invitation and welcome, different sorts of evangelistic activities, missionary worship, and the church as an attractive, loving community.

The residential courses attempt not just to cover technical knowledge but also to give participants a good, renewing experience so that they return home refreshed and reinvigorated for mission and ministry.

Follow-up days and activities have been organized to help clergy apply the lessons learned at the residential course to parish life.

In recent years, with the addition of the diocesan courses, several hundred clergy and other leaders have been attending LyCiG courses every year. Research suggests that churches led by clergy who have been on the course do indeed, on average, experience new growth. The Diocese of Blackburn found that attendance rose in churches whose clergy had attended a course in the three subsequent years. But then the impact seemed to disappear, partly because many clergy had by then moved to another parish. In order to try and embed the lessons in local churches, not just in clergy, the course has been increasingly opened up to church teams in the hope that the impact on church life might be wider and longer term.

In 2014 the LyCiG team surveyed 256 lay and ordained church leaders who had attended a residential course between 2008 and

2013. They were asked to categorize the overall attendance trend in their church or churches in the period leading up to the conference and then after it (Table 8.1 and Figure 8.2).

Table 8.1 Church attendance before and after LyCiG

	Before LyCiG	After LyCiG
Shrank a lot	10	1
Shrank a little	48	5
About the same	84	100
Grew a little	110	134
Grew a lot	4	16

Figure 8.2 Numbers of churches growing and shrinking before and after their leader(s) attended LyCiG

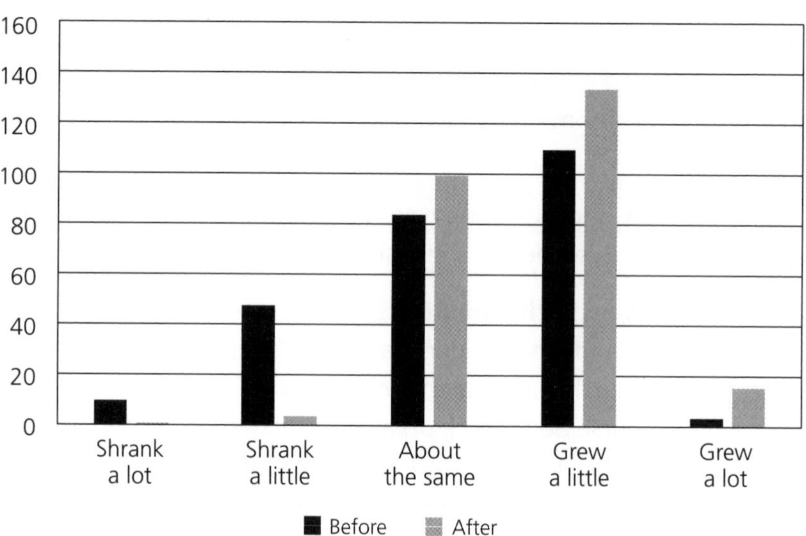

The most striking finding was that the number of shrinking churches came down from 58 to just 6. After their leaders attended a LyCiG course 150 churches were growing numerically and only 6 were shrinking.

Respondents were also asked how effective on a scale of 0 to 10 the LyCiG conference was at impacting the mission of the parish (Table 8.2).

Table 8.2 The effectiveness of LyCiG on the mission of the parish

0	7 responses
1	10
2	8
3	14
4	25
5	55
6	39
7	40
8	39
9	15
10	4

The large numbers indicating an impact of five or more reinforces the conclusion that this training course is highly effective at motivating and equipping church leaders to lead their churches into growth.

However, there still remains the problem of only a few from any one church attending the course and the likelihood of the impact wearing away over time. So the LyCiG team produced a new version of the course in 2014 called *Leading your Church in Growth – Local* to be delivered in situ in a local church with as many members as possible taking part. At the same time, the residential course has been rewritten with the same headings and structure as the local course. So now clergy and other leaders can attend a residential course and benefit from that themselves, but also be equipped to lead the LyCiG Local course when they get back home. This is delivered with the help of course manuals and a DVD with much of the teaching on it.

In this way the intention is to put church-growth teaching and inspiration into the very bloodstream of the local church. It should stimulate, teach, equip and motivate many church members to play their part in leading their church into growth for years to come. Clergy and lay training are integrated together into a whole-church training programme.

LyCiG – Local is too recent an innovation to have been monitored for impact just yet, but the signs are promising and a number of dioceses are taking it up. It is the whole community that needs to grow so it is the whole community that needs to train, and this is a way of doing it.

9

Inviting to grow

> Philip found Nathaniel and told him, 'We have found the one ... Jesus of Nazareth' ... 'Nazareth! Can anything good come from there?' Nathaniel asked. 'Come and see,' said Philip. (John 1.45–46)

Foolishness to Greeks?

Philip's invitation to the sceptical and prejudiced echoes down the centuries – 'come and see'. Abstract talk about a bloke from the equivalent of Rotherham who turned out to be the Son of God, did miracles, taught us how to live, died the death we were heading for because of our sin, rose from the dead and now reigns in heaven with his Father, can initially sound like a tall story today. But an invitation to an unsatisfied lonely, secular consumer to 'come and see' the community of Jesus Christ, feel its warmth, discover the reality of answered prayer and experience God personally can be accessible and attractive. The rest of the theology can follow on later.

The inviting Trinity

One way to explain the love of God for humans is through exploring his invitation to join his Trinitarian community, his welcome into his kingdom and his integration of us into his community of heaven. This invitation, welcome and integration is the very substance of Jesus' good news.

God did not create the human race because he was lonely, like a widow who acquires a dog for company. Father, Son and Holy Spirit already form a perfect community of love. But it is not a closed community. Exclusive and excluding love is not really love at all. Rublev's famous icon of the Trinity has them in an open semicircle around eucharistic bread and wine beckoning us in to join the group. There is a terrible danger that we will spoil the perfect community by our presence, but we are still invited. The eagerness of the prodigal's father in Luke 15 to bring him back into the family expresses God's urgent, unconditional invitation into his kingdom even if we don't deserve it and will cause trouble.

God's open, invitational nature must continue to be reflected in his community as it grows from the original three to include the Bride of Christ. Otherwise the bride will have rejected the very nature of the family she married into. There should be no nimbys in the churches – 'I've got my heavenly mansion sorted so let's keep the others out before heaven gets too crowded.' If we fail to welcome others into the wonderful new kingdom we ourselves have been invited into we may even lose our own places. When Jesus explains the differences between the sheep and the goats in Matthew 25 he says to the blessed of his Father, 'take your inheritance ... for ... I was a stranger and you invited me in'. The righteous answer, 'Lord, ... when did we see you a stranger and invite you in?' and the King replies, 'I tell you the truth, whatever you did for one of the least of these brothers of mine, you did for me' (25.34,35,40).

And so the Christian Church must embody Jesus' revolution of radical inclusivity and hardcore hospitality. 'There is neither Jew nor Greek, slave nor free, male nor female, for you are all one in Christ Jesus' (Galatians 3.28). This welcoming, including, integrating community must offer everyone a new status: 'You are no longer foreigners and aliens, but fellow-citizens with God's people and members of God's household, built on the foundation of the apostles and prophets, with Christ Jesus himself as the chief cornerstone. In him the whole building is joined together and rises to become a holy temple in the Lord. And in him you too are being built together to become a dwelling in which God lives by his Spirit' (Ephesians 2.19–22).

The inviting church

So there is an irresistible urgency laid upon members of the Christian Church to say, like Philip, 'come and see'. This is not an option for enthusiasts but an obligation for all. Yet a recent survey of 4,500 Anglicans sponsored by the *Church Times* found that only a quarter habitually invite people to their church. Frankly, I was surprised it was as many as a quarter, but nevertheless most of us do not have the invitation habit.

Last season my village cricket team was short of players and we nearly folded. We advertised for players and got zero response. Then I went round a few people I knew and invited them to play for the team. Every one of them said, 'Yes, thank you for inviting me.' And now we have a team again. It may be a mix of the inexperienced and veterans like me playing from memory, but a team we are again.

Inviting clergy

Paul Clarke was curate at St Mary, Haughley in St Edmundsbury and Ipswich Diocese. The church was launching a new teatime service for families so Paul suggested an experiment to his vicar. 'While there are two of us with a bit of diary slack could I spend two weeks doing nothing else but visit our baptism contacts from the past few years?' They put together contact details of families that had come at Christmas, plus baptism families and wedding couples – a total of 60 addresses. They did some nice invitation cards for Paul to take round and deliver in person. Sometimes Paul had to make a repeat visit in the evening to find someone in, but he made contact with most of the families that had not moved away. Usually he spent a few minutes on the doorstep saying hello, giving the invite and letting them know the church had not forgotten them. A few families invited him in for a cup of tea and a longer chat, but he was just able to get round everyone in the fortnight. He encountered no hostility, but a lot of warmth from people pleased to be remembered and invited. Key to this was the fact that this was not embarrassing cold-calling – known contacts were being invited to a church service using a visit and an invitation card.

Half the families turned up at the new service (which had an attendance of 70 in its first week) and a year later half of them are still attending church regularly, at least monthly. Two weeks of visiting for the new service had yielded 15 new families – probably the best church-growth initiative that church had ever known.

The parable of the sower and the seed teaches us not to expect everyone in whom a seed is sown to become fruitful disciples, but it does teach us to expect some. Jesus' good soil is one category among four. So perhaps a quarter of the invitees becoming church members is about what we should expect.

I now realize that my own most productive individual initiative for church growth during two decades as a vicar was visiting every one of the hundred people referred to me following Billy Graham's Mission England in Sheffield in 1985. Without my follow-up visit I doubt whether any of them would have joined the church but, following the visit, about a quarter of them did so.

Many clergy feel they never have time for visiting warm contacts and helping them take the next step in discovering their Saviour Jesus Christ. But what exactly is it that is so much more important than this?

An inviting congregation

The research by David Voas, 'From anecdote to evidence', found a correlation between the willingness of a congregation to invite and welcome newcomers and the growth of the church: 'The most direct route to growth comes from members inviting and welcoming family, friends and acquaintances.'

This is not a new or surprising observation. It is the premise of Back to Church Sunday and of the training materials *Everybody Welcome*

(Jackson and Fisher, 2009, everybodywelcome.org.uk).[1] Churches grow when the members invite others to join them. Many people today view churches as private clubs – they need to be invited before they can come along. A question in a telephone survey sponsored by Tearfund found there were around 3 million people in Britain open to churchgoing if only someone would invite them. But, so far, nobody ever has. Three million is only 5 per cent of the population, but finding and inviting them would make a huge difference to church attendance in Britain.

The Diocese of Lichfield made a concerted effort one year to make the most of Back to Church Sunday and about 4,000 new people came as invited guests on the day. Six months later only about 12 per cent of them were still coming, though even that was several hundred people. One reason why more did not stick was that Back to Church Sunday was treated like a church open day; 'Come and see what we do.' The church member was pleased that their friend had come on the day but did not think of inviting them again – now it was up to them. But many people need several invites before they feel confident about coming by themselves. So we need not just an annual opportunity but an all-year culture of invitation – which is what Back to Church Sunday is designed to foster.

Electronic invitation

The business of preparing attractive invitation leaflets and pushing them through every letterbox in the parish is expensive and time-consuming. It may still be worth doing, but usually, today, only at Christmas.

However, new electronic media offer far cheaper and quicker alternatives. The key is for clergy and leaders routinely to ask for appropriate contact details from people they meet – mobile number, email address or Facebook contact. A group text or email can reach large numbers of people in a way that still feels personal. 'It's Messy Church this Saturday, 4 at the hall. Should be great – hope to see you and your family there, love Lucy.' Some clergy and churches feel out of their depth in setting such a system up but there are plenty of companies to do it for them. And most churches will know a teenage geek who could act on their behalf.

One diocese surveyed all its individual church websites and found that half failed to mention their own service times. A church that doesn't invite people to its services even when they are checking out its website would seem to have given up. Warm, inviting, professional-looking websites are no substitute for personal contacts, but may well attract a trickle of church-seekers.

Why are we poor at invitation?

I belong to a tennis club and am very grateful to my friend Mike Chadwick who invited me along a few years ago. In fact I'm doubly grateful to Mike because he ran the Bible class at which I became a Christian 50 years ago. His invitations have shaped my life. However, I am very English. I enjoy going along to play tennis each week, but I have never even thought about inviting anyone else. There is something in our culture, in my psyche as well as perhaps in yours, that makes inviting such a difficult proposition.

Michael Harvey in his book *Unlocking the Growth* (2012)[2] lists the reasons people have given him, as he toured the country promoting Back to Church Sunday, for not inviting friends and family to church:

1. I suffer in my church services and so would others.
2. Our services are unpredictable – I don't really trust them.
3. Our church is boring – it would put my friend off.
4. My friend would not want to go.
5. I don't want to be rejected.
6. We have no non-churchgoing friends.
7. It's the leader's job to fill the church, not mine.
8. My friend said 'no' when I asked them last year.
9. It might damage my friendship.

10. The congregation will think my friend is not 'our' type of person.
11. My friends are not the right type of people for my church.
12. The church is pretty full already – where would they sit?
13. I'm shy so I would find it difficult.
14. Faith is a private thing.
15. I don't want to be seen as strange, a Bible-basher.
16. I wouldn't know what to say – they might ask me difficult theological questions.
17. They might ask me why I go to church.

Church leaders have additional reasons for avoiding the invitation issue:

1. The last 'Invitation Sunday' was a flop – our people are dreadful at it.
2. 'Invitation Sunday' is not our preferred medium for mission.
3. I'm doing my best, don't heap guilt on me for not doing one of an impossibly long list of good things to do.
4. We see new people every week anyway.
5. I am just too busy with other priorities.
6. Our people are tired of inviting once a year.
7. We live in a secular, post-Christian society and people don't respond to invites.
8. Traditional church is not relevant to most people – we have to incarnate fresh expressions rather than invite people to our existing culturally inappropriate services.
9. New people might come but the congregation will put them off. I can't change the culture of the church – I've given up trying.
10. The congregation is too old, the church is a care-home annex and younger people will never join.
11. I'm discouraged and don't really believe anything will work, decline is inevitable and my job is to organize it humanely.

This is a potent cocktail of self-fulfilling excuses, anxieties and defeatism.

What can we do about it?

We know that if we invite enough people to come to church with us, some will come and some will probably meet the living God and stay. But the bundle of anxieties and inadequacies that makes up the average churchgoer, plus the extra issues weighing down many church leaders, usually stop us doing the inviting. Yet invitation stripped of its fears and phobias is a remarkably simple way to introduce people to Christ and his church. We have to encourage a church in which it is normal to say: 'Come and see.'

Archbishop Justin said at a recent conference that there is no reason why the Church of England can't double in size providing its culture changes and evangelism becomes the priority. At a local level the key is that 'Every Christian should routinely invite people to their church, should be informed and confident in their faith, and should be capable of witnessing to it.' How can we move from the reality encountered by Michael Harvey to the vision of Christians routinely inviting people to church held out by Archbishop Justin? Michael Harvey suggests twelve steps:

1. *Vision* – that we can invite, that some will come and some of these will stay.
2. *Modelling* – leaders need to lead by example and invite someone themselves.
3. *Cascading* – every individual in the church should be approached one to one and invited to invite someone.
4. *Friendship* – all church members should be encouraged to have solid friendships of mutual trust that make invitations easy.
5. *Story* – existing church members should be asked to tell their stories of being invited to church.
6. *God's preparation* – consider who you know whom God might be preparing for an invitation.
7. *Practise* – saying the words: 'Would you like to come to church with me?' They get easier to say the more often you say them, first to the mirror then to friends and family.

8. *Prayer* – mobilize the prayers of the congregation for the success of invitation.
9. *Invite* – don't get lost in a quagmire of anxieties, just invite someone; success is an invitation made.
10. *Accompany* – don't tell people they can go to church if they want to, offer to bring them and look after them.
11. *Introduce* – people to your friends and other members of the church family.
12. *Assume* – that they will come again and invite them to church and Sunday lunch next week as well, and the week after that.

It may also be important to attend to the standard of the worship in order to give congregation members greater confidence for invitation. Waiting for church to improve before we dare invite anyone, though, might last us a lifetime.

David Voas makes an interesting point: 'Inviting friends to church does not come easily to most English people, which is partly why it is helpful to have non-threatening half way house events like carol services as a draw. A corollary of the social difficulty of extending invitations is the reluctance to refuse them. Ours is a culture in which asking is a powerful act: it is hard to do but correspondingly hard to decline' ('From anecdote to evidence' report, p. 40).[3]

A warm invitation from a trusted friend can therefore become an irresistible force for good in the life of a person fortunate enough to be invited into the community of God's love.

Welcome

It is dauntingly difficult to join a church. It is hard to join any new human community and many churches are very poor at welcoming the stranger. The sidesman who never smiles, the warden who stops you sitting in Mrs Jones' pew, the congregation who just ignore you, the person who tuts at your children's chatter, and the vicar who loses you in the holy mysteries all conspire to make church an experience you will not be repeating any time soon.

Of course it is not always like this. One reason why the Church of England is arresting its numerical decline is that many churches have got better at welcome. How to do this is laid out in the training course *Everybody Welcome* (Jackson and Fisher, 2009).[4] Churches completing the course have shown that it is possible to increase the retention rate of people trying them out from the national average of 10–15 per cent up to somewhere around 65 per cent. Almost every church in the land would be growing if it achieved a 65 per cent retention rate.

Everybody Welcome is a four-session course for the whole church community, covering every major aspect of the business of welcoming and integrating newcomers into the body of Christ. It deals with the ways in which people find out about and meet the church, with the physicalities of the plant and buildings, with the human welcome and with the longer-term business of integrating people into church life. Someone has only been fully welcomed into the church when they feel like a host rather than a guest in the church community. And the course deals with the setting up of a Welcome Team to take responsibility for ensuring good welcome happens throughout the life of the church.

I find it tempting at this point to repeat the material in the course, but I will confine myself to urging you to check it out (www.everybodywelcome.org.uk). Improving the retention rate of people trying us out is the most productive church growth move most churches can make. So please don't rush off into other chapters before considering its potential impact on your own church. What I will do, though, is tell you a story ...

A welcoming church

St Alphege Seasalter on the north Kent coast had grown from small beginnings and recently acquired brand new church premises. They invited me down to spend a day talking, thinking and praying about the future. I suggested they do three things: 1. take the congregation through the *Everybody Welcome* course; 2. set up a Welcome Team; and 3. write a collect. The collect was to ask God to send them new people and promise God that, when he did so, they would welcome them in his name. I don't always have this effect on churches, but they quickly did all three. They even ran three parallel courses on different days of the week so that nobody could use standard excuse number 1 – 'I'd love to do the course, vicar, but I am afraid I am busy on Tuesday evenings.' They put their collect on bookmarks, asked every member of the congregation to pray it daily, and made it part of the public intercessions at every service:

> God our Father, you grow your church as we proclaim the kingdom of your Son. Increase in number your church at Seasalter as you deepen us as followers and learners of Christ, in the power of your Spirit to the glory of Jesus Christ our Lord. Amen.

I'm not sure copying works, so, if your church wants to pray regularly for new people, you should write your own. Here is another collect that people use as they go through the *Everybody Welcome* course:

> Heavenly Father, you have welcomed us into your kingdom and your heart's desire is to draw every human being to yourself. Grant us clear eyes to see people as you see them, sensitive feet to stand in their shoes, and warm smiles to welcome them in your name. Give us such generous hearts that our church becomes a foretaste of heaven where every soul you send us finds their loving home in the community of your Son our Saviour Jesus Christ, Amen.

And here is the collect from the *Leading your Church into Growth – Local* course:

> God of mission, who alone brings growth to your Church, send your Holy Spirit to give vision to our planning, wisdom to our actions, and power to our witness. Help our church to grow in numbers, in spiritual commitment to you, and in service to our local community, through Jesus Christ our Lord. Amen.

I'm an enthusiast for church growth by collect!

The role of the Welcome Team is to obtain contact details the first time someone comes (otherwise it may be the last!), to introduce newcomers to other congregation members, and during the subsequent week to deliver a high-quality 'Welcome to St Alphege' booklet to their home. The booklet is updated every three months with coming events. One team member has the job of entering contact details and progress indicators on a colour-coded spreadsheet.

Every two months the Welcome Team hold a 'welcome' Sunday lunch on church premises. All newcomers are invited along with a matching group of church members, perhaps families with similar ages of children. Also present are a few church leaders to talk about the church and answer questions. Every newcomer is then invited to join a small group.

Meanwhile, the checklist survey from the course was analysed. This highlighted strengths and weaknesses and enabled the PCC to set priorities for improving welcome and integration.

Immediately the course was finished, the team put in place and the collect being used, the number of people just turning up to Sunday services increased. Perhaps God is more inclined to send us people if he has confidence that we will welcome them properly. And a much higher proportion of newcomers were returning. The church had not previously kept a note of its newcomers but felt that perhaps 10–20 per cent of them stuck. In the first twelve months of the Welcome Team there were 133 newcomers, an average of 2.5 a week. They divided as in Table 9.1.

So the retention rate after one year was at least 53 per cent (the proportion coming at least monthly). It had the potential to rise to 89 per cent if all the people they were not yet sure of stuck. It eventually looked like the retention rate was around two-thirds.

This created major problems. The larger of the two morning services – a contemporary style service at 10.45 a.m. – became uncomfortably full. Two new people were joining every week. Health and safety considerations raised their head. It was becoming very difficult to

Table 9.1 Getting the welcome right

	Adults	Children
Now coming at least monthly	45	25
Not sure yet	17	13
Too soon to tell	10	8
Not attached	7	8
Total	79	54

keep an eye on so many newcomers and help them integrate. The leaders had a crisis meeting and decided to drop the collect for a while in the hope it would give them a breather. It did. We tend to get what we pray for and don't get what we don't pray for. When they resumed their praying they also added a new 30-minute all-age family service called Lighthouse at 10.10 a.m. The hope that many of the old 10.45 congregation would switch to 'Lighthouse' and so relieve the pressure was, however, only partly realized. Some transferred but also many new families turned up for the new service. In its first year it averaged 72 people and at the latest count was up to around 100. So the attempt to accommodate growth by planting a new service just led to yet more growth.

There is more to this story than simply strangers turning up unexpectedly on a Sunday morning. The new and inviting premises house a number of community events, such as a parent and toddler group during the week, and the church is also running Messy Church monthly. So there is plenty of opportunity for invitations to the Sunday services. In that context, prayer for growth, a community determined to be welcoming, an efficient Welcome Team and a new church service have proved a potent church-growth combination. An intentional culture of invitation, hospitality, welcome and integration not only mirrors the nature of God the Holy Trinity and honours his expectations of the Bride of Christ, it also grows the church.

10

Families to grow

> These commandments that I give you today are to be upon your hearts. Impress them on your children. Talk about them when you sit at home. (Deuteronomy 6.6,7)

As I write, it is Monday morning. I spent the weekend speaking at a conference and discovered that the conference-centre manager grew up on the same street as me in Sheffield. Moreover, his dad, Ken, was the leader of my Sunday school back in the 1950s. Ken was still alive, in his nineties, so I asked the manager to pass on my thanks to Ken for passing on his faith to me all those years ago.

One generation from extinction

The Christian faith survives because each generation passes it on to the next. The Old Testament is littered with instructions to communicate our experience of God to our children and grandchildren. In Psalm 78 verses 1–8 the author determines to share what he had learned from previous generations: 'Things … we have heard and known, what our fathers have told us. We will not hide them from their children, we will tell the next generation.' Then he expresses the hope that the next generation will put their own trust in God: 'he commanded our forefathers to teach their children, so the next generation would know [his laws], even the children yet to be born, and they in turn would tell their children. Then they would put their trust in God and would not forget his deeds but would keep his commands.' And then he hopes that the next generation would be more faithful followers of God than previous generations: 'They would not be like their forefathers – a stubborn and rebellious generation, whose hearts were not loyal to God, whose spirits were not faithful to him.'

There have been about 70 generations since Jesus, so Christians today have that privilege because 69 generations have passed on their faith to the next one. In many countries today each generation contains a higher percentage of Christians than the one before. But the Church is always one generation away from extinction. In Britain there has been a lengthy collective failure to pass on the faith to enough of the next generation to sustain the size of the Christian community. The Christian Church has shrunk not because people have left the churches but because a smaller proportion of each generation have joined. Fewer children have been sent to Sunday school and many children of churchgoers have opted out when allowed to do so

Fewer and fewer from each succeeding generation

Figure 10.1 is derived from the British Social Attitudes survey 1983–2011 as conveyed by David Voas in his contribution to the 'From anecdote to evidence' research.[1] As different surveys show slightly different percentages the figures used here are merely indicative, but they tell a clear story.

Declining adult attendance follows on behind declining Sunday school membership through the twentieth century. A smaller percentage of each generation went to Sunday school and so fewer went to church when they grew up. About 85–90 per cent of our church congregations went to Sunday school or Bible class as a child or young person. I can't prove that from a published survey, but I have asked for a show of hands in many Christian conferences I've spoken at and the percentage who started church as a child is always of that order.

Figure 10.1 Percentage with religious affiliation by decade of birth

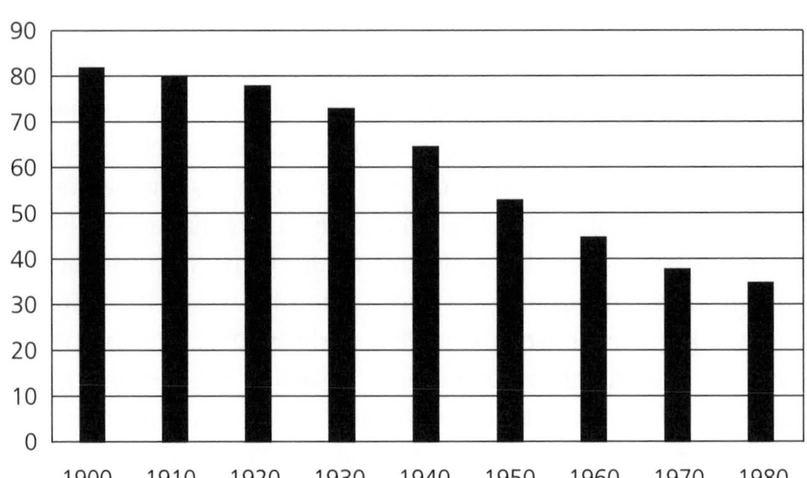

The rise and fall of Sunday schools

In the eighteenth century the formal provision for passing on the faith to young people was catechism classes run by the clergy. These were meant to supplement the Christian education children received from their parents. Anglicans would use the Catechism from the Book of Common Prayer and Dissenters the Westminster Shorter Catechism (which was anything but short). Anglican classes might lead to confirmation. However, the system was hit and miss, even with the middle and upper classes. The Sunday school movement was initiated or popularized by the Gloucester newspaper publisher Robert Raikes around 1780. There was a mix of motives. Some were social – to teach children to read and write, keep vandals off the streets on Sundays, give children a moral compass and create positive citizens who would build Victorian Britain. Others were overtly evangelistic – Sunday schools as academies of faith in which children would become believing Christians.

Sunday schools were aimed at the mass of children in the country, not just a privileged few, and they grew rapidly throughout the nineteenth century (Figure 10.2).

Figure 10.2 Children in Britain attending Sunday school

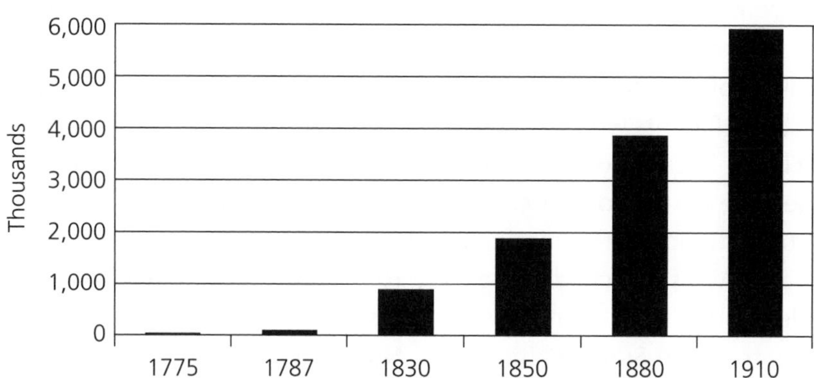

At its peak around 1910 85 per cent of British children (nearly 6 million) were attending Sunday schools. Not all developed their own faith and churchgoing as they grew up. But some did, and this fuelled the rise of churchgoing from the late eighteenth century onwards. Also, the fact that most people had been through Sunday school meant that Christian ethics, morality and world view were widely shared – Sunday school was the foundation on which the feeling that we lived in a Christian country was based.

During the twentieth century Sunday schools declined as fast as they had grown (Figure 10.3).

Figure 10.3 UK Sunday school scholars by denomination, 1900–2000

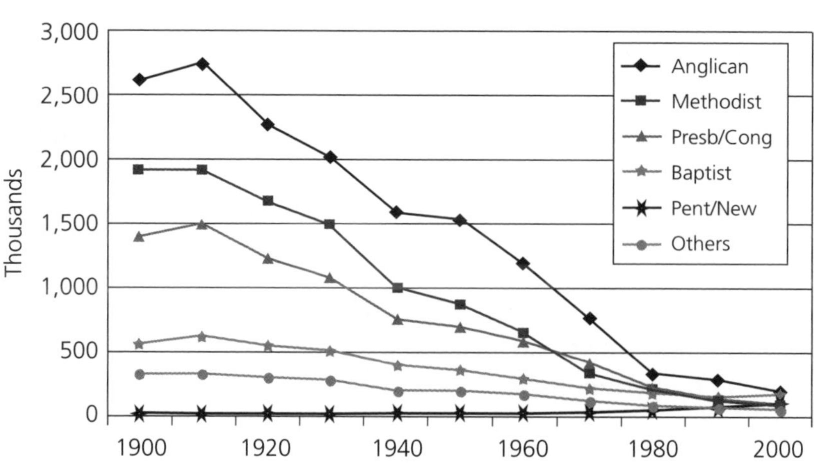

By 2000, after a century of huge social change, Sunday schools were reaching no more than about 5 per cent of children. World War One knocked the old certainties. Universal schooling removed much of the educational motive for sending children to Sunday school. Parents who remembered their own strict or boring Sunday schools became disinclined to inflict this on their own children. It became harder to find enough Sunday school teachers. The move from afternoons to mornings in the 1950s and 60s accelerated the trend. As a small child in the early 1950s I was delighted when I was old enough for Sunday school because there was absolutely nothing else to do on Sunday afternoons. Now children have a huge range of competing possibilities for their time. I used to play out in the streets as a matter of course. Being sent up the road to church with my friends on a Sunday afternoon seemed a perfectly normal extension of everyday life. Not so for today's children who, for fear of traffic and strangers, are rarely let out without supervision.

Evangelism and the young

Human beings are usually fully formed by the age of about 25. This is how God has made us. If we are to form lasting relationships and solid communities we need to be stable and reliable. The writer of Proverbs puts it like this: 'Train a child in the way he should go, and when he is old he will not turn from it' (Proverbs 22.6).

This should not make us despair about the ability of over 25s to change in general and respond to Jesus Christ in particular. We should never give up on people because God never does. My mum was in her eighties before she became a churchgoer. Perhaps one day there will be a mass move of spiritually hungry middle-aged people into the churches.

But the current reality is that most Christians found their faith early in life. Evangelism should focus on the young because they are likely to be far more responsive.

The pie chart below comes from a survey of 1,200 Christians undertaken by the Evangelical Alliance. The pie slices for earlier years may be somewhat exaggerated because the people taking part in the survey were a mix of ages. However, the survey clearly illustrates the truth that most people who become Christians do so early in life. About one quarter of respondents said they had become a Christian by the age of 7, half by 15, three-quarters by 19, 85 per cent by 25 and over 95 per cent by the age of 40 (Figure 10.4).

Figure 10.4 Age at which 1,242 people became Christians

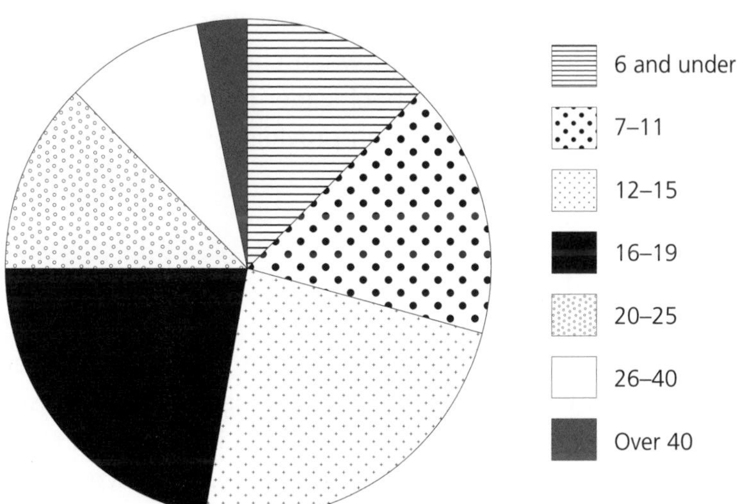

Source: 'Confidently sharing the faith'

Sometimes we imagine that evangelism is primarily about adults with specialist departments for children and young people. The reality is that children and young people are the main event. The future of Christianity will be determined by how well the Church communicates the faith to children and teenagers.

The responsiveness of children

Chapter 12 reports the results of a recent survey of all the churches in the Church in Wales Diocese of St Davids. Churches that had made positive changes to church life and services over the period 2010–13 found their average adult attendance went up about 10 per cent. Churches making no changes saw their adult attendance go down 9 per cent. That seems like a big difference but the changing churches saw their child attendance rise 60 per cent while the no-change churches lost 40 per cent. Child attendance looks hugely more sensitive to what the church has to offer than is adult attendance. It is easy to lose the children when church life weakens or becomes dated, or the Sunday school leader retires, but equally it is possible to attract children through providing something better for them.

Families and church growth

I was sent to Sunday school but most children today would never come to church unaccompanied. If the number of children rises the number of parents or carers has risen as well. Increasing child attendance means increasing family attendance. Evidence shows this is the main growth area in Anglican churches today.

1. A recent report for the Diocese of London, *Another Capital Idea* (Jackson and Piggot, 2011),[2] showed that churches with a high proportion of under 16s were much more likely to grow. In the period 2003–08, churches where children formed less than 25 per cent of their attendance saw their overall attendance shrink slightly. However, 58 churches, 25–30 per cent composed of children, grew 8 per cent; 26 churches, 30–35 per cent composed of children, grew 13 per cent and 11 churches, composed of 35 per cent+ of children, grew 19 per cent. The higher the proportion of families in a congregation the more likely it was to be growing.

2. In the Diocese of St Davids churches reporting an improvement in their provision for children and young people between 2010 and 2013 saw their attendance of children and young people rise 263 per cent. These churches comprise the growth hot spots in that diocese.
3. I asked the leaders of 54 churches attending a course I teach called 'Going for Growth' to tell me their church's attendance trend and also what proportion of their adults are aged under 45 (Table 10.1).

Table 10.1 Percentage of adults aged under 45

	Growing	Steady	Shrinking
Under 10%	2	6	8
10 to 19%	5	4	6
20 to 29%	9	4	1
30% and over	7	1	1

So the majority of churches with at least 30 per cent under 45 were growing but most churches with under 10 per cent were not. In reality a large proportion of the under 45s attend with their children – these are the adult halves of the families. So it is churches with families that tend to grow.

1. Attendance and membership in the Diocese of Leicester have been rising recently. From 2009, Leicester pioneered asking how many people joined and left each worshipping community. Every year there have been more joiners than leavers but the gap is far greater among children. Figure 10.5 shows a bigger difference between joiners and leavers among children in 2013 than among adults. Where churches are growing in Leicester they tend to be growing with children and families.

Figure 10.5 Pattern of church growth in Leicester, 2013

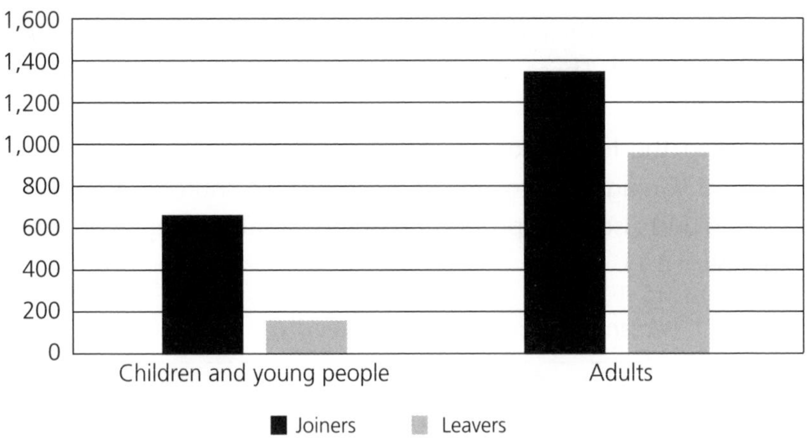

2. Average adult Sunday attendance in Leicester grew by 410, 3.8 per cent, between 2009 and 2013. But child Sunday attendance grew by 184, 11.4 per cent. It is almost universal that churches shrink older and grow younger. As churches grow, their average age comes down because the growth is weighted towards younger people. This is clearly the case in Leicester as evidenced by weekday attendance. Adult average weekday attendance rose from 1,289 in 2009 to 2,433 in 2013, an increase of 89 per cent. However, child attendance numbers went up from 507 to 3,677, an increase of 625 per cent. Now that's the sort of church growth percentage I like, even though quite a chunk of it is actually definitional due to greater inclusion of school services in 2013. But clearly this growing diocese is growing most of all among families.
3. The Diocese of Liverpool has pioneered intentional church growth through fresh expressions. Figure 10.6 shows that nearly half of their fresh expressions in 2010 were centred on families, with some others on children and young people. In addition, many of the other styles of fresh expression will have had families attending them. So it looks like the demographic that composes significantly more than half of the growth through fresh expressions is families.

Figure 10.6 Fresh expressions attendance in Liverpool Diocese, 2010 (3,410 people, 17 per cent of uSa)

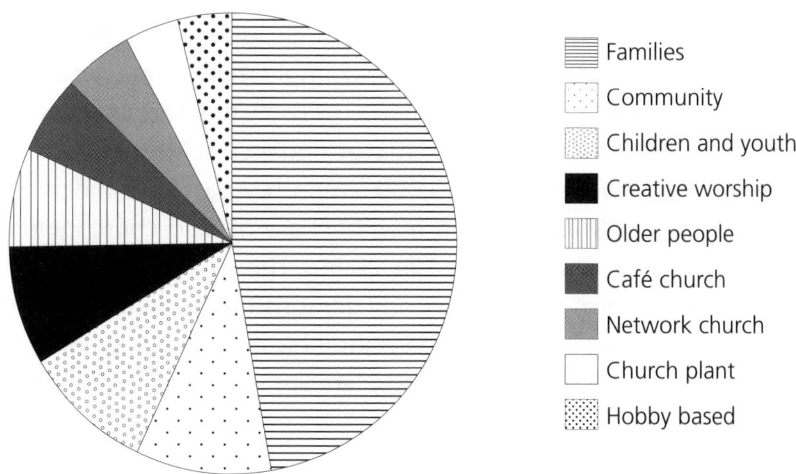

4. The logging of fresh expressions undertaken by the Church Army's research unit and described in Chapter 11 has found that more than half of all fresh expressions across a wide range of dioceses are clearly directed at families, children and young people (Table 10.2).

Table 10.2 Focus of fresh expressions

Messy Church	32%
Child-focused church	19%
Under 5s church	6%
School-based church	5%
Youth church	5%

(There is a little double-counting here as some churches ticked more than one box)

In addition, most other categories of fresh expression, for example café churches, are aimed at the whole population, including families.

Easily the largest church-growth phenomenon numerically in Britain in this century so far is Messy Church. The numbers of Messy Churches in the Church Army sample would have been greater if over half of the examples had not been excluded from the definition of church by their criteria – for example many don't meet the minimum monthly frequency criteria. Messy Church is analysed in Chapter 11 where it is suggested that attendance at Messy Churches may by 2014 have reached 400,000 a month. Apart from the planting teams most Messy Church members are new to churchgoing. (The first Messy Church began in 2004.) The growth of this new families-based form of church clearly demonstrates that it is families that are the most responsive demographic for church growth in Britain today. Where there is growth, families are usually at the heart of it.

Have we turned the corner?

The evidence shows that families and children form the most responsive and promising demographic for numerical church growth today. So, after a century of decline, have numbers started to grow again?

Usual Sunday attendance of children in the late twentieth century went down at about twice the rate as that of adults. When congregations shrink they usually also get older. For example, adult uSa fell 15 per cent between 1989 and 2002 but child attendance fell 35 per cent. From 2002 we have been able to use the October count figures as the best guide because they include weekday attendance. Between 2002 and 2011 adult attendance fell 7 per cent but child attendance only 5 per cent. This is still a fall, but slower than among adults, suggesting that the proportion of children has started to rise slightly. It is also possible therefore that the average age has started to fall. Since 2011 child attendance numbers have been almost stable but churches are recording far more child joiners than leavers. In 2012 there were 23,100 reported child joiners (12 per cent of the child worshipping community) and only 7,400 leavers (4 per cent).

This suggests an 8 per cent rise in the number of child members of the worshipping community in one year.

Child attendance frequency has been going down in recent years as children's lives have become more crowded and weekly Sunday school models have been replaced by monthly all-age and family services, including Messy Church. So fairly steady average weekly attendance is consistent with a rise in the number of child members as more children are coming less often. In addition, not all the fresh expressions of church are getting recorded in service registers and reported on Statistics for Mission forms. Some churches are unsure whether a new initiative is actually 'church' or not, some are not sure whether they will last, some are not well organized enough to do the counting, some are wary of letting their diocese know about them in case the diocese attempts some form of control or taxation via the parish share system.

So it looks as though the Church of England is now seeing increasing numbers of children and families attending worship events including fresh expressions. However, the turnaround is too recent and the statistical data too uncertain to confidently proclaim a major long-term trend change just yet.

How are we bringing back families, children and young people?

To grow numerically churches should focus not on increasing the quantity of the church's people but on improving the quality of the church's life. This is especially true in relation to younger people. Any improvement to the quality of what is offered to families, children and young people is likely to bring more in. Also, churches that adapt to changes in the culture of family life and the evolving demography and lifestyles of their local community will probably attract the families. A list of specific initiatives with positive results includes:

1. Become more intentional

When churches set out a strategic priority to grow with families, children, young people and young adults they have a chance to do so (see Chapter 6). Intentionality is more than just aspiration. The intentional church will follow a plan for focusing its life and resources around the younger half of the population.

2. Renew the culture

The growing-younger church will be updating the whole culture of how it does business including its communications methods. A church of notice sheets and parish magazines is primarily aiming at the over sixties. A church relying on the website and emails will tend to attract the middle aged. A church using Facebook, texting and tweeting is likely to reach teens and younger adults. What the preferred communications method will be for the next generations of teens I have no idea. Churches wishing to reach all age groups will need to be multicultural and use a notice sheet, emails and texting all at the same time.

3. Love children and their parents

My wife has just returned from running the parent and toddler group in the church centre. Most of the families who turn up don't go to church on Sundays but they seem to like us. Christine saw one mum arriving late and frazzled and made her a cup of coffee the way she likes it. Thanking her, the mum said, 'I come here to be loved.' However good the communications culture, however good the premises, however appropriate the service times and styles, if the children and their parents are not loved it is all a waste of time. You can grow the church without a lot of the factors in this book as long as you have love. But you can't grow the church without love. If there are any disapprovers among the congregation when children make noises in services they will need re-educating!

4. Listen to parents and children

A church near us wanted to try Messy Church but was unsure of the best time. So they asked the families at the village school. To the church's surprise the parents said the best time was fairly early on Sunday morning, starting with breakfast. So that is when Messy Church now happens – and large numbers of school families are coming. But there are deeper things to listen to as well. Many parents may not have any deep Christian faith but they are looking for wholesome activities they can share with their children. Others do have a sense of spiritual deprivation in a secular society. Others are keen for their children to have the opportunity of believing in God even if they don't believe very well themselves. A church that listens to the people around it and works with the grain of their aspirations and lifestyles is likely to touch their hearts.

5. Provide good leadership

Leadership is always key to the growth of the church. Children's and youth ministry and all-age worship are particularly dependent on the quality of leadership. To some extent leaders are born and not made, so the church that is serious about the priority of growing-younger will focus its best people on this area. But it will also invest heavily in the training and development of the leaders of the relevant groups and worship events.

6. Join with other churches

Small churches, especially in villages, often feel they do not have the leadership and facilities to offer much to children and families. However, churches can band together to make one good provision. Several village churches can combine leadership to offer a Messy Church or youth fellowship that is on the programme of every church.

7. Set a realistic budget

The priorities of a church are revealed in its budget. Churches have a chance to grow among the younger half of the population when they budget for it. Money may need to be spent on staff, facilities, equipment and events. Better to budget for this than for the families work leaders to go cap in hand to the treasurer on an ad hoc basis every time some money needs spending.

8. Improve the physical facilities

Churches that upgrade their buildings and facilities tend to find that families respond – toilets, health and safety hazards, heating, seating, storage and space to run around are all important. My wife's parent and toddler group meets in our excellent church centre. It is the best building in the area and the group is full to overflowing. Without the facilities there would be no group. People who encounter the church through the group sometimes join the worshipping community as well.

9. Make thoughtful provision

Recently in our church we improved the nappy disposal system in the church centre, we made 'happy bags' with toys and activities for tiny children to use during church services, and we bought some playmats and created a play area surrounded by pews towards the back of the worship space. It was all low-budget stuff but it is much appreciated.

10. Improve the Sunday groups

Although the Sunday school model is a shadow of its former self it is still true that improving the range and quality of what is offered can revive attendance in individual churches. For example, churches with groups for primary school children but not secondary put out the signal that children are expected to leave at 11. Introducing a group for 11s–14s is likely to increase the overall number of children even if there are very few takers at first. One option for churches that no longer have a Sunday school is to create provision and then pray for children to come.

11. Take a look at the monthly family service

Many churches interrupt their normal service once a month with a 'family service'. The results have been mixed. It is hard to develop community and discipleship in a monthly congregation, the regular, older congregation may stay away from the family service and a family service can alienate teenagers. However, in some situations it has been a practical first step and has brought new families into churchgoing. It is probably best to see a family service not as the final destination of a strategy for reaching families but as a step along the way.

12. Try new service times

Sunday morning is no longer a good time for church for many families. Some children have school or sports activities on Sunday mornings, some are still in bed and some have gone to see their other parent. Some parents are working or shopping. Some churches have found that teatime on Saturday or Sunday is better for their locality. One church in a rugby-playing area found it got very few boys on Sunday morning so it changed its family service time to 4.30 p.m. and far more families with boys started coming. One reason for the growth of Christmas Eve Crib Service congregations in recent years is the teatime timing. It is also one reason for the numerical success of Messy Church.

13. Offer all-age worship

Experience with services where the children stay in the whole time with their parents has been mixed. Some parents find coping with the children for an hour in a church service, however good, too stressful and they stay away. In others the older children feel talked down to and rebel. However, a good well-presented format can attract families where the parents are reluctant to entrust their children to unknown group leaders across the road in the church hall. All-age worship can also encourage Christian family life at home and does away with the need to find a large rota of Sunday school teachers. One church needing to fit in an extra service in a crowded Sunday morning programme started a 30-minute all-age service with quick-fire items that was instantly very popular with families.

14. Introduce new styles and fresh expressions

This may have the largest scope for attracting new people into the churches. Styles that are better incarnated into the culture and learning styles of contemporary families appear to be doing very well. Messy Church is the biggest example, but there are other formats also.

15. Try Messy Church

The rise of Messy Church is charted and analysed in Chapter 11. However, it is worth saying that Messy Church is now getting so widespread and well known that it is becoming a recognizable brand. The leadership of Messy Church is not, however, a command and control organization so it is possible to combine the advantages of marketing a well-known brand with some flexibility for local expressions.

16. Employ paid staff

After some years of making grants to about 50 churches to help them employ families', children's and youth ministers the Diocese of Lichfield took a look at the attendance trends in those churches. These churches were at the heart of the whole diocesan turnaround in both child and adult attendance. Growth following the appointment of paid staff is not universal – the paid minster needs to be the right person for the job, well supported by the church, have a good relationship with the vicar, have a job description that is about enabling the church to do the ministry rather than doing it for them, stay for a good number of years and be focused on a fairly tight job description that can be fulfilled to a high standard. However, the growth in the number of paid specialist staff in recent years is clearly one reason for the turnaround in overall numbers.

17. Work through schools

Schools lie at the heart of the church's mission. It is in schools that children and young people are to be found as a group. Many schools are open to the church's contribution to their life and community. Teams from churches, as well as individual clergy, are often able to take assemblies. Church staff and teams who run Christian clubs in schools are able to invite children into church activities and services. Schools often make good venues in which to plant fresh expressions. The Diocese of Blackburn is expanding the number of Church of England secondary schools in its area and finding the funding to employ a chaplain in each one. Clergy and other church leaders with their own children in local schools find themselves in networks of parents and able to make invitations to church events and services. One major reason why younger clergy are more likely to be leading growing churches is the contacts they make through school. Schools can be used to disseminate invitations to special and seasonal events and services. It is the school community who will form the heart of a new Messy Church. Schools often enjoy guided visits to church buildings. Our own village primary school comes into our church building periodically for a prayer event. It's voluntary but most of the children opt to come and seem to appreciate the chance to pray in various guided ways. A good relationship between church and school benefits both enormously – schools are at the centre of the church's mission and often also at the centre of the church's growth.

18. Use seasonal and occasional events

The busyness of family life makes some families reluctant to commit to regular weekly or even monthly worship. But they respond to one-off invitations at Christmas, Mothering Sunday, Easter, Harvest, etc. As well as being worthwhile events in their own right, a well-constructed pattern of annual services can be the platform for more regular involvement for some. Holiday clubs and summer camps can not only deepen the faith and commitment of children and young people but also be a point of introduction to church.

A vision of what can be

The prophet Zechariah had a vision of the post-exile Jerusalem restored to its former glory, a garden of Eden condition, a foretaste of life in the kingdom of heaven: 'Once again men and women of ripe old age will sit in the streets of Jerusalem, each with cane in hand because of his age. The city streets will be filled with boys and girls playing there' (Zechariah 8.4,5). Too many of our churches have the elderly with cane in hand but not the young playing. But when churches find ways of opening up to children and enabling them to play in the streets, corridors and aisles of the church they recover their joy, hope and future. For a whole century the Church in Britain was steadily losing children. But now we are finding ways of bringing them back. This brings all sorts of issues about how to help children and their parents know Jesus for themselves. But it may just be that the vision of boys and girls playing in and around the walking sticks of the elderly in the churches of the land is closer at hand than we imagine. I don't need a walking stick just yet, but by the time I do I very much hope I belong to a church full of the laughter and worship of children.

11

Planting to grow

> Aquila and Priscilla greet you warmly in the Lord, and so does the church that meets at their house. (1 Corinthians 16.19)

Planting and growing churches

I have been vicar of two different church plants. The parish of Ecclesfield near Sheffield was reputedly the largest in the country. The far-sighted Victorian vicar planted several new parishes as the population grew. My own church at St Mark's Grenoside was built around 1884. We celebrated our centenary while I was there. Then I was vicar of a church planted by some French monks about the year 1180 – St Mary Scarborough. That was a while back but it was still a plant because every church there has ever been has been planted by somebody.

Churches do not need specialist buildings in order to be planted, as witness the church in the home of Aquila and Priscilla. They simply need a group of Christians to gather together. Neither do they need to be led by someone ordained – Aquila or Priscilla clearly weren't. And neither do church plants need to be independent units – probably the group in their house was linked with other churches in other homes in the same city.

Planting is the main way in which the Christian Church has grown across the world for 2,000 years. Sometimes existing worship-groups grow larger but group dynamics usually restrict the possibilities. There are surprisingly few individual congregations of more than 120 average attendance in the Church of England. Chapter 4 mentioned the fact that overall church attendance had grown in London by 16 per cent (100,000) between 2005 and 2012. That growth did not come about because congregations got bigger – they didn't. It happened because there were 17 per cent more churches in London in 2012 than in 2005. And the denominations and streams that had grown were the ones that had planted. Most Anglican church planting is of new congregations within existing church structures, but it is still planting.

I wonder what happened when the church in Aquila and Priscilla's house got too big for the house. Did Priscilla send latecomers packing? Did they enlarge the house? Much more likely that some of them went off to another house to start a church there!

We have a fairly new garden. I could hang around for the next 20 years waiting for the existing plants to grow to fill the areas of bare soil. But the climate up in our village stunts growth. So yesterday I bought some new shrubs to fill the ground – that's how my garden will grow.

The two areas of England with the lowest proportion of churchgoers are South Yorkshire and Hull. This is not because the churches in these areas are small – actually they are bigger than average. It is because there are not many of them.

The average congregation size of an Anglican church grows with the population of the parish up to around 3,000. Beyond 3,000 the size of congregation hardly grows with population. Sometimes there is a reverse causation as a large population takes up so much time (for example, with funerals) that the vicar has little time, focus and energy left to lead and grow the gathered church community.

During my time as vicar of St Mary and Holy Apostles Scarborough two Sunday services closed down and the congregations at the two survivors shrank a little. So much for the church-growth expert! Well, actually the church did grow because we also planted three new congregations, which more than made up the numbers and also reduced the average age.

Through a questionnaire I recently put out to all the churches of one diocese I found that in three years average attendance at churches that had not planted a new congregation went down 6 per cent. But at churches that had planted a new congregation it went up 27 per cent. The number of children increased a lot faster than the number of adults. Planting a new congregation enables a church to start with a clean slate. It is often easier to fashion a new event suited to younger people than it is to update an existing one.

I'm not sure how many more ways I can make the same point! Church planting and church growth are not quite the same thing, but often they almost are.

Opportunities for church planting

There is much variety in the field of church planting, and a whole host of opportunities. Here is a list of typical opportunities to watch out for:

1. Some churches keep welcoming new people but never seem to get bigger, perhaps because their main congregation is already at the maximum comfortable size for the building. If the building is 80 per cent full then normally congregations do not get any bigger. Or perhaps it is because the 120 or so ceiling size has been reached beyond which the service and its associated community becomes anonymous and impersonal. If such a church wishes to grow it may need to start a new congregation, with some people transferring so that both the old and the new congregations have growing room.
2. Some churches see the need to offer worship in the culture of a different – perhaps younger – group of people but cannot see how to adapt the existing service without alienating the congregation. Or perhaps there already is some tension between different groups in the service. Such a church needs to plant a new congregation in a different style so that it can attract people from different sub-cultures even if both congregations start small.
3. Some larger churches are able to make a bigger contribution to the overall growth of the church through a transplant into a small or struggling church.

4. Some churches find that most of their members live in one part of the parish, perhaps the one nearest to the church building. It may be worth finding a suitable venue in the other part of the parish for a new worship activity.
5. In some places the population is rising quite fast. Some new churches are needed in new population areas, whether or not they meet in a church building.
6. One strength of the Church of England is its mix of traditions. In many urban areas people can choose from a range of styles within a short journey from home. However, sometimes all the Anglican churches are a similar style or tradition and this restricts overall numbers. A diocese might be able to broaden the range with a new appointment. And if something new begins to emerge from the grass roots the instinct today should be to encourage it. In one town all the Anglican churches were of one tradition in a large team ministry. Anglicans of another tradition were driving to other towns for church. Some of them realized that made them ineffective witnesses in their own town so they started an Anglican fellowship in a home. Traditionally the Anglican hierarchy has seen itself as the guardian of church order and would discourage this. If the new priority is to grow the church such initiatives should be encouraged. The diocese in question has now found a way to officially recognize this new fellowship.
7. The need to help teenagers maintain their faith and church involvement was laid bare in Chapter 10. There has never been a time when it was more important to enable young people to worship with a peer group. Groups of churches all over the country should be getting together to plant youth and young adult congregations. These do not take young people away from the churches where they grew up – most will leave anyway without this provision. Rather they enable young people to stay as part of the church into adulthood.
8. There is a similar need for many more congregations to be set up with the culture, lifestyle and outlook of young adults in mind. It is a good deanery exercise to list all the church services in the

deanery adding the age group the service primarily suits. Can the deanery cooperate to fill the gaps?

Fresh expressions of church

The big breakthrough in church planting in this century has come through the Fresh Expressions movement. This is a dauntingly wide and fast-moving field to cover in a brief summary. There is confusion about definitions of both 'church' and 'fresh expression' and it is hard to get any sort of overall picture of their spread and impact. However, the Church Army's Research Unit has been working with diocese after diocese to bring some definitional clarity, build up lists of fresh expressions of church and interview the leaders.

What is a fresh expression of church?

The Fresh Expressions organization defines a fresh expression of church as a form of church for the changing culture established primarily for the benefit of people who are not yet members of any church. It will come into being through principles of listening, service, incarnational mission and making disciples. It will have the potential to become a mature expression of church.

The Church Army's Research Unit has taken this further, suggesting that a church activity should broadly meet the following ten parameters if it is to be included as a genuine fresh expression of church in the diocesan family:

1. Was something Christian and communal brought to birth that was new and different, rather than an existing group modified?
2. Has the starting group engaged with non-churchgoers? The intention should be to create a fresh expression of church not an outreach project from an existing church. The aim is for the planting team to change, to fit a new culture and context, not to make the indigenous people change to fit into an existing church context.

3. Does the resultant community meet at least monthly? In cases of monthly meetings further questions about how to deepen community, build commitment and increase discipleship should follow.
4. Does it have a name that helps give an identity? An active search, not yet yielding a name, is allowed.
5. Is there intention to be church? This could be from the start, or by a discovery on the way from an initial intention to be a new form of community, evangelism or worship. The key is that they are *not* seen as a bridge back to 'real church'.
6. Is it Anglican, or an Anglican partner in an ecumenical project? 'Anglican' here means the bishop welcomes it as part of the diocesan family, not whether it uses centrally authorized worship texts, or has a legal territory.
7. There is some form of leadership recognized within, and also without.
8. At least the majority of members who are part of the public gathering see it as their major expression of being church.
9. There is aspiration to acquire the four creedal 'marks' of church – one, holy, apostolic and catholic. The sacraments of baptism and communion are a given consequence of the life of a missional community which follows Jesus, but not the sole or even best measure of being church.
10. There is intent to become '3 self' – self-financing, self-governing and self-reproducing. These factors need contextualization, but are some marks of advancing ecclesial maturity. They are not to be interpreted as indicators of congregationalist independency, or breakaway tendencies, but of taking responsibility.

In addition a group should at least be moving towards acquiring the four marks of a good fresh expression:

1. It is *missional* with at least 50 per cent of its members previously unchurched.
2. It is *formational*, making Christian disciples.
3. It is *contextual*, arising out of the target culture.
4. It is *ecclesial*, not a bridge but church itself.

Research into fresh expressions of church

The Church Army Research Unit, led by George Lings, has developed a methodology for discovering key information about fresh expressions of church. Working diocese by diocese the unit conducts a long telephone interview with the leader of every possible fresh expression, discarding those that do not meet the criteria and logging key data for those that do to give a comprehensive account of the key patterns and trends in this emerging movement. Results from the first ten dioceses have now been published.

This chapter offers just a summary of some of the main findings from this research. A full version is to be found on the Church Army's website. In addition the Church Commissioners' 'From anecdote to evidence' programme has financed interviews in the most recent dioceses and a full report on this can be found on the Church Growth Research Programme website (www.churchgrowthresearch.org.uk).

How many qualify?

The clear but demanding criteria meant that slightly less than half of the cases offered by dioceses as fresh expressions of church were accepted as such, about 50 per diocese. Many excluded examples were perfectly good outreach projects or on the way to becoming fresh expressions, or met too infrequently.

How large are the fresh expressions of church?

The average congregation size is 44 with a range of 5 to 500. In Leicester, for example, 17 had average attendance of under 30, 15 from 30 to 49, 7 from 50 to 69 and 6 had 70 plus. This is a widespread movement of many small groups. Many are based on developing deep relationships so they may have a naturally low ceiling size. The main growth route in the Fresh Expressions movement is not existing groups becoming large but planting ever more of them.

How many people are involved?

Average attendance at fresh expressions of church is about 10 per cent of diocesan weekly attendance. However, they add less than 10 per cent to average weekly attendance as many meet less than weekly. So fresh expressions are no longer minor or peripheral – they have become mainstream and are responsible for much of the Church's recent growth. The large variety in the incidence of fresh expressions both within and between dioceses suggests that there is huge scope for further growth simply from other areas catching up with the early adopters.

When did they start?

The systematic surveying of dioceses began in 2011. Around half were begun in the most recent three years and three-quarters in the most recent five. The growth of fresh expressions is recent, rapid and accelerating.

What are the main types of fresh expressions of church?

Messy Church account for around a third of the examples, with other child-focused formats contributing a further fifth. Café Church, church for special interest groups, cluster-based churches, network churches and community-development plants form the next more numerous categories. What is most striking is the variety. Messy Church is the most common but it does not dominate, partly because over half of the Messy Churches referred by dioceses did not pass the inclusion tests. However, the overall emphasis is very much on families, children, young people and young adults.

What sort of people are involved?

Around 40 per cent of those attending fresh expressions of church were aged under 16, compared with 17 per cent in traditional parish churches. Many of the adults are the parents and carers of these children, also at the younger end of the Anglican age spectrum.

The leaders of fresh expressions believe that about 25 per cent of their members are pre-existing Christians, many of whom were the planting team, 35 per cent have come back to church through the fresh expression and 40 per cent are new to churchgoing. Fresh expressions are adding to the church community rather than redistributing it.

Where have fresh expressions of church been planted?

Fresh expressions have been planted across all socio-economic settings. Around a quarter are village or rural, with the rest well distributed between urban, housing estate, suburban and town situations. About half were primarily neighbourhood-based and 40 per cent primarily network-based.

What do we know about the planting teams?

Most planting teams are small – about 75 per cent containing three to twelve people and a further 10 per cent one or two people. This is good news because it means that even small churches can plant.

The typical motive of the team has changed over the years. In the 1990s a desire to reach unreached areas of the parish or new housing areas was common. More recently the main motive has been to reach unreached people groups. The older model replicated provision of church in new areas, the newer one enculturates new forms of church for new types of people.

What impact have the planting teams had?

On average the fresh expressions contain about an additional 2.5 people for every planter. Most of that growth is new or reclaimed young churchgoers. When it comes to growing with new people and winning new generations nothing else comes close to the planting of fresh expressions of church.

What do we know about the leaders?

Half the leaders were ordained and there were also a few Church Army evangelists and readers. However, 40 per cent of the main leaders were lay people. Mostly these have no church badge or office, no training for the role and are unpaid. Their proportion has risen from around 10 per cent of the early plants to almost half of the most recent. That so much of the planting and growth of the Church of England is being directly led by a large army of unrecognized, untrained and unpaid lay people should be a cause for rejoicing. The response of clergy and dioceses should be not to control and restrain but to offer the support, encouragement and training these leaders deserve.

It is hard to estimate the impact of leadership training on the growth of fresh expressions because most leaders have not had any. However, it looks like leaders who have done a 'Mission-shaped Ministry' (MSM) course from the Fresh Expressions organization, or a church-planting module are more likely to see growth. Around 35 per cent of their fresh expressions continue to grow significantly beyond the start-up stage compared with 20 per cent of those led by people with no training. But over 60 per cent of churches that have an outside consultancy continue to grow significantly – perhaps the priority training agenda should be the training of consultants.

Where and when do they meet?

The church building is the venue for around 40 per cent of the fresh expressions, and the church hall for around 20 per cent. The remaining 40 per cent use a variety of secular public buildings and houses.

The proportion meeting on Sunday varies by diocese and style but is around 40 per cent. Under fives, cell church, clusters, midweek church, older peoples' church and special interest groups are more likely to meet on weekdays. Messy Church is 50–50 weekend and weekday.

Just under half meet monthly, 10 per cent meet fortnightly and the remainder weekly. Weekly events are harder to sustain, fortnightly ones are hard to predict due to five-week months and may lose people as a result, monthly events have trouble building community and discipleship. Yet all three are proving to be viable.

Mortality rates

Just under 10 per cent of the fresh expressions of church discovered had died. In an era of experimentation with many small and vulnerable groups this is encouragingly few.

Continuing numerical growth

The Sheffield team were able to chart continuing numerical growth in fresh expressions more than two years old. Defining numerical growth or decline as being at least 5 per cent per annum, the team found that around a quarter continued to grow, about a half plateaued or fluctuated and around a quarter began to shrink. So overall numbers remained about the same. Many of the churches are still new and there may be longer-term patterns to discern, perhaps as some get a second wind. But the best route to numerical growth currently looks like doing a lot of planting, getting groups up to their natural size and then planting some more.

Weekly fresh expressions are more likely to continue growing while monthly events are more likely to plateau quickly. Fortnightly events are more likely to start declining, perhaps partly because it looks as though a weekly pattern is the best for long-term growth. This is no surprise – there are good reasons why churches have met weekly ever since the resurrection of Christ.

About a third of the leaders were spare time, a fifth part time and half full time. Those led by full-time or paid leaders were slightly more likely to start declining after the planting period and slightly less likely to grow than those led by unpaid spare timers. This may have something to do with the paid leading differing styles of fresh expression of church from the unpaid, but the finding is still striking. The fact that unpaid spare-time leaders experience trends as good or better than those experienced by paid leaders means that there is no financial limit on the growth of the church through planting. The limit is set by the availability of willing and able volunteer spare-time leaders. This should encourage those exploring unpaid focal ministry as a leadership model for smaller parish churches (see Chapter 7). When it comes to leadership development for the future growth of the Church, lay training may be as important as clergy training. Falling stipendiary numbers may even provide growth opportunities if unpaid and lay people are trusted to lead churches.

Perhaps the professional full-time leader tends to do the ministry and the members become dependent. The train has one driver and many passengers. The spare-time unpaid leader involves everyone in ministry or the church does not function. The train has a full working crew.

The Diocese of Leicester has absorbed the twin lesson that many fresh expressions are best led by unpaid volunteers but still benefit from expert consultancy support. They have appointed three Pioneer Development Workers to support, encourage and resource unpaid pioneers and fresh expression leaders with the aim of establishing and maturing as many authentic fresh expressions in the diocese as there are existing churches. Each development worker will be rooted in their own fresh expression and so be a current practitioner. But their main role will be to provoke and support a diocesan-wide movement.

If this vision materializes then three posts will have helped generate the planting and growth not of three fresh expressions but of 320. This looks a far more promising way of directing scarce funding into pioneering planting than appointing paid leaders for individual initiatives.

The planting of fresh expressions has brought a major new dynamic to church growth. There is great variety of both style and setting. Mostly the planting team and resulting fresh expression are of modest size and continuing growth is coming mainly from further planting. Increasingly existing fresh expressions will do the planting. A large proportion of the leadership are unpaid and lay and they are doing very well. Numerically the largest brand is Messy Church and it is high time to turn to this now.

Messy Church

The first Messy Church was created in an Anglican church in Portsmouth in 2004. The format was popularized through the books written by Lucy Moore, the BRF website, 'Messy Fiestas' put on around the country and simple word of mouth.

In line with general experience, the average Messy Church grows fairly quickly to its natural size. Overall growth comes mainly through planting new groups. Most groups are led by lay people, meet monthly and are a planting initiative of a local church. A few are ecumenical or other joint projects.

There have been differing views about whether Messy Church really is church. However, a standard monthly Messy Church run along the lines recommended by BRF easily passes the Church Army's 'fresh expression of church' criteria. Messy Church is a public event called 'church' that involves Christian learning, community, prayer and Bible. A creature that quacks like a duck and waddles like a duck is a duck. Messy Church involves learning by doing rather than simply by listening, families learning and worshipping together rather than being separated off, and eating together like they did in the book of Acts rather than filing off home after the blessing. It is not conventional church, it is a fresh expression of church, but it is still church.

Nevertheless, just over half of the Messy Church events put forward by dioceses did not get classified as fresh expressions of church. Many did not meet often enough. Others were Messy-style events intended as outreach or halfway houses rather than being church themselves. Messy Church is not a command and control organization so there is no imposed uniformity. Some authentic expressions do not use the brand-name, others use the name but fall short of being fully church.

As with other forms of fresh expression, there are major issues in Messy Church connected with how conversion and discipleship are enabled. Often it is the children who make a quicker and bigger spiritual response – how can that be handled when their parents or carers are more wary? And how can a stage-of-life church become a whole-of-life church? It is hard to build community and discipleship with only a monthly event. Yet usually something more frequent is impractical because of the demands on leadership time and imagination. How can a Messy Church congregation be integrated in some way with traditional congregations? And how can a Messy congregation be part of the leadership of the whole church, join the PCC, and contribute financially?

Some Messy Churches are experimenting with extensions to the original concept designed to enable community, conversion, discipleship and whole-of-life growth. Monthly Messy Church can be linked with Messy Café or Who let the Dads out? or nurture courses or other, less time-consuming models of church. Much more experimentation is needed to enable congregations formed around a monthly Messy Church to meet more often and grow spiritually as Christian communities.

These issues have arisen in a form of church that has grown incredibly rapidly from scratch in only ten years. The numerical success has taken everyone involved by surprise and all are struggling to catch up. One definition of mission is 'finding out what God is doing and joining in'. God is the grower of the Church and the energy and vigour of the growth of Messy Church has his fingerprints all over it. Anyone in the Church of England who is serious about mission will be wanting to find out what God is up to in Messy Church and joining in in some way, even if that is simply praying for it.

How big is Messy Church?

A lot has been written about Messy Church issues recently and there are various resources available from the website (www.messychurch.org.uk). Rather than going over the ground again this section simply charts the numerical rise of Messy Church. Since 2009 the website has encouraged local churches to register and the growth looks like Figure 11.1.

Research by BRF suggests that attendance at the average Messy Church is around 55, half and half adults and children. So total attendance at registered churches in February 2014 was around 125,000. But not everybody comes every time. General experience is suggesting that the average church may have, at a guess, around 80 members. So membership of registered Messy Churches in February 2014 was around 180,000, half and half adults and children. The number of registered churches has been rising at the rate of around

Figure 11.1. Number of registered Messy Churches in February each year

500 a year (10 a week) since 2011. If this growth rate continues then by, say, February 2015 we would expect membership to have risen to around 220,000 people.

Apart from the planting teams the evidence so far collected suggests that the great majority of Messy members are new to churchgoing. This growth is not recycled Christians, it is of unchurched people. Many, of course, have not yet made a clear commitment to be a Christian, but have equally clearly begun some sort of journey.

Around 60 per cent of the registered churches are Church of England, giving a Church of England attendance of 75,000 in February 2014 with membership of 110,000. The impact on average weekly attendance is much less than this because most Messy Churches only meet monthly and some even meet at the very start or end of October, outside the four-week Statistics for Mission survey period. So the addition to average weekly attendance will be around 17,000. Half of all Messy Churches meet on weekdays, so the impact on usual Sunday attendance will only be around 8,000. Clearly these traditional attendance measures of the size of the Church of England are just not picking up the great bulk of this new church growth.

Not all Messy Churches have registered on the BRF website. Surveys of what is happening on the ground in local areas suggests that there may be as many as two unregistered for every one registered. If this is true then in February 2014 there were more like 6,600 Messy Churches with an attendance of 360,000 and membership of 530,000. This may or may not be an exaggeration and we have here reached the limit of guesswork. But we can safely say that Messy Church in 2014 has at least a quarter of a million members and perhaps more like half a million. And its membership is growing at the rate of between 50,000 and 100,000 people a year.

I hope you did not switch off at all that figuring. If you did I hope to get your attention back by saying that there are more people going to Messy Church in the UK today than to the Methodist Church. This is the biggest single churchgoing growth phenomenon in this country since the rise of Sunday schools and Methodism at the end of the eighteenth century. We do not know how much more growing room Messy Church has, but I suspect it is a lot because of its patchy nature on the ground. Some dioceses have few Messy Churches, others have many. There are over 100 in the Diocese of Lichfield alone.

The most promising way in which Messy Church can navigate its major issues and find ways of becoming a whole-of-life disciple-making church is through it becoming a much more intentional learning community enabled by electronic media. A Messy Development website forum routinely logged into by every Messy Church leader in the land would be an enormous engine of spiritual, discipleship and numerical growth. So if you have any responsibility for a Messy Church please register on the website and plug into a learning community.

I will grow my church

The growth of Messy Church illustrates that Jesus' great promise to grow his Church applies just as much to the UK in the twenty-first century as to everywhere and anywhere else. If we can see major numerical growth with one form of fresh expression of church we can see it with other forms. Keep working with what God is doing today but also keep looking out for the next big thing he has up his sleeve!

12

Changing to grow

> Unless you change and become like little children, you will never enter the kingdom of heaven. (Matthew 18.3)

Change is what Christians and churches do

Jesus' warning that we need to change to enter the kingdom of heaven gets to the heart of what it means to be Christian. A Christian is constantly trying to become less of a sinner and more like Jesus, to lose the self-sufficiency and pride of a competitive adult and put on the trust and humility of a child. However, Jesus' warning is made not to an individual but to his whole group of children, plural. A Christian community should constantly try to change in order to enter the kingdom of heaven. It shakes off its sinful nature to become better reflective of the perfect community of the Holy Trinity. A Christian church is trying to put aside the pride and self-sufficiency of competitive adults and put on the humility and trust of children.

So a church community that has given up trying to change has given up growing the kingdom of heaven and given up trying to be Christian.

The only constant is change

The churches of Britain have lived through many periods of great change followed by times of stability. Anyone attending the same church from 1530 to 1560 would have noticed violent swings in worship, theology, leadership and power, including a reformation, counter-reformation and new reformation settlement. Along the way it is entirely likely that their bishop had been burned at the stake. The Pope had become alternately the Vicar of Christ, the Devil incarnate, the Vicar of Christ again, and then a slightly lesser devil.

Anyone attending the same church from 1635 to 1665 would have experienced similar upheavals in the Civil War, culminating, if they lived in London, in their church building burning down.

Anyone living in one of the new northern cities from 1850 to 1880 would have been awestruck by the impact of population and economic growth and the proliferation of new churches.

Periods of decline and decay in the churches have been followed by periods of growth and renewal. The eighteenth-century horror of enthusiasm in religion was entirely understandable as a reaction to the excesses of the Civil War. Yet a period of decline and decay in the Church was followed by the rise of Methodism, Sunday schools, the Evangelical Revival and the Oxford Movement.

Our own era of change has been gentler than in the past. Your bishop has probably not yet been burned at the stake for his or her beliefs ...

My little secret

I don't actually like change. I just think it is needed if the Church is to share the unchanging gospel in a changing world. Whenever I can I sneak up into the loft to run my model railway where it is eternally summer 1959, the trains are pulled by steam engines and I am in control. It is everything the real world is not.

When I went to Sunday school in the early 1950s it seemed like a period of Christendom stability. It was not without its confusions, of course. The Methodist minister was Mr Pope and the Church Steward Mr Bishop. But the Sunday school was full, and half the population came to the local park for the annual 'Whit Sing' of popular hymns. Right and wrong were determined from on high, mediated by the Church and accepted by the people. They didn't always live by the rules but they accepted what the rules were.

Since those days Christian morality and ethics have been largely rejected in favour of opinion polls. In many parts of the country it looks like Christendom has died. The postmodern consumer chooses their own mix of beliefs, buys their own social identity and tells their own story – 'I did it my way'.

I used to think that 'truth' had something to do with facts but apparently it no longer has – truth is whatever you experience it to be. If fairies down dingly dell are true for you that's fine with me. Or it would be if I were not an unreconstructed dinosaur blundering about in this strange postmodern post-Christian secular relativism in which Christian truth claims have become intolerant bigotry and Jesus a swearword. There now, I've got that off my chest and I'm feeling a little better. You see, all this change is quite unsettling for a pensioner like me, and I'll take my sedative now, nurse, if you can spare the time from texting.

Changing church and changing people

So those of us who have lived through this era of social change find it hard to understand and master. The Church of England is undergoing a sea change in its self-understanding from 'A pastoral church caring for a Christian nation' to 'A missionary church to a post-Christian culture'. We are lurching unsteadily from one world to another. The journey is taking a couple of generations and is most unsettling.

The role of the clergy is also changing. Clergy job descriptions less and less describe a parish pastor or congregational chaplain and more and more a leader in mission and enabler of the ministries of all believers. And the majority of clergy no longer lead one church, they oversee several. One day it is anticipated that clergy selection and training processes will notice this fact.

Huge change has also come upon lay church members. Once they were passive recipients of the ministrations of 'ministers'. Now they are expected to be ministers themselves. Church was an event you attended in your Sunday best, now it is a community you belong to in your leisurewear. At the same time as church has become more demanding of its members, their lives outside church have become more stressful. Back in 1959 going to church helped fill the emptiness of Sunday. For many Christians today, church feels like one more pressure in an over-pressured life.

Back on my model railway those model people arriving at its six well-attended churches are turning up out of habit, duty and loyalty. Frankly they are glued to the floor and have no choice. Such automatic attendance can no longer be relied on. If a church's services fail to satisfy the spiritual and social longings of the people they are not glued to the floor and may not be there next week. Quality matters, and this may be no bad thing.

Postmoderns treat churches like helicopters. They keep their distance for fear of being sucked in by the rotas. Churches structured around long lists of jobs, rotas and office holders, where the vicar's job is to find any old square peg to shove into a vacant round hole to keep the old show on the road, are struggling. My generation tried to fit into the fixed world they found around them. Younger generations of consumers believe the world should fit around them. Postmodern church life should be shaped around the gifts, energies and lives of the people rather than the other way round.

Up in the loft, the model people filing into my cardboard churches in 1959 look up to those important authority figures called clergy. Out in the real world today people are respected less for the position they hold and more for the authenticity of their lives. People take less notice of the vicar's sermons and more notice of how Christians live. Testimony is more powerful than ever. My little people experience community and belonging in their back-to-back streets and extended families. Today's people more likely seek community, friendship, love and belonging in church. In the 'Bricks and Mortar' section of *The Times* recently was a guide to finding the perfect village community. It listed eleven features needed for a good quality of village life, one of which was an 'active church'.

Churches still draw people. The Holy Spirit is still at work. Human hearts are still restless till they find their rest in Christ. But the motivations and processes have changed. Churches that work with the grain of societal change tend to grow and those stuck in a 1959 timewarp shrink.

Traditionally, we understood church growth to be about getting more people to join us. The culture and patterns of the church are fixed and we seek more people to join in. So long as the church is attractive in the first place this attractional model of church might work well, providing the people of the local community are broadly like those who go to church. But what if they are not?

Incarnational church

You can attract iron filings with a magnet but trying the same trick with aluminium leads to disappointment. Many people are not at all like churchgoers. They know nothing of the Bible, hardly anything of the Christian faith, and react badly to church services. Some are astonished that they have to dress in warm clothes in church, or that the toilet facilities are primitive or non-existent. And they do not take kindly to being constantly told to stand, sit, sing, and listen to me. The Sunday morning timing is impossible because the 9-year-old needs to get to football, the 14-year-old is in bed and Mum is setting off to ring the supermarket cash till. And none of the family want to spend precious time on Sunday sitting on a wooden bench in what appears to be a care home extension. The church magnet will never work for aluminium people.

However, the evidence in Chapter 11 shows that incarnational church can work well in aluminium country. An incarnational church is not predetermined but emerges out of the people and context it is trying to reach. Around half a million people have started going to Messy Church in the last ten years. When the church no longer expects the people to jump the cultural chasm to come and join it but goes out in new culturally accessible forms, people respond. Church shaped around the not-yet members rather than the preferences of existing members is likely to be both changing and growing fast.

Trad and new?

Churches should not make the 'either-or' mistake in which modernizers try to enforce change and traditionalists resist it. Church music, worship and style need not be battlegrounds in a multicultural church serving a multicultural world.

Moderns and postmoderns, Radio 1 and Radio 3 listeners, introverts and extroverts, computer-gamers and railway modellers, Goths, ravers, retired wing commanders, trainspotters, teen texters, venerable twitchers, and twenties tweeters all live together in our multicultural society. Rather than revolutionize an existing service many churches have found it better to add a new one in a different culture. Multiplex church can thrive and grow without disenfranchising those who meet with God in traditional ways. We can have one service for texters and another for trainspotters. Of course the texters will be unable to sing, being too busy with pithy comments to look up at the screen. I can tell you now that the trainspotters will not sing either. But at least they will write the hymn numbers down in their notebooks.

A church service in which all ages and types of people are integrated harmoniously together is, literally, a foretaste of heaven. Unfortunately they are as rare as hens' teeth. Academics call the need for a range of services for different sorts of people 'The homogenous unit principle'. In Yorkshire, where I come from, it is called 'Not putting all t' ferrets int' same sack'.

Settling the change debate

A gentleman with a flourishing ministry of discouragement came up to me one day and delivered a short sentence that clearly had some unspoken sections in brackets attached. In order to assist I will supply the unspoken sections in full: 'When the Reverend Oldman was vicar' (unlike the lightweight clown we now have as our vicar i.e. me) 'and we had the Prayer Book' (unlike the comic strip we now have) 'the church was full every week' (and now we all know it's empty). I was of the view that the changes would grow the church. I had looked in the old service registers and knew the old timer was suffering from selective memory syndrome. The church had only ever been full for special occasions. In fact, partly through adding another congregation my interlocutor never attended, attendance in my time had doubled. But still the contention remains – changes don't prevent decline, they cause it.

The argument over change and decline is easily settled by statistical survey. A church lists any recent changes and gives its attendance numbers three years ago and today. Attendance change at unchanging churches are then compared with changing churches. The results of five such diocesan surveys were reported in *The Road to Growth* (Jackson, 2005, p. 58).[1] The result is decisive and universal – churches making changes grow and those that don't shrink. Ten years on, the pattern is the same. A 2013 survey of all the churches in St Davids Diocese in south-west Wales revealed the following:

Q: What significant changes have been made to church life in the last three years?	
No changes: 92 churches	Attendance down 9%
At least one change: 67 churches	Attendance up 16%

Such a startling difference in just three years emphasizes the power of change, any change, in the recovery and renewal of churches. But the relationship between change and child attendance is even more startling than it is with adults (Figures 12.1 and 12.2).

Figure 12.1 Percentage change in adult attendance, 2010–13

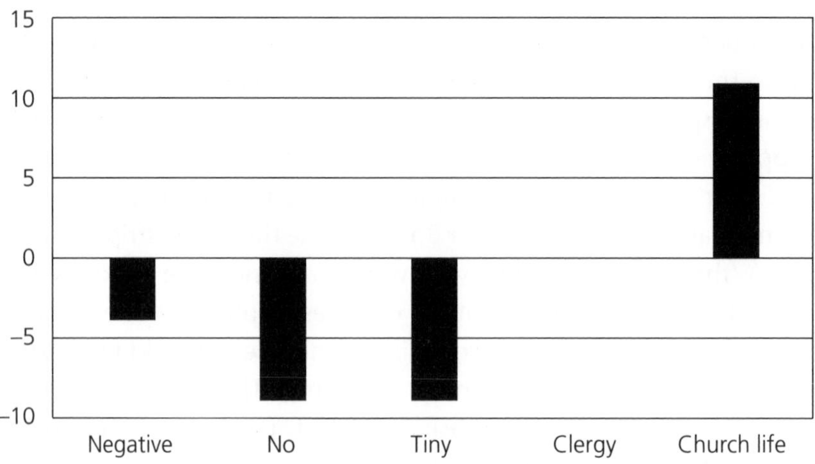

Figure 12.2 Percentage change in child attendance, 2010–13

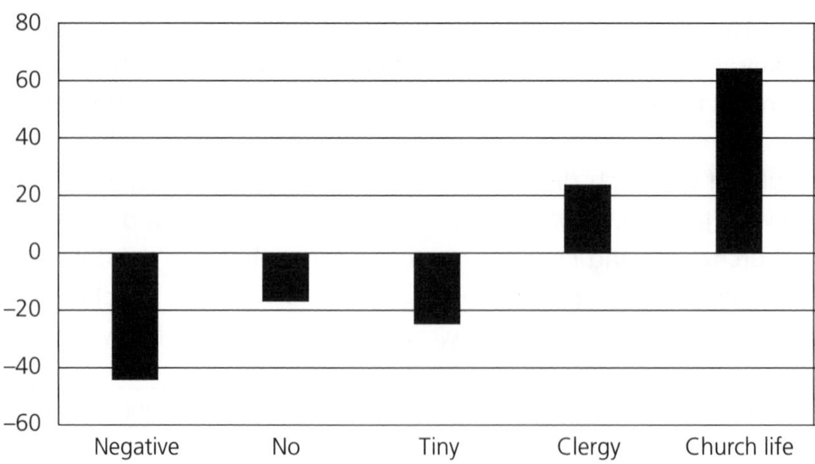

Negative changes included the loss of services or premises as part of the general decay of church life. Tiny changes were those too small to have a measurable impact. Clergy changes (gaining and losing vicars) cancelled each other out. Church life changes, however, were associated with significant numerical growth of just over 10 per cent of adults and 60 per cent of children. This compares with a loss of 20 per cent of the children in no-change churches. It is hard to overestimate the relationship between change and the numbers of children and families involved in church life. Those most responsive to both the failure to change and the achievement of change are the young and their parents.

Types of change that deliver growth

There was no screening here by type of change. Any deliberate change in church life or services was included. It is the ability to change that means a church can grow. No one change-category is the magic ingredient. Nevertheless, the types of change mentioned by growing churches do follow a consistent pattern. The research in five dioceses underlying Chapter 6 of *The Road to Growth*[2] suggested that effective change associated with church growth came in eight categories:

1. Planting new congregations.
2. Worship becoming less stiff, more relaxed, with better quality music.
3. Better provision for children and young people.
4. Improving the welcome and integration of newcomers (opening the front door).
5. Providing better small groups and pastoral care (closing the back door).
6. Regular use of evangelism, basics or nurture courses as part of an overall strategy.
7. More lay involvement in leadership.
8. Improvements to buildings.

These changes are about improving the quality and relevance of what is offered. It is not gimmicks that grow churches but improvements. Surveys in the last decade have found similar things. In St Davids 33 churches reported planting a new congregation. Their combined adult attendance rose 16 per cent and their child attendance 176 per cent. All-age attendance rose 27 per cent compared with an average drop of 6 per cent in churches that did not plant. Most of the newly planted services were aimed primarily at families, hence the dramatic rise in the number of children.

Sixteen churches reported making their service styles less stiff, more relaxed and contemporary. Adult attendance rose 25 per cent and child attendance 152 per cent. An additional twelve churches reported improving their provision for children and young people in other ways and these saw a 16 per cent rise in the number of adults and a 263 per cent rise in the number of children.

Similar growth was reported by churches that improved their welcome and integration of newcomers, their pastoral care provision, and their leadership spread. The 45 churches regularly using nurture courses also grew.

The churches collectively reported some modest overall attendance decline in the three-year period, yet those adopting appropriate changes saw significant growth. The diocese was not growing numerically, as some other dioceses in England are, not because the same things don't work – clearly they do – but because a smaller proportion of the churches had adopted them. What is needed for overall diocesan growth is for more churches to adopt similar changes.

The times they are a changing

It was reported in *The Road to Growth* (p. 49)[3] that attendance trends differed greatly between different service times. Most of the decline in church attendance since the 1960s was from Sunday evenings and early morning communions. Many of these services have now died. Main Sunday morning services had held up quite well and there was some growth in weekday congregations. These trends continue. The survey of St David's Diocese found 235 Sunday morning services but only 55 on Sunday evenings (Figure 12.3).

Figure 12.3 Diocese of St Davids numbers of congregations

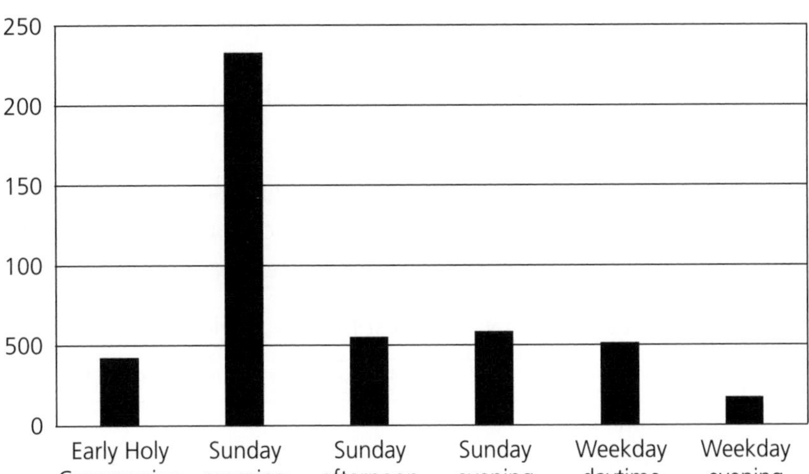

Figure 12.4 Diocese of St Davids numbers of congregations, 2010–13

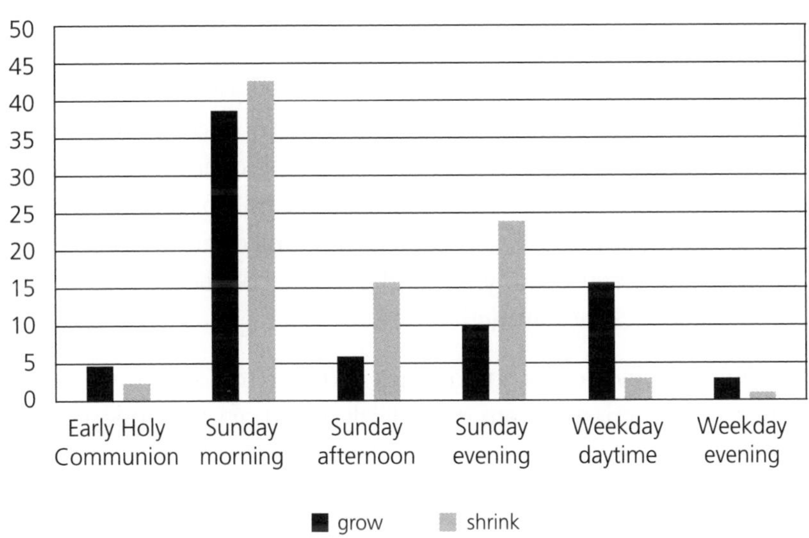

Morning services were more likely to grow and evening services to shrink. Sunday afternoons were mainly traditional services in churches within multi-church benefices. The time had been forced upon the congregation by the timetable of the peripatetic vicar and in most cases shrinkage appears to result. Weekday services, however, were growing well. Weekday attendance has been rising slowly as a proportion of the Church of England for many years. It accounted for 14 per cent of average weekly attendance in 2002 and 18 per cent in 2012.

Over the last ten years there has been a new service-times development. A questionnaire I used for a training course revealed the following spread of growing and shrinking services (Table 12.2).

Table 12.2 Spread of growing and shrinking services

Service time	Number growing	Number shrinking
Early Holy Communion	3	10
Main Sunday morning	30	17
Sunday late afternoon/ teatime	5	0
Sunday evening	3	12
Weekday daytime	14	4
Weekday evening	3	0

The new development is Sunday teatime, a good new time for many families. School and sports activities are over, the shops have shut, children have returned to Mum after a visit to Dad, the toddler has had her nap and is ready for action, families are getting a little fractious and need occupying, and the offer of food, worship and community becomes attractive.

So churches alert to changing times and able to adjust their service patterns and schedules are more likely to attract new people than churches whose service times are dictated either by a long-forgotten past or by the schedule of the vicar. Flexibility of service times is one of the key advantages of the 'Focal Minister' ministry arrangement advocated in Chapter 7.

> Habit is habit and not to be thrown out of the window by any man, but coaxed downstairs one step at a time. (Mark Twain)[4]

We have recognized that change inevitably hits churches from both external and internal sources. Passivity in the face of change leads to victimhood, but proactive churches have the chance to flourish and grow in a changing climate. They may need to change their service styles, times and patterns and to change or broaden their culture to cater for new generations. They will certainly need a drive for quality in all aspects of church life and buildings.

So strategic leadership for change is a precious asset for a church. Most changes will have some sort of rocky ride and partial acceptance. Leaders cannot afford to try to please everybody and need courage to drive through change in the face of opposition or uncooperativeness. But the good strategic leader can still come unstuck if the pastoral implications are neglected or poorly understood. Simply knowing what changes are needed does not make change straightforward. Human beings find change difficult and stressful. It is often controversial. Many a church has suffered not because it left change off the agenda but because its process of change went wrong.

I used to be vicar of a church where the PCC met in a first-floor room. We would have a good PCC meeting in which all agreed to make a certain change. A group would then gather underneath the window on the pavement to have their real meeting – discussing the results of the night's business. They never realized I hung about at the open window above them before I locked up, listening in. So they never knew that I heard all their complaints about the changes they themselves had just made. Real human beings are complicated creatures!

So winning the argument and the vote for change is not enough. Blank stares, muttering, foot dragging and subtle sabotage can turn any good plan into an unworkable mess. As well as making the external change, people also need to make the transitions inside their own heads that will enable them to adjust their habits, handle their emotions and be reconciled to what they have lost. The biggest issues are usually not to do with the shiny new things but with leaving behind the treasured old ways and familiar habits.

This is why churches try to do too many things. It is far easier to get agreement to add something new than to drop something old. If an element of the church's life or ministry does finish, it is often because it has dwindled away to almost nothing or else the leaders have died or despaired. A thinly spread church trapped in its past initiatives simply reeks of failure. Healthy churches are focused not frantic. Therefore, in order to become healthy, churches need good processes of change that enable the old to be let go of positively and the new to be embraced enthusiastically.

People buy into the leader before they buy into the vision

Change is best led by leaders whom the people have learned to trust. Sometimes a wise new leader will spend time being trust-worthy in smaller things before unveiling some grand scheme. It may be good to get a couple of small successes under the belt of a church community before it embarks on something ambitious. Churches often grow best when the main leader has been in post for between five and twelve years. After five solid years the people trust the leader and the leader knows the people.

There are, though, exceptions to this. In high population-turnover areas with few long-stay church members a new leader can become established more quickly. And most new clergy or other leaders get a honeymoon period. Perhaps the church has been waiting for change for a long time. The old vicar had stopped innovating years ago and then there was a twelve-month vacancy. So the process should start immediately and trust will need to be built along the way. Eighteen months after I became vicar of a Grade 1 listed church in Scarborough we had reordered the building and planted a new congregation.

One problem for new leaders of settled communities is that they are unaware of the history. They suggest a small and sensible change and some people react as though the four horsemen of the apocalypse have trampled into church. The presenting reason for their extreme reaction is not the real reason – this is hidden deep in their church or personal history. So new leaders will want to find long-stay tutors who can help them understand what makes the church and its people tick the way they do today. Time will need to be spent one to one to uncover, understand and deal with the unreasoned negatives triggered by an innocent suggestion.

Endings and losses

It is usually a bad idea to make the case for a change by rubbishing the past. This is usually taken either as personal criticism or as cruelly uncovering personal failure. Antagonizing half the people and depressing the other half is no foundation for moving forward together. We can talk about how these things were good in their day but, now that times have changed, we need another approach. The pews were a great improvement on private boxes when installed in 1864 but in our day comfy chairs and a carpet will be more effective missionally. The past is to be honoured and built upon not rubbished and discarded.

But a consensus for change may only build if there is dissatisfaction with the present as well as vision for the future. If people think the church is fine as it is they are not going to respond well to any future vision however fantastic it is. Dissatisfaction may need to be fostered but that is sometimes better done through focus on Jesus' high standards and ambitions rather than on the church's low ones.

In helping people to have a good process of change, start not with the shiny new outcomes but with the endings and losses, with letting go of the old. One mark of whether a MAP is authentically guided by the Holy Spirit is whether or not it includes elements of sacrifice. Is the existing church community willing to sacrifice something of what it likes for the sake of reaching others? Or are they just consumers planning to enhance and protect what they already like? Learning to embrace loss and sacrifice is part of the business of growing up as Christians. But, in order to get to that state of maturity, most congregations need leaders who understand their emotional processes and help them to deal with change and loss sensitively.

Stalwart George

George is a middle manager in a large company. He has been on the PCC for many years and is well respected. He started coming 40 years ago because he fancied a girl. They married in church and both their children were baptized there. George held many jobs in the church, including a stint as Sunday school superintendent in what he thinks were its glory days. He was treasurer for ten years and is proud of the 'rainy day fund' he built up. His wife died of cancer five years ago and her funeral was in church. George sits in the pew he always sat in with her. When he looks towards the chancel steps, in his mind's eye he either sees his wife resplendent in her wedding dress or else stiff and still in her coffin.

The new vicar is talking to the PCC about reordering the church, replacing the pews, turning the worship space round 90 degrees, adding some rooms for children's groups and costing a pretty penny. However good the argument for the reordering it is likely to unleash strong and difficult emotions in George, creating fresh feelings of grief and loss. It may feel like an insult to his wife's memory, a desecration of the key sacred moments of his life. Unless George can be prepared pastorally, listened to sympathetically, journeyed with lovingly, enlisted to work on the project positively, then it may be too much for him and for others. The architect's plan of the new building is no more important to the future of the church than is the pastoral plan for George's transition.

The sad sidesmen story

The sidespeople for the Family Service are introverted pensioners who have served faithfully for 20 years. Now they are getting tired and wanting to give up. The vicar finds some families to take over and the wardens create a new 'welcome desk' for them to operate from. The outward change is a great improvement. Everyone prefers being welcomed by a smiling 7-year-old to a surly 70-year-old. Therein lies the problem. The pensioners have overheard people saying how much better things are now. Old hurts and insecurities surface. Self-esteem takes another knock. Ceasing to be useful at church comes to symbolize the whole process of life closing in. Fuelled by their inchoate emotions, and rewriting history, they grumble about being no longer wanted. Some stop coming, others spoil the atmosphere. A change that should have contributed to the growth of the church is causing division and decline.

The vicar realizes what is going on and embarks on a process she should have started earlier, for prevention is always better than cure. She meets with the pensioners and gets them to tell her their church life-stories and how they feel now they no longer have official roles and jobs. She gets them to articulate their feelings, whether of anger, disorientation, loss, sadness, anxiety, withdrawal, depression or anything else. Simply talking about it acts as a safety valve. Being given a good listening to is wonderful therapy.

The next Sunday they have an official handover ceremony followed by a party. The pensioners are credited with getting the church to the stage it has now reached. The vicar asks them to help her run a training event for the new families and to make some 'play bags' for young children unaccountably bored with her all-age sermons.

So the pensioners, instead of feeling dumped, are enabled to make a healthy transition to the next stage. They had never wanted their old jobs back but they did want their sense of belonging, usefulness and self-esteem back. Belatedly, the church has done that for them so all can move positively on together.

In the transition zone

This is the stage when the new has not yet settled down and you are not quite sure whether it is going to work. Anxiety levels get high, old weaknesses emerge in full flower, some people get overloaded and ill. But there are many creative opportunities and the church is much more open to new people joining. Creative, innovative people are energized and in their element. You had thought the church might start growing once the change had bedded in, but it is actually the process of change that provokes the growth. This is why when a congregation needs to move out of its regular building for a few months while a rebuilding takes place the congregation grows numerically. When the transition is over and the congregation is back in the box of its improved building the hopes for further growth are often disappointed.

It is important in the nervous transition zone to have an early success to bolster confidence and morale, so it is no bad thing to build that into the planning! Celebrate success and cultivate a culture in which successes are expected and worked for. It is often best to try things for a few months and then review them than to go instantly from a previous immovable steady state to a new one. Celebrate the end of the probationary or experimental period, give thanks for the past and for the transition period before enabling people to dedicate themselves to serving God together in the new era.

Corporate and personal change processes

Having good processes of change is every bit as important to the growth and health of the church as having good content. The transitions matter every bit as much as the outcomes. It is usually better to install good systems for change in a church than to rely on the ad hoc instincts of the leader on each individual occasion. One of the purposes of MAPs is to make the business of instituting and managing change more corporate, less personal, more strategic and less reliant on individual initiatives. When a church community has its own MAP for developing the life of the church then part of that plan should be that the process of change and transitions is managed well – decisively but sensitively.

If the vicar gets the personal blame every time someone experiences a difficult change then eventually too many people will be holding something against them and their goodwill capital will all have been spent. They may need to move to another parish. It is better for the process of change to be the corporate will of the body of Christ, led by a vicar but broadly owned and implemented by the whole team. And the team will care just as much about the processes and transitions as about the outcomes. Then the full potential of intentional change in the life of a church can be realized for its future growth and flourishing.

13

Spending to grow

> The Twelve were with him, and also some women who had been cured of evil spirits and diseases: Mary (called Magdalene) from whom seven demons had come out; Joanna the wife of Chuza, the manager of Herod's household; Susanna; and many others. These women were helping to support them out of their own means. (Luke 8.1–3)

How fascinating that Jesus' own financial backers were women, at least one of whom, Joanna, must have been wealthy! The Son of Man had nowhere to lay his head, yet still there was a financial side to the business of bringing the kingdom of heaven into the kingdom of this world. Judging from the paucity of references to it, finance was not seen by the Gospel writers as a major factor. Money is never the main ingredient needed for churches to grow. Sometimes it is hardly needed at all. Yet it can critically constrain what is achievable. And, just as Jesus taught about money more than any other single subject, so churches worry about money more than any other single subject. When talking about the growth of the church we cannot ignore how the growth is financed.

Local churches

Planning and budgeting

The priorities of a local church, diocese or denomination are revealed by the diaries of its leaders, the agendas of its meetings, and the budgets of its activities. It is said that the majority of Anglican churches have a bigger budget for church flowers than for the whole of their youth and children's ministry. Many churches have to revolutionize their priorities if they hope to grow. Many do not even have amounts allocated to key budget heads for the year to come. These tend to be 'Magic Roundabout' churches as described in Chapter 6. If a PCC member asks for money the answer may well be determined by the attitude and worry-level of the treasurer. Where there is a preset budget the amounts available for different aspects of church life can be set by the strategy of the church to achieve the strategic priorities. Where there is intentionality about the future, a vision and plan to achieve it, then the need for budgets to enable each aspect of the plan to be activated become obvious. A church serious about growth will set a serious budget for growth.

Reviewing the spending pattern

Every church should occasionally review its past spending to work out what its financial priorities have actually been. Often the largest item has been parish share. Some other items, such as insurance, may also be predetermined. In fact some churches feel that they have very little 'free' money available to spend on 'optional' things like mission initiatives. Even if the PCC feels that the spending pattern does not reflect its own decisions the exercise is still helpful. At the very least it should uncover the frustration of budget constraints appearing to make genuine priorities impossible. In some churches the fact that most expenditure is spoken for before any PCC decisions are made may actually be a strange comfort, absolving the PCC of responsibility to set priorities. Such a church needs an injection of genuine desire to possess the tools to grow. Only then will it stand much chance of acquiring them.

If, on reflection, a PCC realizes it easily agreed a large amount of money on some new stops for the organ but then agonized about a small amount on evangelism, it will need to acknowledge where its priorities truly lie. That may be the first step towards rebalancing them.

When a church has a realistic budget for its spending heads it should also have a budget-holder for each aspect, either an individual or small group. Their job is to spend their budget as effectively as possible in pursuit of their element of the strategy. The budget holder has spending power over their own budget and should only go to the PCC during the year to ask for an increase. They should report to the PCC annually on how they have spent their allocation. That way the PCC is freed from micro-management and can focus on the main spiritual and strategic framework of the church's life.

Giving people budget-holding responsibility is an excellent way of helping them grow as church leaders and contribute to its growth.

Giving trends

Considering the long-term decline in church attendance and the greatly increased costs of the clergy, the Church of England has done well to stay afloat financially in recent decades. The main reason for this success is the increase in personal giving (Table 13.1).

Table 13.1 Giving to churches (real terms in 2011 purchasing power)

Year	Tax-efficient giving (millions)	Weekly average total giving per ER member
1970	£42	£2.10
1980	£62	£2.70
1992	£147	£5.10
2001	£244	£7.00
2011	£276	£8.40
2012	£283	£8.70

Source: Church of England, Finance Statistics, 2011

In 2012 78 per cent of all parochial income was voluntary giving. Other sources such as investment income and fundraising can be important but the churches are mainly reliant on the giving of their people and the people have not let them down.

However, we cannot expect personal giving levels to continue rising for ever to compensate for declining membership. Although some of the slow-down in the upward march of giving is the result of the recession, perhaps the limits of per capita giving are now being approached (Table 13.2).

Table 13.2 Annual average increase in giving in real terms (real terms in 2011 purchasing power)

	Tax-efficient giving p.a.	Total giving per ER member p.a.
1970s	5%	3%
1980s	11%	7%
1990s	7%	4%
2000s	1%	2%

Any further real-terms increases in parochial giving may need to rely less on the increased generosity of the remaining people and more on an increased number of people. The long-term solution to the financial needs of the churches is more people. This is not the main motive for churches to seek growth but it is a very happy outcome.

Giving attitudes

Many churches discover that 'money follows vision'. When churches find a new vision and purpose, perhaps through a MAP, they tend, literally, to buy into the vision. Churches focused simply on 'the trivial round, the common task' find the people do not 'furnish all we need to ask'. But where there is excitement, ambition, vision and strategy the people respond.

While I was vicar of St Mary and Holy Apostles Scarborough we realized we needed to employ a children's and youth minister in order to make further progress. But the church seemed fully stretched financially. So we had a Gift Day one Sunday. We set minimum targets for the amount of money to be pledged and the number of people doing the pledging. Only if both targets were met would we proceed. It was made clear that all offers should be in addition to existing giving. On the day both targets were hit exactly and the extraordinary precision of this made us feel God was in the process. New vision had called forth new faith and giving and a youth and children's minister was duly appointed.

Some churches with financial needs turn first to fundraising. Sometimes this can be positive, drawing in people outside the church and pulling the church community together in a shared and perhaps pleasurable activity – the church fete. But fundraising can become an end in itself, displacement activity from the real mission of the church. It can exhaust people by its repetitive nature and discourage them by the small amounts raised – the church fate. Repeated appeals for their money can put the local community off the church. And a focus on fundraising can stop Christians from taking responsibility for their own giving. The attitude becomes not 'How much should I give?' but 'Who can we get the money off this time?'

Underlying this is our fundamental attitude to money and giving. Many Anglican churches use the offertory prayer: 'All things come from you and of your own do we give you.' Churches where that prayer is genuinely meant will never be held back by money. God is the creator and owner of all our wealth and income. Giving some of it back to him through the church is a joyous act of gratitude and love. What better use for our money could there possibly be than extending the kingdom of heaven on earth?

Jesus taught more about money than any other subject, including apparently more religious ones like prayer. Read one of the Gospels and see what I mean! Some churches, however, find the subject so difficult it is almost taboo. Unless church leaders preach and talk about giving then how are the people to learn about it? And the matter of giving is a perfect example of the truth that example influences people more than exhortation. Unless clergy and leaders are giving seriously themselves they cannot expect church members to give seriously.

In most churches giving is not evenly divided between the congregation. It looks like over half of giving comes from 20 per cent of the givers – see 'Giving Insight', a report from the Churches Together Stewardship Network, 2011.[1] Often it is not the better-off or more prominent people who are the large givers. Giving varies less with income levels than with faith levels. Many clergy do not ask the treasurer to tell them how much individuals give. Personally I found it much better to be in the know. It is then possible to keep in perspective the cautious voices on the PCC giving £1 a week, and to take seriously the vision of the quiet sacrificial giver.

The parish and the diocese

Historically, the main financial interface between parish and diocese has been the parish share. Every diocese has its own unique allocation system. Many dioceses have a habit of changing or tweaking their system every few years. However, there are three main types.

1. The formula

A formula is applied to every church, parish or deanery to determine their share of the share. The main elements are usually attendance, membership and income modified by prosperity and other factors. Some formulae have grown so complex it is hard to understand why the share of a certain church has risen or fallen. But essentially the formula approximates to a poll tax or income tax. There are many problems with the formula approach, outlined in Chapter 13 of my book *The Road to Growth* (2004).[2] Some churches become very careful about their statistical returns, entering numbers that will yield a share they can handle. Others are bemused and disaffected by arbitrary rises nobody from the diocese can explain. Some are prevented from offering more than the formula amount because that is the nature of the formula – 'not a penny more, not a penny less'. Other churches become entangled in 'debt' to their diocese because they can't afford the amount the formula demands of them. Parish life becomes bedevilled by share arrears. The first response of the diocese to the growth of a church becomes not 'congratulations, how can we help you grow more?' but a demand for extra money even though the new people have not yet learned Christian giving. Increasing share with attendance or membership is not just a disincentive to grow, it also strips off the surplus that growing churches need to help them keep growing in the future.

It is hard to see how a diocese that claims to have a strategy to help churches grow but still has a formula share system can possibly be telling the truth.

2. Paying your costs

Here the clergy costs of a benefice plus some proportion of joint costs make up its share. This 'cost-based' system may be modified by a relative prosperity factor but generally the idea is you get what you pay for. This has a number of advantages. Church members are encouraged to pay the costs of their own church, or at least as much of them as they can manage. Benefices are incentivized to grow rather than shrink. There is no penalty for telling the whole truth on the Statistics for Mission form. If a benefice is chronically unable to pay its own way then the problem is solved by pastoral reorganization so benefices are modified until all become similarly sized self-sufficient units financially.

However, churches are still presented with a 'not a penny more, not a penny less' demand. It is hard to make allowance for benefices where there is growth potential but which cannot yet pay their own way. Unless there is strong cross subsidy through relative prosperity factoring, clergy may be withdrawn faster from areas of deprivation than areas of prosperity. The arrears problems remain.

3. Contributing what you decide

This system attempts to introduce Christianity into diocesan finances. Instead of a system of enforced taxation dictated by the central diocese this relies on mutual trust and Christian giving. Each church is informed about its costs to the diocese and asked to come to its own view about how much it can afford to pay – all its costs or more or less. If the total of offers is insufficient there may need to be another round until the numbers add up. Churches paying more than their own costs are freely offering Christian giving to others. Churches chronically unable or unwilling to pay their costs may, if other churches are not generous enough towards them, need to have their costs reduced through pastoral reorganization until they do meet them.

The concept of 'arrears' disappears along with that of 'taxation'. There is absolutely no need to think about share when filling in the Statistics for Mission form, growth makes it easier to meet costs and new surpluses can be harnessed for the next round of growth. Generous churches with good income are not restrained from giving more than a formula dictates and churches are free to help each other out.

In view of the polemic in favour of moving away from formulae towards an offers-based system in *The Road to Growth* (2005),[3] I confess to finding the recent growth in dioceses adopting this system quite gratifying. Basing share on offers rather than demands takes the risk of treating churches as though they were composed of Christians. Does treating people like mature Christians mean they will behave like mature Christians? The evidence accumulating from a number of dioceses suggests that this is indeed normally, though not universally, what happens.

Access to capital

In the secular world businesses need good access to capital if they are to thrive and grow. Sales and turnover rarely grow unless investment has been made. Churches are much more than small businesses, but the same realities apply. Any diocese wishing to support the development of its parishes should see the offering of grants and loans to entrepreneurial churches as a core component of its strategy. The Mission Development funding stream from the Church Commissioners provides many dioceses with the required funding source. Some dioceses find their own capital. The Diocese of Leicester is applying the proceeds of the sale of several surplus parsonage houses to its Growth Fund. The Diocese of Exeter recently made available 'A million for mission' out of its reserves to support parish initiatives.

This morning my writing of this chapter was interrupted by an email from another diocese saying they had received a multi-million-pound legacy. Could I suggest what they should do with this unexpected largesse? I have to confess I found this such an entertaining request that it engaged my attention for the rest of the morning. This is a diocese that had recently adopted a mission and growth strategy following years of decline. My response was threefold:

1. Through one person's extraordinary generosity, God has given the diocese money at this time because it is taking mission evangelism and growth more seriously. It is God's job to grow the church and God is providing the tools to do the job. So rejoice that, in the grace of God, the churches of the diocese will grow and flourish in the future. But the diocese will have to respond to the generosity of God with focused faith and ambition.
2. Resist siren voices to fritter the money away on building projects, employing a few more clergy for a while, diocesan vanity projects, a general reduction in parish share to make life easier for everyone, or help for redundant churches and old graveyards that ensure a comfortable decline. Similarly resist prudent but visionless voices to keep the capital and just use the interest or to put the capital on one side as a rainy day fund – it's raining.

3. The diocese has a core strategy to stop shrinking numerically and grow. The money should support that strategy. The best way of doing this is to establish a Growth Fund to which any unit of the diocese can apply for funding. The main grant-making criteria would be to support initiatives that show a plausible link from the spending of the money to the growth of the church. All the entrepreneurs in the diocese should be implored to make plans and put in bids to the fund. Let parishes, deaneries and the arms of the central diocese compete with each other on a level playing field to ensure the money gets used in the most effective way possible for provoking the growth turnaround and achieving the strategic goal. It will take a few years to get all the money out into the diocese growing the churches but there is enough money in this legacy to kick-start the growth everyone wants to see.

I wonder what the diocese will do!

There is accumulated wisdom across the country about good practice in diocesan grant-making and the use of mission funding. One day your author hopes to gather this together and disseminate it.

Money for planting

Most dioceses have put money into a few fresh expressions plants in recent years. Sometimes these are initiatives such as youth and young adult churches beyond the reach of individual churches. However, as these usually require a full-time paid planter they are expensive and few in number. The great majority of church plants are inevitably birthed and funded by local churches. It is usually a more efficient use of limited diocesan funds to offer grants and other financial encouragements to parish-planting rather than pursuing the central diocese's own initiatives. Modest start-up grants can provoke more widespread fresh expressions growth than mega-money for a single project that will probably fold anyway once the initial funding runs out.

The diocese and the national church

It is clear that national church money is capable of provoking growth if it is directed accurately for that purpose. The Mission Development Funding stream from the Church Commissioners to the dioceses has enabled a lot of church growth; see *Investing in the Church's Growth* (2008).[4] Chapter 14 of this book makes it clear that the growth of cathedral attendance since 2000 has only been made possible by the generous funding of cathedral clergy posts from the Commissioners. This growth is based on a multiplicity of services throughout the week that is well beyond the capacity of just one clergyperson to sustain.

However, it is beyond the capacity of the national centre to identify the most efficient ways of spending its growth-money at local level. The same principle applies to national money as to diocesan – it is best to invite bids from a grant-pool and so to allow everyone to compete on a level playing field. The superiority of the encouragement of enterprise over a system of central planning for growth can be seen in economies all over the world. Central funds are best used to encourage entrepreneurs rather than finance the brainchildren of officials.

Some of the most potent forces enabling new church growth are national initiatives from local entrepreneurs. Examples in recent years include the *Leading your Church into Growth* courses, Back to Church Sunday, Messy Church, and initiatives such as 'Arrow' and 'Growing Leaders' from CPAS. These initiatives tend to be chronically short of funding to enable them to reach their full potential. They do not need to be taken over or controlled from the centre. That is usually the kiss of death. But national initiatives for growth do need access to national church growth money. A national Church Growth Fund to go alongside the diocesan ones would probably be the best contribution of carefully targeted funding the national church could make to the culture of enterprise that will grow the church of the future.

The women who supported Jesus' ministry out of their own resources changed the whole history of the world through their carefully targeted giving. Some Christians have responsibility for national or diocesan funding, many PCC members have responsibility for spending by local churches. But all of us have some measure of power and responsibility for the spending of our own money. Whether by regular giving or one-off gifts or legacies together we have the capacity to provide the Bride of Christ with all the funding God will ever need to grow his church and bring in his kingdom.

14

Cathedrals to grow

Every day they continued to meet together in the temple courts. (Acts 2.46)

You are welcome to your cathedral

My wife and I were on holiday in the Netherlands. One day we, or at least my wife, enjoyed some city-centre shopping before wandering into a great square at the far side of which appeared to be a cathedral. As we approached it the crowds melted away and we were on our own in front of a large, locked door. We decided on circumnavigation to find a way in. It was an enormous building and a long walk, with locked doors and barred windows appearing from time to time. Finally, 90 per cent of the way round, was an unlocked door and in we went.

We found ourselves in a deserted cloister with a 'no entry' sign, but a left turn brought us to a glass booth occupied by an unsmiling lady selling entry tickets. We were the only customers. 'Are you over 65, it's cheaper if you are?' she asked my wife. My wife was not over 65 and was not amused. We appeared to have gained entry to a museum of ancient church silver and clerical garments occupying medieval anterooms. Tiring of rotting mitres I wandered down a gloomy corridor and tried a huge blank door at the end of it. There were no signs or markings. Surprisingly, the door creaked open and there at last was the worship space itself, vast, dark and pervaded by a strong odour of ancient incense like stale sweat in a gym. There were no staff, guides, life, colour or discernible facilities and, apart from a carved 'stations of the cross', no Jesus. The most interesting things were the ancient tombs in the crypt. We emerged depressed, wishing we had never visited this crumbling museum and understanding why the locals obviously never did.

'Such potential, such waste, such defeat,' I mumbled to my wife. 'If only one of our good cathedral deans could get their hands on this place, it could be transformed. Let's hit the shops again, anything is better than this, even shopping.'

Back across the square we entered a bookshop occupying a redundant church building. Maybe on our next visit the cathedral will be a department store – St John Lewis.

From a cathedral whiffing of death, we can now turn to the growing life and ministries of our English cathedrals.

Attendance at English cathedrals has grown

Cathedrals are complex institutions. Like parish churches, attendance at services is not the only measure of their effectiveness. But cathedrals are part of the attendance turnaround in the Church of England. The statistics that follow come from the 'Cathedral Statistics 2013' section of the Church of England's website.

In 2012 the 42 cathedrals were responsible for 3.7 per cent of Church of England average weekly church attendance – up from 2.3 per cent in 2002. In eleven years average weekly attendance at regular services rose 43 per cent from 26,500 to 37,800. Such growth is important itself but also illustrates how churches grow in general. It is true that cathedrals are different from other churches, but there are also commonalities and there is much overlap between the factors involved in cathedral and parish church growth.

Has attendance grown on Sundays or weekdays?

Sunday congregations have held up well but the main growth has been on weekdays – almost all the growth between 2002 and 2013 was accounted for by weekday attendance (Figure 14.1).

Figure 14.1 Total attendance at English cathedral services

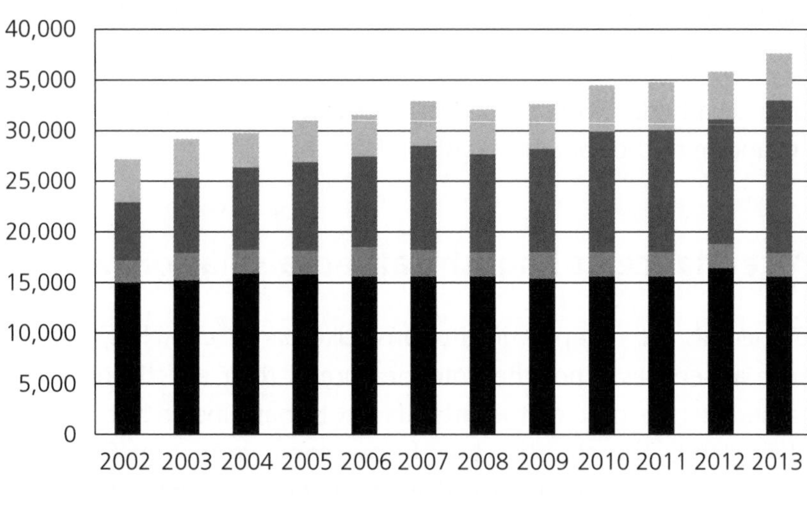

Attendance returns for some cathedrals look pretty inconsistent year on year. Some of the recorded growth, especially in the earlier years, may have resulted from changed or improved counting and reporting methods rather than growth on the ground. On the other hand, one or two recent headcounts suggest that cathedrals might still be underestimating their attendance. The statistical data contains problems but there has clearly been genuine overall congregational growth on weekdays. This assessment is reinforced by a range of other cathedral statistics which have risen significantly (Table 14.1).

Table 14.1 Cathedral statistics

	2002	2013	% growth
Adult weekly attendance	20,700	30,900	49
Child weekly attendance	5,800	6,900	19
Christmas attendance	106,500	124,300	17
Easter attendance	49,500	53,300	8
Child baptisms aged 0–12	520	570	10
Teenage and adult baptisms	120	220	83
Marriages	270	290	7
Funerals	350	390	11
Children attending cathedral schools	9,160	9,310	2
Cathedral choristers	1,810	1,940	7
Cathedral volunteers	11,930	14,700	23

Perhaps attendance has risen because cathedrals are well placed to benefit from the switch to weekday churchgoing. In the same period Sunday attendance at parish churches fell 10 per cent but weekday attendance rose 13 per cent. Cathedrals are open to the public all week through, have well-established routines of weekday services and are well enough resourced with clergy to enable multiple weekday services. It is perhaps no surprise that weekday numbers have risen fast when increasing numbers of people either feel too busy or tired on Sundays or else have lost a 'Sabbath' view of churchgoing. It is also helpful that weekday services tend to be quite short (say half an hour), a length of time people feel they can fit into their busy lives.

Which cathedrals have seen the growth?

Attendance has not risen uniformly in all cathedrals. Between 2007/08 and 2011/12 the nine cathedrals in London and the South East saw a 34 per cent increase in their attendance while attendance at all other cathedrals fell 2 per cent. The South East is the region where churchgoing trends are the strongest generally, and where economic dynamism, inward migration and population growth are concentrated. The socio-economic setting and geographical location of the cathedral is clearly an important factor in its attendance trend.

However, it is possible for cathedral attendance to grow rapidly anywhere. Average weekly attendance of adults at all services in Bradford Cathedral rose from 214 in 2005 to 610 in 2010.

There are also significant growth differences between the different types of cathedral buildings and foundations. In recent years the six large internationally known cathedrals (Durham, York, St Paul's, Canterbury, Salisbury, Winchester) have seen far more attendance growth than the others. It looks as though part of the appeal of cathedral worship lies not in the mere fact of designation but in the size, history and magnetic quality of the building itself.

Large congregations or multi-congregations?

Cathedral attendance growth has not come about through the swelling of giant congregations. Cathedrals are extreme examples of the 'multi-congregation' model of church. The average cathedral has 24 services a week and a total attendance of 850. This means that the average cathedral congregation size is 36. Cathedral attendance numbers are large because they attract lots of small crowds, not one big one.

This is also how many parish churches have grown, though not usually with as many services as cathedrals manage! The implication for all churches is clear – growth can come from planting new worship events on any and every day of the week. Multi-congregational church, as exemplified by cathedrals, is quintessentially Anglican because the Anglican ethos is that we are there for everyone. A multicultural 24–7 society needs a multicultural 24–7 church. Naturally, cathedrals tend to have their own niche cultures but their service style variety is growing and their 24–7 offering is second to none. Cathedrals suggest to the rest of the church that week-long multi-congregation is a great way to grow.

Research into cathedral growth

A team from St John's College Durham was asked to research cathedral growth as part of the 'From anecdote to evidence' Church Growth Research Programme set up by the Archbishops' Council and Church Commissioners. The full report by John Holmes and Ben Kautzer can be found on the Commissioners' website[1] and is due to be published by Cranmer Hall. Some of the most interesting findings are summarized below.

What types of services have seen the growth?

The Durham team received questionnaire responses from 36 of the 42 cathedrals showing numbers trends at each one of the regular services (Figure 14.2).

Figure 14.2 Attendance trends at cathedral services (numbers of services)

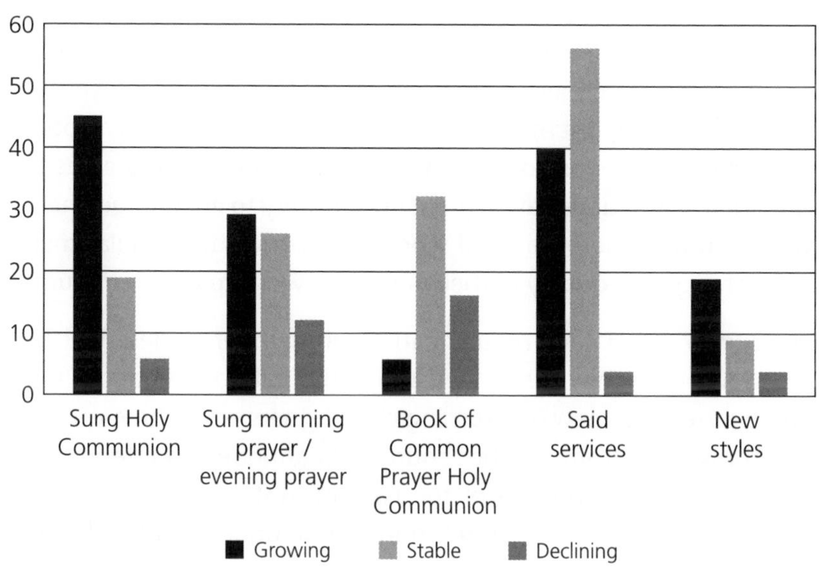

The only category with more declining congregations than growing were Book of Common Prayer services. This suggests that cathedral growth is not coming through adherence to traditional-language services. Rather, a range of new services begun in the period in question has contributed significantly to attendance growth. These include weekday communions and choral evensongs as well as new styles such as healing services, Taizé and fresh expression events. Chapter 12 showed that churches with fossilized services tend to shrink and those that innovate and plant to grow. The same is true of cathedrals.

What sort of people are cathedrals attracting?

A questionnaire from the Durham team of all regular congregation members in four cathedrals during one week found that just over half of respondents were retired, with an ethnic mix that was overwhelmingly white of UK origin. If these largely white and elderly congregations are in any way typical, they present a clear challenge to cathedrals to attract a wider age and ethnic range, perhaps with a wider range of worship and community styles.

The proportion of occasional and one-off visitors is a lot higher than in parish churches, with only half the congregations being regular, committed worshippers. Some one-off worshippers will have been tourists from afar, but most were local. Eighty per cent of all respondents who gave a postcode lived in the same postcode area as the cathedral. Cathedrals have a great opportunity to encourage one-off visitors to become occasional worshippers and then regular members through the quality of their welcome, worship and community.

The survey asked each regular cathedral member to describe their situation when they first joined the cathedral congregation. Only one-quarter were new or returning churchgoers while three-quarters had transferred from another church or continued to attend both. This is the exact opposite of the case in fresh expressions, where three-quarters are new or returning churchgoers and only one-quarter transferees. For those looking strategically at where overall church growth is likely to come from, therefore, putting resources into fresh expressions may be a more promising investment than cathedrals. Fresh expressions present a clear challenge to all traditional churches, not just cathedrals, to find ways of attracting those currently not attending any church.

Why do people choose cathedrals?

The congregational survey in the four cathedrals used a question from an earlier study of two cathedrals (Francis and Williams, 2010, pp. 39–40).[2] This classified motives in four categories – place, worship, people and anonymity. The 'place' motives (feeling of peace, connection with history, contemplative atmosphere), the 'worship' motives (music, choir, style of worship, preaching), and the 'people' motives (friendly atmosphere, friendship) scored highly among cathedral worshippers, but the 'anonymity' motives (anonymous to congregation and clergy, not having to take on responsibility) had low scores and appeared to be important to very few. There will always be some who start sitting behind a pillar and gradually over the weeks slide along a pew into the sight of the clergy. But they seem a minority even in a cathedral. What most people are looking for is warmth and friendship, not isolation. If this is true in cathedrals how much more true in parish churches!

So it looks as though the main elements of cathedral drawing power are:

- an environment that helps people feel at peace, to be contemplative
- the music, choir and style of worship
- a friendly community.

These answers reflect people finding their way to God stimulated by great architecture, centuries of prayer, good quality music and preaching, and a friendly, supportive cathedral community.

The importance of choir and music is both about the quality and the style. Cathedrals should never compromise on quality. But if some are attracted by top-quality music in one style then it is likely that others can be attracted by top-quality music in a different style in the same quality venue. In order to grow their congregations cathedrals do not need to change their 'Radio 3' music, but they can add other styles in a multi-congregation, multi-music-culture church. There seems no reason why cathedrals cannot attract new groups and generations with high-quality music allied to the attractions of the building and community in a range of styles – jazz, rock, gospel, modern worship or whatever.

Why have cathedral congregations grown?

As usual, the list of factors involved is quite long. The following have emerged from statistical evidence, conversations with cathedral deans, and observations of good practice. This list of reasons why cathedral attendance has grown in the last ten years suggests how it might grow further in the next ten years:

1. Cathedrals are well placed with their open buildings and daily services to cater for the switch to weekday churchgoing.
2. They have grown through expanding the number of services they offer throughout the week. Some cathedrals have changed their service times and patterns better to fit with the rhythms of their local communities, for example changing from a mid-morning to a daily lunchtime Eucharist.
3. Cathedrals have expanded the range of their service styles. For example, in many cathedrals, the largest service of the week includes family-style worship and children's groups. Further expansion of the range may offer the biggest scope for future growth.
4. They have been able to offer so many services because they are relatively well staffed with clergy.
5. Cathedrals have not been subject to the same debilitating cuts in staffing and amalgamations as the parish churches because

their funding has come direct from the Commissioners and been protected.

6. Cathedral buildings that offer a numinous atmosphere where people can find beauty and inner peace are perhaps an increasing draw in a frantic age.
7. High-quality music, choirs and preaching, a rich depth of regular daily worship, draw people in.
8. Cathedral congregations thrive not as isolated, anonymous individuals but in the soil of a friendly community. It helps in this that cathedral congregations are not one giant community but many small ones. Although growth is possible anywhere, cathedrals grow best in areas of high population and socio-economic vibrancy.
9. Cathedrals have become more intentional about mission. The culture is changing and mission has moved up the priority list. This cultural shift has been essential to making the most of the opportunities available to cathedrals and it needs to continue if cathedral congregations are to continue growing.
10. Better hospitality and welcome. This is a vital aspect of the culture shift. Cathedrals have been improving their attitudes and facilities for welcoming visitors, hosting events, and cultivating community in congregations. Some have invested in improving the welcome embodied in their buildings, for example by replacing great solid wooden doors with glass ones. The number of cathedral volunteers, key to good welcome and hospitality, has risen steadily.
11. Many cathedrals have developed the way they create a climate for the spiritual seeker to take a step forward with sacred spaces, votive candles, prayer cards and so on. Wells Cathedral sold over 50,000 votive candles in 2011.
12. Some cathedrals have increased their civic profile and range of special services. The number of special services at Bradford Cathedral increased from 28 in 2009 to 51 in 2010. Some of those who appreciated their own special service seem to have returned for regular services.

13. The architecture and artefacts of a great cathedral can make it a natural venue for cultural and artistic events, bringing in large numbers of people to enjoy the building. An invitation to explore the beauty of a cathedral should be an invitation to explore the wonder of God.
14. The number of schoolchildren visiting cathedrals in organized parties rose 15 per cent between 2002 and 2012. Some cathedrals invest heavily in their educational ministry, employing education officers. There may be little immediate impact of this on cathedral attendance, but perhaps a long-term impact on people who responded warmly to cathedral visits in their formative years.
15. Several cathedrals say that congregations have grown because of new provision for children in worship. Some are admitting children to communion before confirmation. Some cathedrals report an increase in confirmations and in the provision of Christian basics courses.

Almost all of these engines of growth lie within the compass of cathedral leaderships to change and develop.

Cathedrals have their own unique role and special opportunities within the dioceses, but their roads to growth are full of the same principles that apply to every church. There is huge scope for further growth through the application of these good practices adapted to the unique situation of each cathedral.

What are the threats to further attendance growth?

There will always be threats from the usual suspects – undue preoccupation with building maintenance, ancient monument-mindsets ousting mission-thinking, financial crises causing staff to be laid off, 'Temple' theology, that God is to be found primarily in the building, disharmony between the clergy or other leaders, and so on.

However, one particular threat is almost bound to grow year by year. Congregational growth in cathedrals is hugely dependent on their clergy staffing levels because of the sheer numbers of services involved. The Church Commissioners pay the costs of a dean and two canons in most cathedrals, which between them employed 153 deans and residentiary canons in 2002 and 145 in 2012. Much of this slight drop is probably caused by vacancies rather than a reduced number of posts.

It is unlikely that cathedrals can continue for ever to be protected from the clergy cuts that afflict parish churches in almost every diocese in the land. Ringfencing national cathedral subsidy leading to an increasing imbalance between the protected and the unprotected leads to increasing pressure arbitrarily to reduce cathedral support financed centrally. *Resourcing Mission for a 21st Century Church* (2006)[3] recommended that the money flow from the Commissioners to the cathedrals should be included in a block grant to each diocese, leaving the diocese to make the decision about the balance of funding between parishes and cathedrals. That way the decisions are made by local people responsible for paying for them locally and a more efficient distribution of resources is more likely. Dioceses may choose to increase provision for their cathedral or to reduce it. But in the long term, cathedrals will be more secure under such a system than they are at present when the funding regime can change through national church decisions unrelated to their local needs. Cathedrals that can develop their own funding streams to pay for their own clergy will be far more secure in the twenty-first-century church world.

Greater churches

In 1991 a group of incumbents of large, cathedral-like, churches got together for mutual support to form the Greater Churches Network. Their shared characteristics include large church buildings and visitor numbers, a wider ministry than the normal parish church, paid staff and an open church each day. Greater churches tend to be historic buildings with a representative focus in their locality and diocese. They face similar challenges and opportunities to cathedrals but without the same financial support from the Commissioners or the 'cathedral' label. Many are part of multi-church benefices.

There are currently 41 members of the network, though their situations and natures vary considerably. One significant development has been the awarding of 'Minster' status to 14 large urban churches around the country, beginning with Dewsbury Minster in 1993.

On average the greater churches put on four services a Sunday, like cathedrals, and eight on weekdays, a lot less than cathedrals, partly because of their lower staffing and volunteering levels. It is possible that more of their weekday services are of the low-key 'join the clergy in saying the Office' type than is the case in cathedrals.

It is difficult to compare the attendance trends of greater churches with those of cathedrals. The questions asked are different – cathedral weekday attendance figures are yearly averages, greater churches are a four-week count in October like other parish churches. The response rate is not good and the data standard for multi-church benefice greater churches is too poor to use at all. However, given those limitations it looks as though attendance at greater churches may have declined somewhat up to around 2007, then grown back since.

Greater churches may have lacked the consistent growth dynamic of cathedrals because they lacked the same capacity to plant and develop growing weekday congregations. However, over the last five years it looks as though this has started to happen. Weekday attendance looks to be around two-thirds higher in 2012 than 2007. The cathedral experience suggests that greater churches have the potential to grow weekday attendance a lot more, providing they can find the people to lead them.

Learning from and supporting each other

It may be no coincidence that greater church numbers have started to turn around as the network began to focus more on common mission issues. It seems universal that where churches and clergy connect with each other, learn from each other, support each other, and think together about strategy and intentionality, their congregations tend to grow. This was an observation in the report *Another Capital Idea* (Jackson and Piggot, 2010).[4] Both the Association of English Cathedrals and the Greater Churches Network should feel encouraged to develop their role encouraging sharing good news, pooling good practice and offering mutual support.

Incremental growth

Much of the recent competitive success of British cycling under David Brailsford has been put down to an incremental approach to quality. Attention to a whole series of detailed improvements to bikes and training, none of which are very significant by themselves, have added up together to give team UK a competitive edge.

Sometimes church growth comes not in a giant leap as a result of a single major development, but slowly, steadily, driven by a succession of small improvements that together, over time, build into significant change. Small steps can make big differences. Cathedral leaderships across the Church of England have been making progress through a succession of apparently minor improvements that over time have built up momentum. Examples include displaying 'church open' signs, putting out more votive stands, installing glass doors at the west end, announcing a service over a loudspeaker before it begins, inviting visitors to join in, running a nurture course and making better use of social media to advertise services and events.

Driving up the quality of buildings, services, events, ministry, relationships and community through an intentional programme of many small-scale improvements can be a very effective way for any church to grow numerically and steadily over a period of time.

15

Dioceses to grow

'Out of the eater, something to eat; out of the strong something sweet.' (Judges 14.14)

A necessary crisis?

The diocese had been losing money for ages, reserves dwindling. The chair of the board of finance knew economies had to be made, but the bishop wouldn't hear of clergy cuts. Keeping the clergy on the ground was the only mission and growth strategy he knew. But cutting clergy numbers was the only rescue strategy the finance chair knew. Impasse. Eventually, the bishop retired and the chair of the board of finance seized his chance at the next bishop's council meeting.

In a tense atmosphere he laid out the financial realities, demanding a decision. Clergy costs accounted for 90 per cent of the diocese's expenditure. Unless clergy numbers were reduced the diocese was heading for bankruptcy. The calculations had been made – cut 50 clergy posts over 5 years, diocesan expenditure would be level with income and all would be well.

The chair was right – current expenditure was unsustainable – but his reasoning was flawed because removing 50 clergy would also cut income. This was clearly shown in Chapter 7. And, if attendance decline was left to continue unabated, then income would go down even if 50 clergy were not lost. But would council members see the flaws and point them out?

Fortunately the diocesan missioner had the ability to see the flaws, the courage to point them out and also the sense to find a way forward. Simply opposing cuts would have meant defeat. The financial urgency and the smell of fear in the bishop's council were too strong. Instead, the missioner said, 'The trouble is, unless all the clergy are completely ineffective, if we cut 50 posts, churches will shrink and income will go down. Then we'll have to cut more posts and lose more income indefinitely until there are no more clergy and churches left. I accept we have to make some cuts but we also have to develop a mission strategy to help the churches grow. Otherwise we're just organizing our own decline and eventual death.'

So the bishop's council made two decisions that day – to make the clergy cuts but also to invest in a new strategy for mission and growth. In the following five years the cuts were made, decline was almost halted, and the financial deficit beast slain. More recently, the growth indicators have all been going upwards. The sweet honey of new life has emerged out of the strong deficit that was eating up the life of the diocese.

Riddle solved!

A short history of diocesan mission strategies

Until recently most dioceses did not consciously adopt strategies to aid the flourishing and growth of the churches. Diocesan leaders chose and paid the clergy, collected money from the parishes, and maintained the status quo and the parish system. They maintained stability rather than provoked change.

Sometimes a bishop would pursue his own strategy. When David Lunn was Bishop of Sheffield in the 1980s his aim was that 'every parish would be a good parish'. He looked for good young clergy to bring that about and supported them when parish old guards objected to change. To keep the momentum of a good incumbency he kept vacancies short – about three months. He supported Billy Graham's 'Mission England' mission to Sheffield in 1985. Church attendance was greater at the end of his time than the beginning. But this was a personal strategy of the bishop, not a written, agreed, publicized, corporate strategy of the diocese.

The first diocese to develop a written mission and growth strategy was London in the 1990s. A few others (Leicester, Lichfield) followed in 2004/05, then others (Bristol, Salisbury, Birmingham, Blackburn, Exeter) in 2008/09 and more in 2010 (Liverpool, Norwich, Rochester, Chelmsford, Southwell). Since then the majority – though by no means all – of the dioceses have either adopted a written strategy document or are working on one.

These dates are offered tentatively because sometimes it is unclear whether a diocesan document really is a rounded growth strategy or when it first came into operation. Some documents make little difference on the ground. I may have missed developments in some dioceses. But once there was a pioneer, then a trickle, then a stream and now a flood.

Should mission strategy be core diocesan business?

The absolute core church activity is to worship God. But mission or evangelism leading to the growth of the church is not a second-order optional extra for enthusiasts. If we are overwhelmed by the love of God for the world then we overflow with the love of God to the world. That is why David Bosch said that it is not the Church of God that has a mission in the world but the God of mission who has a Church in the world. God's mission of saving love to the whole of creation is at the heart of his being and agenda. It flows out of him both to and through the Church. The Church is not the only route by which God's missional grace flows into the world, but he has chosen and appointed the Church for this purpose. A diocese is not a financial organization or employment vehicle, it is a mission agency serving the extension of God's kingdom. The primary task of diocesan leaders is not to manage decline, employ the clergy, preserve an institution or fight internal ecclesiastical battles, but to lead the mission of the Church out into God's world. It is the very DNA of the Bride of Christ to pour out the love Christ pours into her over the world Christ poured out his blood to save.

When Archbishop Fisher succeeded William Temple as Archbishop of Canterbury in 1945 the priority apparently changed from 'The conversion of England' to 'Reform of Canon Law'. Speaking at General Synod in 2013 in connection with the founding of an evangelism task group to re-evangelize England, the Archbishop of York said, 'Compared with evangelism, everything else is like rearranging furniture when the house is on fire. Tragically, too often that is what we are doing. Reorganizing the structures, arguing over words and phrases, while the people of England are left floundering amid meaninglessness, anxiety and despair.'

From now on we should never again make Fisher's mistake – the main thing must be the main thing until Christ comes again.

Pooling wisdom

Anglican dioceses spend much time paralleling each other across the spectrum of their activities. The people holding parallel positions in different dioceses may rarely learn from each other. This means that the Anglican Church is not a very efficient learning organization.

To help dioceses pool their wisdom for growth strategy, the St John's Nottingham Centre for Church Growth organized two consultations for those responsible for framing and delivering strategy. What follows is a distillation of the collective wisdom of the two gatherings, beginning with principles for good diocesan practice in helping churches grow.

Start with vision

Vision comes first. Vision is where you want to go, strategy is how to get there. You cannot plot a route until you know where you want to go. A diocesan vision should capture what the diocese wants to become and achieve. It should summarize its core priority and distinctive calling discerned from God. Vision is best expressed as a short, memorable phrase expanded with some brief straplines. A visual logo helps emphasize the vision phrase. Examples of current vision titles are:

Going for Growth	(Lichfield)
Transforming Church	(Birmingham)
Growing Hope	(St Davids, Church in Wales)

London's current vision has a title and three straplines:

Capital Vision 2020
Confident in speaking and living the gospel of Jesus Christ
Compassionate in serving communities with the love of God the Father
Creative in reaching new people with the power of the Spirit.

A good vision document will be discerned and agreed by the whole diocese, not simply be the private brainchild of the bishop. The explanation will commit the diocese to aspire to grow and also to change in order to grow. It will include a diocesan prayer for the vision, circulated to help every individual and church to pray.

Listening is key

The core vision and strategy for achieving it are likely to be discerned through a multiple-listening process:

1. To God. The appointed leaders of the diocese should enlist the help of 'anointed' listeners to the voice of God.
2. To the national church and its leaders. Diocesan strategies are unlikely to vary wildly. The Archbishops have given a strong lead. The priority is to grow the church spiritually, numerically and in its capacity to serve the nation.
3. To church members. Trust the Holy Spirit to be at work in the people as well as the leaders. Good vision and strategy come bottom up as well as top down and the vision needs wide ownership.

4. To the people of the area – it is important to address the issues that concern them.
5. To our partners in other churches – we need to work together where we can.
6. To the current situation, being realistic about what a diocese can and cannot achieve.

Good strategy is always worthwhile

Strategy is an intentional set of interlocking changes intended to achieve the vision. Change is inevitable. One diocese reflected that '47 per cent of our stipendiary clergy will have retired in ten years' time. This alone should help concentrate our thinking. Change is going to come whether we like it or not. Our challenge is to be masters of this change, discerning where God might be leading us.'

It is possible to do strategy badly. 'Consultation exercises' should not be 'sell exercises' in disguise. Cost-cutting exercises should not be dressed up as mission exercises to sugar the pill. Strategy is not telling everyone to do the same thing, imposing uniform change on unwilling parishes. Anyone interested in comparing directive central planning with the encouragement of enterprise as ways of delivering growth should study the contrasting fortunes of North and South Korea. And strategy is not about expensive diocesan vanity projects. Churches, not dioceses, grow churches. So effective central diocesan strategy is about supporting churches not controlling them.

Principles of good strategy

1. The alternative to bad strategy is not no strategy, it is good strategy. Good strategy provides a helpful environment in which existing churches can flourish and new ones be born.
2. Good strategy is long term. It should evolve but not be ditched when a new bishop arrives or a snag appears. Fifteen years is a

good time span. It can take five to ten years before the growth indicators turn around.

3. Good strategy is SMART – specific, measurable, achievable, realistic and timed. It is not about holy platitudes. The diocese should have the honesty to evaluate and courage to adjust when things are not working.
4. Good strategy is impatient with mediocrity. It focuses not on forcing numerical growth but on supporting growth in the quality of church life. Healthy churches grow naturally, so help the churches to be healthy and God will do the rest.
5. Good strategy needs good process as well as good content. Processes should not be a top-down steamroller, but promote healthy, adult relationships and value individuals. Sometimes, a unifying, energizing process can do more good than the content of the subsequent strategy.

Good strategy is clear about what the diocese can do. The four main categories are:

1. *Reform the elements that hold churches back* – shortening vacancies, changing poll-tax share systems, cutting down ineffective boards and committees, reducing overheads, tackling a hoarding mentality on the Diocesan Board of Finance or a conservation mentality on the Diocesan Advisory Committee.
2. *Add new and helpful elements* – adding new mission and growth posts, offering 'growth fund' grants, arranging good practice exchange, offering helpful conferences and training opportunities.
3. *Improve the way the diocese supports the clergy* – making better processes for finding entrepreneurial ordinands, offering more direct training in how to be a leader in mission, recruiting clergy in tune with the existing diocesan strategy, shaping realistic job descriptions with growth in mind, highlighting clergy with growing churches.
4. *Make direct parish interventions* – asking parishes to develop Mission Action Plans, funding and organizing Lent courses on growth, sending leadership teams on *Leading your Church into*

Growth courses, organizing a good diocesan Back to Church Sunday.

Can every diocese grow?

Dioceses differ – some are in the less economically dynamic parts of the country, remote from London, away from the main trade routes, lacking in population growth and seeing the more able segment of their population move away. Others are in the more favoured parts of the country, seeing population growth and net inward migration. So is it harder to grow churches in the less dynamic places than it is in London?

Table 15.1 divides dioceses into four groups according to their rate of population growth from 2001 to 2011. All dioceses have seen some population growth, but the amount varies considerably between 15 per cent in Ely and hardly anything in Hereford. Figure 15.1 suggests that attendance change in the four groups of dioceses did indeed vary with their population trends. Those with the biggest population growth had the least attendance loss, and the decline in attendance per thousand population was fairly uniform across the groups of dioceses.

So population growth looks like it helps church growth, but does not guarantee it. David Voas's survey for 'From anecdote to evidence' found that population growth was only mildly significant for attendance trends. In Canterbury Diocese population rose 11 per cent but usual Sunday attendance shrank 22 per cent and average weekly attendance 18 per cent. In Carlisle population rose just 3 per cent but usual Sunday attendance shrank only 13 per cent and average weekly attendance 7 per cent. External factors affect but don't determine attendance trends – internal church factors are often key.

Table 15.1 Population growth by diocese, 2001–11

Group 1 Rapid growth		**Group 2 Steady growth**	
Diocese	% pop Growth	Diocese	% pop Growth
Ely	14.8	Bradford	8.6
London	12.9	Winchester	8.4
Southwark	11.7	St Albans	8.2
Canterbury	11.1	Birmingham	8.1
Bristol	10.8	Guildford	8
Chelmsford	10.7	Oxford	7.8
Leicester	10.7	Chichester	7.6
Peterborough	9.8	Coventry	7.6
St Ebbs	9.8	Southwell	7
Lincoln	9.3	Wakefield	7
Manchester	9.3		
Average	11%	Average	7.80%

Group 3 Modest growth		**Group 4 Little growth**	
Diocese	% pop Growth	Diocese	% pop Growth
Salisbury	6.9	Exeter	5.5
Bath	6.7	Derby	5.2
Truro	6.6	Newcastle	5
Norwich	6.5	York	4.7
Rochester	6.5	Chester	3.7
Sheffield	6.4	Blackburn	3.4
Portsmouth	6	Carlisle	3.3
Worcester	6	Durham	3.3
Lichfield	5.9	Liverpool	2.4
Ripon	5.8	Hereford	0.6
Gloucester	5.7		
Average	6.30%	Average	3.70%

Figure 15.1 Percentage change in groups of dioceses with different rates of population growth, 2001–11

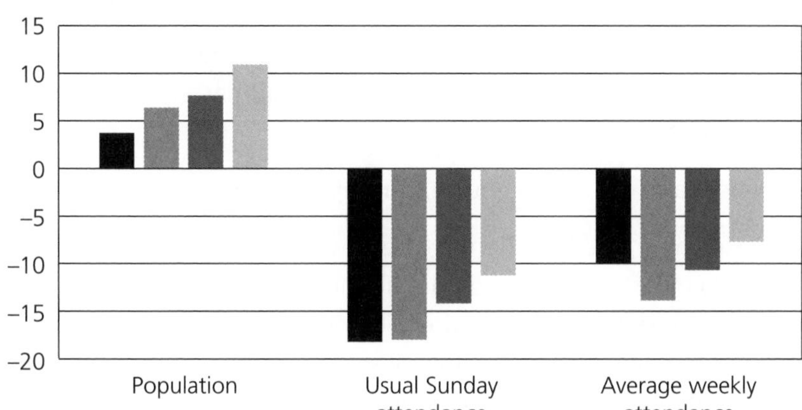

Elements of a good strategy

As well as working out some principles, the consultations also identified key elements in good strategy.

1. Pray – hit the ground kneeling

Most diocesan strategy documents start with prayer. Listening prayer is needed for guidance and discernment about the strategy, and intercessory prayer for the strategy to succeed. But also prayer deepens relationships with God and develops Christian disciples. Sometimes we become the answers to our own prayers. If a strategy calls people to pray then the diocesan leaders should lead by example. Diocesan meetings should move on from a perfunctory opening prayer to praying seriously together as the heart of the business.

Being a praying person was not always universally seen as advantageous for a bishop. When he retired in 1961 Archbishop Fisher called on the prime minister, Harold Macmillan. 'I have come to give you some advice about my successor,' said the Archbishop. 'Whomever you choose, on no account must it be Michael Ramsey, the Archbishop of York. Dr Ramsey is a theologian, a scholar, a man of prayer. Therefore he is entirely unsuitable as Archbishop of Canterbury. I have known him all his life. I was his headmaster at Repton.' Macmillan replied, 'Thank you, your Grace, for your kind advice. You may have been Dr Ramsey's headmaster, but you were not mine.'

Michael Ramsey was, of course, duly appointed.

Dioceses may need to identify the best growth opportunities into which to direct their limited human and financial resources. A good guide is to look for places where there is a group of local leaders praying regularly together, already some evidence of the Holy Spirit transforming lives, and people willing to pay the cost of mission and growth.

Specific prayer initiatives a central diocese can consider include:

- Whole days of prayer, praying specifically for renewal and growth.
- A day of fasting or a week of prayer when there are no church events but all Christians are encouraged to pray at home for evangelism in their communities.
- Spiritual MoTs for individuals – 'start by stopping'.
- Time of lament – to feel God's heart for a broken world and empty souls.
- Diocesan email or text prayer messages to a network of intercessors.
- A diocesan prayer card (bookmark?) to give to every church member containing the diocesan strategy prayer. Ask everyone to use the prayer at home and every church to use it in the public intercessions at every service.

The Diocese of St Davids in 2013 issued such a bookmark containing the logo, vision statement and prayer for the diocesan turnaround strategy (Figure 15.2).

Figure 15.2 St Davids' bookmark with logo

O God our Father, you lead us on ways both new and unknown: teach your church in our Diocese of St Davids to live the good news given to us in Jesus Christ Lord and Saviour; make us to be light in your world and equip us to be partners in your mission so that others will find their way to you. Amen.

2. Aim at cultural transformation

Specific actions may be ineffective unless the culture of the diocese and its churches are changing. Sometimes people are afraid to change or experiment because they think change is disapproved of. Some Anglicans feel bound by 'rules' that exist only in their own imaginations. Some like it that way because restrictive rules take away personal responsibility. But a bishop can change the culture simply by articulating the need to change and inviting or inspiring people to experiment. 'We will think better of you for trying new things that don't work than for not trying at all.'

Diocesan culture can be shifted through appointing dynamic people rather than safe people to key positions. Rather than making appointments to keep a tradition balance, dioceses should always appoint the best person to deliver the strategy.

In some dioceses the centre is viewed with suspicion – the main impact of 'the diocese' on churches having been, 'They take more and more money from us and give us less and less in return.' And churches suffer from 'diocesan initiative fatigue'. One way of reversing this debilitating culture of resentment and suspicion is to establish a Diocesan Church Growth or Diocesan Mission Fund to which parishes can apply for funding help (see Chapter 13). A large fund well administered and well spread around can change the culture as the diocese becomes 'The people who help us achieve our dreams' not 'The people who take all our money'. The central diocese has to show with its actions that it genuinely supports the growth of the churches for that is how partnership is built – and a growth fund is the best way to demonstrate this.

Good strategy is built on trust and honesty, not on power and competition. People buy into the leader before they buy into the strategy. Even bishops cannot bank on a great deal of loyalty simply by virtue of their position – in this postmodern culture diocesan leaders need to earn trust and loyalty by virtue of who they are as Christian human beings.

Large and growing churches can be unpopular among their neighbours, and the culture of deanery chapters can be defensive and dysfunctional. But the new growth-culture needs deaneries and dioceses to celebrate growth stories and to circulate them around for encouragement and learning. Any culture of competition needs replacing with a team understanding so that all rejoice whoever scores the touch downs and kicks the conversions.

3. Base strategy on good theology

Strategy should arise out of theology rather than theology be used to justify a predetermined strategy. Carefully nuanced theology to keep everyone happy tends to be bland and blurred. Instead it should express in clear and exciting ways the good news the church has to share. It needs to fit the contemporary context but focus on Jesus not the church. The threefold growth ambition (spirituality, numbers and community ministry) is both theologically coherent and unifying. 'Discipleship' language can also be true to all traditions.

4. Unite the team around the strategy

A diocesan mission or growth strategy is not something the mission people do while everyone else carries on as normal. It is the core strategy of the whole diocese and every office-holder should know their place in it and feel included. The role of the stewardship officer might be, 'To help church members grow spiritually through encouraging generous giving, and to help churches develop the resources they need for evangelism and service in their local communities.' The role of the Diocesan Advisory Committee might be, 'To promote buildings that are conducive to the numerical growth of the churches, to which people respond well spiritually, and which can serve local communities effectively.'

The diocesan bishop must oversee and be identified with the central strategy, but should also appoint a member of their central staff team to head up the strategy day to day. This could be an assistant bishop or archdeacon. Equally it could be a 'growth officer' or 'director of mission' but such a post-holder would have to be a member of the senior staff team, otherwise the strategy would not be given central importance or its progress discussed at routine meetings.

5. Celebrate what is being achieved

A vicar recently commented, 'I have been in this parish 20 years, in which time the church has grown enormously and this in a diocese that has shrunk numerically more than almost any other. Yet until our new diocesan bishop called on me the other week, nobody from the diocese had ever shown the slightest interest in how or why we had grown or whether there might be any lessons or inspiration for others.'

In the new culture of a diocese focusing on growth, such churches need to be identified and learned from, their stories told around the diocese, their success celebrated, and inspiration shared.

6. Recruit the right people to the right jobs

Clergy with mainly personal ministries have become a luxury dioceses can no longer afford. Starting with London in the 1990s many dioceses now look for people who will be not parish pastors or congregational chaplains but leaders in mission and enablers of other people's ministries. The clergy role in a diocese with an ambition to reverse decline is to deepen existing disciples and make more of them – to grow churches in depth and breadth. So dioceses should recruit and train ordinands capable of leading churches into growth. They are likely to be more entrepreneurial, less safe, less conformist, than previous generations, younger, and to have experience of being a lay member of a growing church.

In one diocese every candidate for a clergy post is asked their view of the diocesan strategy and how they would implement it in the local church. Only clergy who seem genuinely committed to the strategy are appointed. But their track record is also important – clergy currently leading growing churches being more likely to be appointed.

People should be recruited to diocesan posts not to fill a position but to undertake a task. If the core task of a new bishop or archdeacon is to be a leader in mission then the diocese should search for someone who has already shown themselves to be a good leader in mission in parish life.

7. Support the whole people of God

Diocesan representatives and parish clergy are not the Church. They are appointed to serve the people who form the churches. Supported by their diocese and clergy it is the people of the churches who will grow the churches.

The most effective training support for church growth is that which is offered to the whole church community, not just to leaders or clergy. For example, the *Leading your Church into Growth* residential course began as a course for clergy only. Then it became a course for clergy plus a few key leaders. Now it has been rewritten to include a 'LyCiG – Local' course delivered locally for the whole church community.

8. Engage with the churches through Mission Action Plans (MAPs)

Many dioceses are now asking their churches to produce and implement Mission Action Plans. MAPs are simply a process or framework for mission, so the content of a MAP is not prescribed. That is a matter for each individual church. But MAPs tend to be more effective when the diocese can provide accompaniment along the MAP journey, engaging with content and delivery as well as simply receiving written plans. In many dioceses MAP has become the instrument of choice for stimulating growth in the parishes, as described in Chapter 6.

9. Prioritize areas of need and opportunity

It is easy to argue that the greatest need for evangelism is among the younger half of the population. Church participation rates decline with every age cohort. The key priorities and opportunities for the future of the churches are to retain the churchgoing young and to reconnect with the secular young. Much of today's church growth is among families.

The British Social Attitudes survey suggests that most people experience little change in their religious beliefs and practices once they reach their early 20s.

The guidance notes for the Growth Fund in the Diocese of Lichfield state that applicants should show a plausible route from the spending of the money to the growth of the church especially among people aged under 40. The diocese has also invested in a Messy Church Development Worker. Until recent years, child attendance in Lichfield was falling rapidly but now it is rising – by 3 per cent in

2012 and 4 per cent in 2013. There are around 100 Messy Church congregations in the diocese. Children provide one-third of the joiners, and probably their parents account for a further third.

Clearly, the area of greatest need for church growth is also the area of greatest opportunity.

10. Communicate well

Sometimes diocesan staff seem to live in one church world and local congregations in another. If a diocese is to have an effective strategy for helping churches grow the two worlds must come together. Partly, this is a communications function. A diocese may have a wonderful strategy on paper, but if the churches don't know about it the impact will be limited. Some dioceses have reduced their communications effort, or focused it mainly on external communications with the media. A diocese with a growth strategy needs to focus on developing a healthy two-way communications process with the churches to embed and develop the strategy in the culture at every level.

11. Reshape structures and re-imagine ministry

It is unlikely that the old wineskins of diocesan structures, boards and committees will be suited to the new wine of a diocesan growth strategy. It may be better to replace all non-statutory bodies with implementation groups for the different areas of the strategy. Where statutory bodies cannot be replaced they may need refocusing with the help of new personnel.

With declining numbers, over-clericalized models of ministry are no longer appropriate. The main element in re-imagining ministry is to embrace 'every Christian' ministry. This will include lay and unpaid leadership of churches (see Chapter 7). In the future many churches may have leaders rather than incumbents. The cure of souls will become the responsibility of the whole church community, not just the vicar.

12. Encourage church planting and fresh expressions

Probably the majority of church growth across the world for 2,000 years has come not from the enlargement of existing congregations but from the creation of new ones (see Chapter 11). Specific encouragements a diocese can make include:

1. For every vacancy or pastoral reorganization, survey planting opportunities and include in parish profiles and job descriptions.
2. Use archdeacon's visitations and other opportunities for finding out what is happening – keep lists up to date and have someone responsible for doing so.
3. Use Bishop's Mission Orders, made possible by the Mission and Pastoral Measure 2011, to provide recognized oversight for new forms of church.
4. Include church and congregation planting and fresh expressions ministry in Continuing Ministerial Education courses.
5. Create networks, buddying or mentoring links for planters within or across diocesan and denominational boundaries.
6. Set aside a proportion of the diocesan budget for start-up grants.
7. Collect and disseminate good news stories through diocesan events, publications and websites.
8. Specifically encourage non-evangelical plants.

In the latest incarnation of its mission and growth strategy ('Capital Vision 2020') the Diocese of London has moved from an era of opportunism in church planting to an era of strategy. A wider range of planting types has been identified and targets set for the number of plants in each category each year. These include new church buildings, transplants from other churches, new services within parishes, new congregations meeting in schools, new congregations meeting in 'unreached' estates, new network churches and new missional communities. A planting oversight team has been formed, processes for exploring possibilities, undertaking planting and assessing results have been identified, budgets set and funding models explored.

13. Minimize vacancy losses

Vacancies longer than six months are a major occasion of attendance loss. This is especially acute in medium-sized and large churches. One diocese has managed to reduce its average vacancy length from eleven months to nine and halved its vacancy losses. Any diocese serious about numerical growth needs both short and good vacancies. Vacancies can be opportunities for reflection and a change of direction, but there will be a price to pay if this means lengthening them. Dioceses could circulate the booklet *Growing through a Vacancy* (2013).[1]

14. Make financial policy the servant of the strategy not the master

Diocesan finances are opaque and complex, not the natural expertise area of clergy. Dioceses in financial trouble tend to be dictated to by the finance people. In one diocese the chairman of the Board of Finance was a retired building society executive. He ran diocesan finances like an old-fashioned building society, with deep, safe, reserves and cautious spending. Nobody on the bishop's staff team had the expertise to challenge this. Mission was strangled through lack of funds. Eventually a new chair was appointed with a business background. He said to the bishop, 'We are sitting on a lot of assets and our budgets are flexible. How can we help you resource your strategy? You tell us what you need money for and we will find it.'

Diocesan budgets should not be constructed simply through inflating existing budget heads but looked at afresh each year with flexible headings. The starting point for the annual round should be a conversation between the finance director and the bishop – 'In order to pursue the strategy next year, what spending priorities should we budget for?'

Parish share systems based on a formula including attendance or income data effectively become taxes on growth and protect churches from the consequences of decline. So they work directly against any growth strategy. Better are systems that are based on parish costs, better still are systems based on offers and agreements. These encourage and reward growth, enabling churches to retain the financial surplus numerical growth can supply in order to reinvest in further growth. The nature of the share system may not be the most important of growth factors but it is also a potent symbol of whether or not a diocese is serious in its growth agenda.

The Mission Development Funding stream from the Church Commissioners is being used effectively in many dioceses in the making of grants towards parish mission initiatives. Some dioceses are now adding their own funding. Encouraging entrepreneurship in the parishes in this way looks to be a better generator of growth than flagship diocesan projects.

15. Be guided by research findings

The Church of England has been good at implementing untested bright ideas and poor at checking the subsequent reality against the theory (see the spread of team ministries). Policy decisions should be made on the basis of evidence, not hunch or anecdote. Good evidence comes from a good database. Each diocese should develop their own database, tied in to the evolving national 'Statistics for Mission' database.

16. Measure growth properly

Any strategy for numerical growth has to monitor indicators of growth to assess progress and work out what factors are shaping the growth. As Chapter 1 showed, attendance measures are an increasingly poor proxy for the size of the Church. The new sections of the 'Statistics for Mission' form asking about the size of the worshipping community and the numbers of joiners and leavers should in time provide better indicators, much closer to any theologically coherent definition of the size of the Christian Church.

Is there evidence for the effectiveness of diocesan strategy?

There is sometimes no cut and dried answer to the question 'Does your diocese have a strategy for mission?' I may have missed developments in some dioceses. But here is a tentative list of 'earlier adopters' of written, agreed diocesan mission and growth strategy:

London	1990s
Lichfield	2004
Leicester	2005
Bristol	2008
Salisbury	2008
Birmingham	2009
Blackburn	2009
Liverpool	2010
Norwich	2010
Rochester	2010
Southwell	2010

The turnaround in London Diocese following the adoption of a new strategy in the 1990s under Bishop David Hope is well documented and is best seen in the graph of Electoral Roll numbers. Rolls tend to be well maintained in London and they are the preferred diocesan growth measure (Figure 6.1 in Chapter 6).

The growth of the Diocese of London is clearly partly associated with general church growth in London (see Chapter 4), but the turnaround is much greater than that in Southwark Diocese.

In Lichfield Diocese, attendance decline slowed considerably in the early years of the 'Going for Growth' strategy following 2004. More recently, October average attendance excluding school services has started to rise by around 2 per cent per annum and the excess of joiners over leavers suggests a growth rate of around 3 per cent per annum. It seems to have taken about eight years to achieve positive growth.

The statistical record in Leicester Diocese is problematic for the earlier years of the period, but a turnaround appears to have begun in 2007, with consistent growth from 2010. Average weekly attendance in October has been growing at about 5 per cent per annum since 2010 and the excess of joiners over leavers at about 4 per cent per annum. As in Lichfield, it is weekday worship that is leading the growth.

The 'Transforming Church' strategy of the Diocese of Birmingham began life in 2008 as a long-term process. There was little evidence of turnaround from the statistical indicators up to 2011, but the 2012 and 2013 indicators were largely up – for example there were 5 per cent more adults in October 2013 than 2011 and the excess of joiners over leavers suggested a worshipping community 7 per cent larger in 2013 than 2011.

It would seem slightly early days yet to compare the group of eleven dioceses with a strategy by 2010 with the others. However, their combined usual Sunday attendance grew 2 per cent between 2010 and 2013 compared with a drop of 6 per cent in the other dioceses without an obvious strategy. The October average adult weekly attendance of the eleven 'strategy' dioceses grew 4 per cent between 2010 and 2013 compared with a drop of 4 per cent in the others. The excess of joiners over leavers in the eleven dioceses in 2012 and 2013 combined was 7 per cent of the worshipping community compared with 4 per cent in the others. Prior to adopting a strategy this group of eleven dioceses had a rather worse attendance trend than the other 32, so some early evidence of turnaround is beginning to accumulate.

It will be important to continue to monitor trends in dioceses with strong strategies, but the evidence to date does indeed suggest that a strategy for growth is likely to achieve it, though not necessarily immediately and not automatically.

Part 3

What is working under the surface?

16

Angels and growth

> 'To the angel of the church in Ephesus write: These are the words of him who holds the seven stars in his right hand … I know your deeds, your hard work and your perseverance … Yet I hold this against you: You have forsaken your first love.' (Revelation 2.1,2,4)

Angels?!

I was sitting in the vicar's stall next to the pulpit with Philip my curate opposite while someone else was preaching. Suddenly Philip's jaw dropped open and he performed double takes. There seemed to be a commotion in the congregation as well. 'Did you see it?' Philip asked at the end of the service. I had seen nothing, as usual. 'Seen what?' I asked. 'The angel, standing on the bottom pulpit step with its back to the preacher, arms folded, aggressive, guarding it. It was small, about three feet high.' A member of the congregation had also seen it and came up to tell me the same thing. 'Well it's good to know we have a guardian angel,' I said, 'even if it is a midget. But a bit scary that we need one.'

It is unclear whether the writer of Revelation had a literal angel in mind; he could be referring to the leaders of the churches or to their collective being. The Bride of Christ is perhaps being treated as a living thing itself. Churches have personalities, characters, their own besetting sins, joys and strengths. These corporate features of a church can persist from generation to generation. Perhaps the approach and attitudes of one generation are caught by the next one, and so get passed on down the decades. Perhaps history keeps repeating itself because a particular sort of people live in the parish. Perhaps it is something to do with the unseen spiritual battle between the kingdom of heaven and the kingdom of this world fighting it out for the effectiveness, the soul, of this manifestation of the Bride of Christ. So perhaps there really are church-angels getting their orders from Jesus. The one certain thing is that it is rarely easy to understand what is going on behind the scenes in churches, how they really tick and what the controlling forces are. Clergy, churches and dioceses may stumble against these behind-the-scenes goings-on more often than they realize. If we want our churches to flourish we may need to deal with them.

Breaking the chains of the past

Sometimes, the long-term culture and fundamental character of a church – the 'angel of the church' – will trump any amount of good ideas and practices brought in by a brave new leadership. Growth needs more than changing the things we do together – there is a deeper project, to change the people we are together. Change is always a project for individuals, but also for the essence and culture of the church, its identity, character, besetting sins and weaknesses – for the angel of the church.

One church was drafting the job description for its new vicar. It was a long and impossible list of the things the church would demand of them. Although couched in contemporary language by people comparatively new to the church, those with long memories realized it was basically the same as all the previous lists of expectations of previous vicars. And every previous vicar had suffered exhaustion and ill health due to every major job and burden being dumped upon them. The 'angel' of this church needed identifying before the job description could be rewritten to make it realistic. A new section was also added about the love and support the vicar should expect from the church congregation. Now the church and its future clergy may have a chance of breaking the cycle that has held them in chains for generations. The old culture may well try to reassert itself, but at least a new era will have dawned officially and the new approach has a chance of becoming the new culture.

Another church revered the Reverend Johnson who had been its first vicar at the end of the nineteenth century. The folk memory of this hero persisted even after the last person who knew him in the flesh passed away. The vicarage was not even called the vicarage – etched on the sturdy posts holding up the grand gates at the bottom of the vicarage drive were the words 'Johnson Memorial'. Every subsequent vicar was compared with 'Saint Johnson' and found wanting. No change from the ways he had taught the church was achieved without a battle. It became used to its periodic internal warfare. Those who survived in the church were those robust souls who rather enjoyed a good squabble, quieter ones quietly left. The past fought the future and the past won.

This church was only going to thrive and grow in the contemporary world if its cycles and patterns were broken, if the baggage of its history was cleaned out. Eventually, the grand old vicarage was sold and a modern house bought to replace it. The monumental battle over this cost the vicar his health and his relationships with the congregation. He left before he could occupy his new vicarage. But at least his successor, no longer living inside a memorial to his distant predecessor, could start with a cleaner slate, the past's hold over the future weakened.

Growing ears to hear

The writer of Revelation wrote to the angel of each of seven churches identifying their strengths and weaknesses. He didn't dream up the content of the letters himself, he obediently wrote down the words he heard Jesus say in his vision. So these brief letters cut straight to the heart through the spiritual insights granted. Sometimes we need a similar level of spiritual insight in order to identify and understand the angel of a church. This can usually only come through some serious listening prayer: 'Whoever has ears, let them hear what the Spirit says to the churches.'

Things at 'St Luke's' were not right. Trouble kept breaking out. When the vicar spoke from the chancel steps rather than the pulpit he got into trouble from the denizens of the back pews because he obstructed their view of the altar cross. People felt uncomfortable in the chancel. Various people prayed and independently identified the altar cross as a source of trouble. Mystified, the vicar took a close look at it. It was subtly twisted so that there were no right-angles left, and the animal representations of the four Gospel writers were pockmarked and grotesque. One even carried a pitchfork. The vicar was out of his depth but the vicar's wife prayed intensively for whatever hold the altar cross had to be broken. The next Sunday morning the verger announced in great agitation that a stress fracture had opened up at the base of the altar cross. Alone in the church the vicar eyed it up at close quarters. As he did so the brass stem of the cross snapped in two and the top half banged down on the altar with a great thud in front of his nose. There was agitation to get it repaired, but the vicar offered to buy a replacement himself. Everyone could sense a breakthrough. The chancel became a place it was good to be in. Church life improved no end. The vicar never really understood what it was all about, but was grateful that prayer had uncovered the strange spiritual problem and dealt with it.

Mercifully, many churches are free from all these things, with healthy pasts and communities. In these churches good practices tend to bear fruit. But in other churches the deeper things need dealing with if the usual growth practices are to stand a chance.

Diagnostics

Clergy and other new leaders usually arrive in churches that have long histories they are largely ignorant of. It is important to piece together as much of a church's history as possible, to ask the people who have been around a long time to talk about it, and to look in old records and parish magazines to catch a flavour. People sometimes exhibit strange overreactions to minor events, changes and proposals in church life. Usually there is something deep in their past controlling this. It may be something personal, or it may be embedded in the corporate history of the church so that several people have the same mysterious reaction. If the church is to move forward it may be necessary to burrow underneath the presenting reaction to the root cause.

In any church it may help to undertake a diagnostic exercise to get at the nature of its strengths and weaknesses so that the strengths can be exploited and the weaknesses put right. I spent a day with a church looking at its processes of invitation, welcome and integration of newcomers. They sensed there was a blockage, but what was it? I described the processes of jumping over the hurdles to become a member of a church community as being like the Grand National steeplechase. The question was, in your church which is Becher's Brook – the hardest, biggest hurdle at which most people fall? The seven hurdles we looked at were:

1. *Discovering that you exist.* Some church buildings are well hidden and locked in the week, the worshippers living a distance away. There is an out-of-date notice board and no website.
2. *Meeting church members.* Church members are not well plugged into the local community and rarely admit they go to church. When there is a special service or event at church like a carol service they stay away because it is not their regular service. Even when locals come into the church building they can't meet the members.
3. *Attending an initial service or event.* There is no culture of invitation. If someone plucks up courage to come to a service will they know which door is open and what time the service is? There is a big fear factor for many people when it comes to going to church.
4. *The initial welcome and friendliness.* Perhaps the sidespeople never smile or explain to newcomers what to do. Perhaps the person taking the service never guides them through it. Perhaps at the end of the service nobody speaks to the strangers.
5. *Making new friends.* In some churches the initial welcome is friendly enough but it is hard to get beyond that superficiality

into genuine friendship. This can be especially difficult when even regulars don't come every week. Some people attend a church for a few weeks or months but then mysteriously leave. Usually this is because they have been unable to make any friends.

6. *Small groups and belonging.* It is comparatively easy in some churches to attend events and services, but harder to find a way into belonging to the community. Are there small groups open to new members, or do the groups all seem closed off to newcomers, or are there no groups at all?
7. *Making a contribution, full identity.* In order fully to belong to the church a person's mindset needs to change from that of being a guest in the church to being a host. This usually means being given a role and responsibility. In some churches these are monopolized by people who have been there a long time. They may complain that nobody else does any of the jobs, but actually they don't really want to share them with others.

I had laid out seven physical 'hurdles' in a line across the church hall and asked the 70 members present to go and stand by the hurdle they considered to be Becher's Brook in their church. Figure 16.1 shows how they are they divided up.

Figure 16.1 The church handicap hurdles

Hurdle	Number
• Discovering that you exist	3
• Meeting church members	8
• Attending an initial service or event	7
• Initial welcome and friendliness	7
• Making new friends	45
• Small groups and belonging	0
• Making a contribution, full identity	0

The first four hurdles had a few people but a great scrum surrounded the hurdle labelled 'making friends'. Absolutely nobody went to the two hurdles after this one because every runner and rider fell at the friendship hurdle! Here was a 'friendly' church full of people looking for friendship but not finding it, and recognizing that newcomers would not find it either. The fact that so many recognized the need for friendship and felt its lack showed there was a widespread culture in the church that stopped the people achieving their desire – friendship, community, belonging. And if the people could not even develop friendship with each other how could they develop friendship with God? A church that is merely friendly with people is likely also to be merely friendly with God.

So the diagnosis enabled the church to understand its problem and hopefully find the motive and confidence to move forward in friendship. Each individual had previously assumed it was just them – 'the others must be friends with each other but I have been left out'. Once they realized that this inhibition stopping friendliness moving into friendship was universal – part of the church's DNA or angel – they hopefully had the nous to take the steps to deepen their relationships. Then they would become a community that embraced others in friendship and be able to flourish and grow. The simple act of identifying and naming 'the angel' was enough to rob it of much of its power to harm.

Robert Warren's book *The Healthy Churches' Handbook* (2004)[1], referred to in Chapter 2, contains a helpful section about identifying and naming the angel of a local church. It also offers a way of scoring seven marks of a healthy church. Going through that scoring exercise enables any church to identify its own underlying strengths and weaknesses and so address them.

Culture eats strategy for breakfast. If a church has a serious problem with an aspect of its cultural and spiritual health then its strategies for growth are unlikely to work. It will need to address its ill-health first, then it will have the ability to grow.

The power of repentance

If a besetting sin or weakness is identified then the church has a tool for dealing with it. This tool changes cultures, mends weaknesses and deals with legacies from the past. It is called repentance and confession. We provide a confession in church services to enable individuals to wipe the slate clean, restore their relationship to God and go into the week as forgiven people. We have the same resource available to the collective unit of the church. Sometimes an act of confession and repentance is the way to deal with issues from the past. This may need a lead from people not involved in the issue at all, but standing as representatives of the church community, perhaps the current leaders, or the bishop or archdeacon.

In Revelation 3.19,20, John lays out the route to victory over the sins of the lukewarm church in Laodicea: 'Those whom I love I rebuke and discipline. So be earnest and repent. Here I am! I stand at the door and knock. If anyone hears my voice and opens the door, I will come in and eat with that person, and they with me.' A church with issues that need solving should take them seriously (be earnest), repent of past sins and weakness, listen out for what Jesus has to say, welcome him in afresh, and then share a new intimacy with him.

One church had earned a bad name through a 'believers only' baptism policy, brusquely administered. So a lot of parish families had experienced 'rejection' by the church on the only occasion they had approached it. Under a new vicar the church recognized its mistake and repented of it. They posted a letter of apology into every letter box in the parish. This went a long way to restoring the church's good name and has been a factor in its recent growth in depth and numbers as families have once again felt welcomed by the church however uncertain their current faith situation.

There is an argument for tackling 'angel' issues during a vacancy between vicars. Perhaps the baggage from the past can be dealt with spiritually with the help of bishops or archdeacons using formal or informal ways of repenting and starting afresh. Perhaps a vacancy is a good time for a church community to do an angel or healthy churches exercise that identifies the community issues separately from those surrounding its clergy. Perhaps it is a good opportunity to clear the decks so that the church can see what type of new incumbent it needs to lead it forward. Perhaps it is better to try and deal with the past in a vacancy so that the new incumbent does not have to do this. Instead they can focus on being a positive leader in mission driven by future vision rather than past baggage.

To tackle or to ignore?

It can be dangerous to ignore a church's past baggage or old sins, but equally dangerous to give them too much prominence. Unseen dark spiritual forces may feed off fixation but starve when deliberately ignored. A church for ever trying to deal with its past is for ever locked into it.

One church, debilitated by conflict, wrote into its MAP that this had to be resolved before new progress could be made. But then a key individual moved away. Quickly the conflict that needed sorting became irrelevant, in the past, a bad memory. It became wiser simply to move on rather than rake up the past. The MAP was revised because the church found new unity, not in reconciliation processes for a now irrelevant conflict, but in pursuing new mission opportunities together.

The real danger lies in being unaware of the past, of the culture, of the unseen forces, of the angel of the church. Once church leaders are aware of these things then wisdom and guidance are needed to discern the best way to live in the light of them. Sometimes it is best to tackle something head on, sometimes it is best to leave it behind in pursuit of fresh vision – 'Forgetting what is behind and straining towards what is ahead, I press on towards the goal …' (Philippians 3.13).

17

Guidance, prayer and growth

> While they were worshipping and fasting, the Holy Spirit said, 'Set apart for me Barnabas and Saul for the work to which I have called them.' (Acts 13.2)

Church growth results from listening and guidance

Though Luke's history of the early Church is known as the Acts of the Apostles it should perhaps be called the Acts of the Holy Spirit. On the surface it was the elders of Antioch who sent out Barnabas and Saul on their historic first missionary journey. They sensibly decided to start in Cyprus, the birthplace of Barnabas. But under the surface, behind the visible world of humans, another force was controlling events. It was God the Holy Spirit who said that these two should be sent out as missionaries. Personally I find it easier to visit the dentist than to fast and pray, so finding guidance is not a soft alternative to making our own minds up. Following that guidance would involve Saul in suffering, hardship and imprisonment. But spiritual guidance was certainly more effective than a purely human initiative would have been.

The Spirit said the two pioneer missionaries were to be set apart 'for me'. They were to be his servants, his pieces to be moved about the chess board of the ancient world as the chess player determined. And they were to do 'the work to which I have called them'. Their job was not to think up their own itinerary and strategy but to find out the Holy Spirit's and follow it. This would not prove easy. There were times when they were baffled and frustrated as in Asia in chapter 16, until eventually guidance arrived from the 'man of Macedonia', and they were able to proceed.

The Holy Spirit did not randomly choose Saul. The whole of Saul's previous life, becoming a Pharisee at the feet of Gamaliel, persecuting the Church, that remarkable business outside Damascus, his apprenticeship years in the Church, were all preparation for his main calling. It was not Saul who consciously prepared himself for a future he could not imagine – it was God the Holy Spirit who shaped his whole life up to that pivotal prayer meeting in Antioch.

The Christian life is God's mystery tour

By first profession I was an economist. In the 1960s I sat at the feet of Keynes' surviving friends at Kings College Cambridge. I became a Government economic adviser in the 1970s in the Heath, Wilson and Callaghan era. In the late 1970s I began to feel a call to ordination in the Church of England even though at the time I was a deacon in a Baptist church. I went about testing the ordination call in the way best calculated to invite rejection, but I still somehow got accepted and went off to retrain as a vicar. The Church of England, of course, had no idea what to do with an economist and I had to start again from scratch. While I learned over the years of college, curacy and incumbency how to be a vicar, the economist in me slumbered. I couldn't understand why God had led me down one path then another, with no seeming connection. I was on one of God's mystery tours. You may have been on one yourself.

Then one day I realized that our diocesan office held files of the statistical returns sent in annually by the parishes. They were not yet computerized but at least the calculator had been invented and I saw an opportunity to bring the economist out of cold storage, working out the impact of Billy Graham's 1985 Mission-Sheffield on attendance in Sheffield Diocese – the result was 10 per cent growth! It dawned on me that the two halves of my life could make sense together. I remained a vicar for many years, but gradually developed ways of analysing church statistics for the purposes of understanding church growth until it became my full-time calling.

The Holy Spirit had set me apart for the work to which he had called and prepared me over many years.

My previous church growth books were getting dated and people started asking if I was going to write a sequel. I had some material, but wasn't keen because it's awfully hard work! Eventually I decided to pray for guidance: 'Should I write a book or not?' Sitting down on my prayer-chair, I brushed against the Bible on the table next to it. It fell as I sat down and bounced open on my lap. Just one chapter began on the double page so revealed and I instantly read its opening:

> 'This is the word that came to Jeremiah from the Lord: This is what the Lord, the God of Israel, says: "Write in a book all the words I have spoken to you."' (Jeremiah 30.1,2)

This is quite the fastest answer to prayer I've ever received and is the reason why you are now reading this book. It is also, incidentally, the reason why my model railway remains unfinished.

In case you are thinking guidance comes easier to me than yourself, I should add that, normally, I'm as uncertain as the next person about what God might be saying. I know I've got to write this book but I've no idea what comes next!

It's tricky separating out the words God 'has spoken to me' from those that are just my inconsequential ramblings, but I comfort myself with the thought that such sifting, dear reader, is now your job, not mine. What I am certain of is that God the Holy Spirit is taking the business of growing Jesus' Church so seriously he is prepared to use whatever tools come to hand for the purpose, even me.

It's God who makes things grow

I'm a warm-weather gardener. But I enjoy pottering about, prodding things into life in the spring, weeding and watering in the summer. I have absolutely no idea, however, how and why the different plants and seeds grow and produce flowers and fruit. God has created them with that capacity and each seems to obey the creator's rules. I have never yet seen gooseberries on the raspberry canes or pansies on the laburnum tree. And there is one universal rule – all the healthy plants in my garden are growing and all the unhealthy plants are dying. Just like churches.

That difficult church in Corinth was dividing into factions. One lot claimed to follow Paul, the founder, and the other Apollos, whose gifted preaching had led to its subsequent growth. But Paul would have none of it – I planted and Apollos watered, we have the same purpose, we are allies not rivals, we are just two simple gardeners who made a contribution at different times. We gardeners don't grow churches. We simply provide the conditions for growth. It's God who makes it grow for it is only God who makes all things grow (1 Corinthians 3.1–9).

In these last three chapters we are exploring church growth as an act of the Holy Spirit. But we should be wary of neat functional distinctions between the persons of the Holy Trinity. The growth, maturing and beautification of the Bride of Christ is the responsibility of every member of the Holy Trinity. It's wholly Trinity. Church is a set of relationships with the Holy Trinity as well as with each other. Luke shows that the growth of the early Church was provoked and organized by the Holy Spirit. Paul says in 1 Corinthians 3 that it is God the creator-Father who grows the church. And Jesus says in Matthew 16.18: 'I will build my church.' He will build on the rock of church leaders like Peter, but he is the builder and that is why the powers of death and the gates of hell will never overcome it.

If it's God who grows the church can we all relax?

Yes we can! Because we just have to focus on getting the conditions for growth right, improving the health and quality of church life and allowing God to do the rest. Growing the church is a divine project not a human one.

No we can't! Because God chooses to rely on human beings for the success of his divine project. If the gardening is poor the plants wither and die. All Christians have an obligation to commend Jesus to others by imitating him, making disciples of all nations, witnessing to the reality of our faith, loving our neighbours and growing to maturity as spiritual beings living in the kingdom of heaven. As we do these things together we grow the church.

I listened to a bishop preach a sermon recently in which he said not to worry if the Church shrinks, that is fine because God knows what he is doing. But it is not fine if a church is dying because it is unhealthy, a poor quality witness or a failing custodian of gospel treasures. Paul said, 'Woe to me if I do not preach the Gospel' (1 Corinthians 9.16). I wake up each morning feeling 'Woe to me if I do not do church growth', because that is my calling. Every Christian should feel, 'Woe to me if my life does not attract others to Christ and his community', because that is every Christian's calling.

So perhaps we can relax but we certainly can't sit back and expect God to do everything. We think and work as though what we do is all-important in growing the church and trust and pray as though what God does is all-important. Part 2 of this book was about what we do as humans up on the surface, Part 3 is about what God is doing under the surface and how we can join in. The proper balance between the human and divine, between on stage and behind the scenes, is not 50–50, it is 100–100.

Can we fully explain growth patterns by factors we can measure?

In recent years the Church of England has started to prioritize understanding the visible causes of church growth and decline in order to finds ways of preventing decline and provoking growth. Statistical research has even produced equations in which a series of 'explanatory' variables partly explain variations in church attendance or membership.

There is a potential theological problem here. If we were able to produce an equation that fully explained the different growth patterns of different churches would we have eliminated the 'God grows the church' hypothesis? Church numerical growth has been fully explained by visible human factors such as the quality of the clergy, the socio-economic setting, and the range of ministries the church offers. So there is no need to search for the mystery of God as there is no mystery left to explain.

This is the same question asked by science as the mysteries of creation are steadily understood – who needs the God hypothesis any more? It is sometimes said that the survival of the Church of England, despite all its failings and everything thrown at it, is proof of the existence of God. It's a powerful argument. But if we can produce accurate statistical models using human factors that fully explain church growth and decline then that argument looks a dead duck.

There are two answers to this problem. The first is that, even if we were to fully 'explain' growth in an equation we would only have found the proximate causes and associations. God will lie behind these just as he always has. The gifted vicar growing her church was gifted and given her vocation by God. God led her to the church in which her ministry would thrive and prepared the hearts of the people to work with her. This answer is just the same as the answer to the charge that science has removed the need for God as an explanation of why things are as they are. There will always be a scientific or research description of the processes involved, to the 'how' questions. But there will never be a scientific or research answer to the ultimate 'why' questions. Learning to describe the processes by which God works shows us that God is awesome not absent.

But also, so far, the equations have only 'explained' a modest proportion of the variance in numerical growth between different churches and probably only ever will. Churches are composed of human beings, each a complex, flawed and unique image and likeness of God. We will never be able fully to model the interactions of a large number of these fathomless beings as they generate the subtle complexities of a Christian church. And we will never be able fully to follow the mysteries of God working away in his Church. God is God and we are not, so we will never fathom all his ways. Nor will we fathom the ways of his enemy the devil.

So there will always be holy mystery as to why one church is thriving and another struggling. However, both multiple and single variable numerical analysis demonstrate that even patterns subject to holy mystery are not wholly mystery. God grows the church but how the church behaves determines how well he can grow it. We now understand how different behaviours have different outcomes and it is our responsibility to choose the behaviours that lead to growth.

Here is the formula for church-growth success – or your money back!?

Unfortunately, the uniqueness of every church setting and community, plus the holy mystery implanted in the DNA of the Bride of Christ, means that there are no general or guaranteed solutions to the growth puzzle. I cannot tell you how to grow your church. But I can tell you the things that seem in general to be associated with growth. This book offers some sort of toolkit but you will have to work out which tools to try and how to work with them, seeking your own divine guidance for your own unique situation. There are no 'off the peg' solutions, only tailor-made ones, no self-invented solutions, only God-inspired ones. And there are usually no cheap and cheerful solutions, only costly, sacrificial ones.

Guidance – old issue, new application

The problem of how to find and recognize divine guidance – and the development of wisdom about it – is as old as the hills. Read Proverbs for example. What we mainly find in the Old Testament is expressions of trust in the providence and guidance of God, whatever the situation. 'If I rise on the wings of the dawn, if I settle on the far side of the sea, even there your hand will guide me, your right hand will hold me fast' (Psalm 139.9,10).

This trust and wisdom has usually been applied to our individual lives. This is directly relevant to the growth of the church – Barnabas and Paul received guidance and direction for their individual lives but the result was the growth of the church. The new dimension in many churches today is the quest for guidance and direction for the future of the church itself. This has been provoked by the rise of parish MAPs and diocesan strategies, and also by the development of corporate church leadership.

In Chapter 6 I said that the primary wisdom for finding a good MAP is to pray for guidance about what specific mission God is calling the church to. Top of the list of elements of good practice in diocesan strategy in Chapter 15 was to pray – hit the ground kneeling! This involves both listening prayer for the discernment of strategy and intercessory prayer for the success of strategy.

Once upon a time the vicar – the undisputed embodiment, leader, almost owner, of the church – would make up his own mind what to do and get on with it. Today the vicar is better understood as the enabler of the ministries of all. The vicar's leadership is no less vital, but the arts of such leadership are more subtle than they used to be! Rather than making them on the church's behalf, today's vicar has to lead the church into making its own decisions. It is the church corporately, not just the vicar individually, that seeks the mind of God.

So here is a checklist of some ways of seeking guidance for a local church, for its strategy, MAP and future:

1. Plans are established by seeking advice (Proverbs 20.18)

Read books, check the websites of other churches, take advice from the diocese, learn from the experience of other churches, ask a specialist to help you. Go through a training programme such as LyCiG – Local. Do not funnel all the advice or training through one person or even a small group. Enable all the church to access advice so that wisdom is shared not monopolized.

2. Your word is a lamp to my feet and a light to my path (Psalm 119.105)

Be alert to what the Bible might be saying to you. Devise a sermon series on guidance or on the letters to the seven churches in Revelation, or make it the subject of small group meetings. Invite members of the church to report passages of Scripture that have spoken to them about the future direction of the church.

3. Agabus stood up and, through the Spirit, predicted that a severe famine would spread over the entire Roman world (Acts 11.28)

This prophetic word resulted in the collection for the church in Judea. Action was taken as a result of the Spirit-inspired insight. Expect God to speak through individuals; test, discern and recognize prophetic insights about the future. Agabus was not the most prominent Christian of the day, but on this occasion God spoke through him. Be open to the key breakthrough coming through someone who is not one of the church leaders.

4. The apostles and elders met to consider this question. After much discussion … (Acts 15.6,7)

The question was the future of the church – would it be a sect of Judaism with a circumcision entry requirement, or would it be a new religion for all? A large group got together to consider the question and had much discussion. A church seeking direction for the future should consider and discuss it, not meekly accept whatever a vicar or other leader might impose on them. Arrange a day or evening conference, invite written contributions from those who get intimidated by crowds and meetings. Ensure that the whole church is involved in setting the policy because then they will own it.

5. James spoke up: 'Brothers, listen to me … It is my judgment that we should not make it difficult for the Gentiles who are turning to God.' (Acts 15.13,19)

At the end of the discussion the leader of the church summed up the discussion and announced his judgement about what would now happen. Finding a new direction for a church today should not simply be decided by majority vote. The church's leaders have a twofold responsibility – both to enable a good process that involves all and to give a lead in terms of the outcome.

6. After they had fasted and prayed, they placed their hands on them and sent them off (Acts 13.3)

The new direction for the church in Antioch – sending missionaries – was the result of prayer and fasting as well as a word from the Holy Spirit. A church cannot be serious about finding guidance for the future unless its members pray and fast for it. Call a series of prayer meetings, or 24 hours of prayer, invite people to take this seriously enough to fast, and expect God to respond to serious and sacrificial prayer. Then don't just wander along aimlessly once a new direction or plan has emerged – commission people to get on and do it!

7. Many are the plans in a person's heart, but it is the Lord's purpose that prevails (Proverbs 19.21)

In some churches there may be competing agendas or divergent visions. Ask people to put aside their own preconceived plans to seek the Lord's purpose. Of course, the two may sometimes be the same, but that needs to be tested. Be cautious about accepting at face value the person claiming divine support for their pet project. If necessary form a small group of leaders to weigh competing or individual plans and discern what really does seem to come from God.

8. Commit to the Lord whatever you do, and your plans will succeed (Proverbs 16.3)

Do not remain paralysed by indecision because you are not absolutely certain you have heard God right. Don't allow the elusive perfect plan to stop a good one. Make a decision and commit it to God and he will honour that even if you have missed a trick or two. There will be time to learn and change tack as things unfold.

Intercessory prayer and growth

A church needs not only to listen to God to find new plans and direction, it needs to pray to God for their success. Whereas listening for guidance is a periodic requirement, intercession for the mission of the Church is a continuous requirement – even during August.

There is no substitute for prayer when it comes to accessing the behind-the-scenes power of God for growing the church. Paul and Silas had been flogged and put in prison. They could have been plotting their way out, maybe an escape bid, maybe a legal defence. By midnight they could have been catching some sleep. Instead they were praying and singing hymns. The resultant earthquake shook the foundations of their prison, unfastened the chains that bound them and caused the conversion of the jailer and his family (Acts 16).

It is still prayer that breaks the unseen chains that bind and imprison the Church today. As we developed the new strategy for the Diocese of Lichfield called 'Going for Growth' there were some visible elements helping to slow and even reverse the decades of decline that preceded it. But the behind-the-scenes impact of new prayer may have been just as necessary. One of the bishops wrote a prayer that was circulated round every church to be used in the public intercessions every week:

> God our creator and redeemer, help your church to grow in holiness, unity, effectiveness and numbers. Draw us closer to you and those around us. Give us enthusiasm in our faith, and wisdom in sharing it with young and old. Open our eyes to new opportunities, our lips to speak of you, and our hearts to welcome the stranger. Grow your kingdom in us and in the world, through the intercession of our Lord Jesus Christ and in the power of the Holy Spirit. Amen.

Two years after the prayer was circulated, he and I went on one of our regular day-visits to a small group of churches. The team at St Paul Wednesbury told us a story. Attendance at the church had been declining for a long time. But for a whole year they kept a copy of the prayer on the altar in church and used it as one of the intercessions every Sunday. During that year new people had kept on turning up unexpectedly – and staying. The church grew from an average weekly attendance of 63 to 95. Then one day the prayer went missing and they forgot about it for the following year. The flow of new people dried up. In the year of our visit average attendance had drifted down to 86. They had just made the connection and reinstated the prayer.

This story should not be used to justify a chocolate bar view of prayer. You put your prayer-money in the slot and get your church growth chocolate out of the draw. But I know of similar stories and so might you. We have accumulated enough experience between us to know that when a church prays seriously for its own growth in holiness, unity, effectiveness and numbers, these things are more likely to happen.

So, no church hoping to grow should be without a prayer element in its strategy. Make sure that when your growth plans are devised or revised a plan for prayer suited to the tradition and situation of your own church is at the heart of them. As it is so easy for the prayer effort to sag, keep refreshing it as time goes by. Log any specific answers to prayer as an aid to faith and to further prayer. Make sure the prayer element is present in the public life of the church as well as in the private lives of its members. And, if you are a church leader, model such prayer both in your own life and in the running of the church's business. If your church has a Mission Action Plan your PCC will need to discuss its progress at most of its meetings. If your PCC prayed for the progress of the MAP for as many minutes as it discussed it, verbosity might be restricted and progress accelerated!

In this chapter we have focused on the way that searching for guidance and praying for success in the mission of the church interacts with the behind-the-scenes work of God the Holy Trinity. In the final chapter we will focus more specifically on the work of the Holy Spirit and how we align ourselves with it in the growth of the Church.

18

The Holy Spirit and growth

> He said to me, 'Prophesy to these bones and say to them, "Dry bones, hear the word of the Lord!"' ... tendons and flesh appeared on them and skin covered them, but there was no breath in them.
>
> Then he said to me, 'Prophesy to the breath' ... So I prophesied as he commanded me, and breath entered them; they came to life and stood up on their feet – a vast army. Then he said to me: 'Son of man, these bones are the people of Israel.' (Ezekiel 37.4,8,9,10,11)

Now hear the word of the Lord

Mostly this book is about good practices that result in the numerical growth of the church. But how far can you go with good practices alone? Ezekiel was told to prophesy to the dry bones he found strewn over the valley floor. These bones were the people of Israel, God's people, the equivalent of the Church today. They were disconsolate – 'Our bones are dried up and our hope is gone', they said, because they were living in exile in a foreign land. Similar feelings flow through many churches today that find their numbers and life drying up in the newly foreign land of a secular society.

Tremendous things happened when Ezekiel prophesied to the bones – they rattled together, tendons and flesh appeared and skin covered them. They became passable imitations of human beings. Even moribund, dry bone, disconsolate Christian churches can become passable imitations of the body of Christ through good intentionality, leadership and practices. Churches can grow and flourish more than might be expected when they respond positively to those, like me, who prophecy to the bones.

But, says Ezekiel, there was still no breath in them. They were passable imitations of human beings but they were not breathing, they were corpses. So God tells Ezekiel to prophesy to the breath. The Hebrew word translated by 'breath' is 'ruach', which means wind, breath, spirit or life-force. Ruach is God's Holy Spirit, the breath of God who breathes God's life into the world. So Ezekiel is told to ask God's Holy Spirit to breathe new life into the corpses littering the valley floor. Only when he did this did breath enter the bodies and they stood alive on their feet – a vast army ready to do battle on behalf of God in a pagan world.

Perhaps a church doing all the right things and growing numerically may yet be no more than a lifeless skeleton. Prophesying to the bones gets us only so far. Unless we prophesy to, deal with, call upon and receive God's Holy Spirit afresh then a new and vast army of God's people will never arise from the dry valley of our secular world to transform it into the verdant pasture of the kingdom of heaven.

Luke makes the same point at the start of Acts. Between Ascension Day and Pentecost he tells us there were 120 believers but on the very first morning the Holy Spirit arrives 3,000 were added to their number.

Rowing boat or sailing sloop?

Suppose your church is a rowing boat and you are not making progress in it against the current. What can you do? You can try rowing harder but most church leaders are pretty fully stretched anyway. Rowers can put in a spurt by upping the number of strokes per minute but they pay for it later, exhausting themselves prematurely.

You can try rowing smarter. My son rowed at university. He wasn't the biggest but he was a very technical rower with a precise, efficient technique. I know this because he told me so himself. I used to pay a pre-baptism visit to the home of every baptism family. Then I switched to gathering a group of them together – it was a better use of my time, I was rowing smarter. I also find I row smarter, get more efficient in the use of my time, if I take time at the start of the day to pray about it. Sadly, all too often I launch straight in – too busy, too stupid to pray!

You can also recruit more rowers. Most churches have a few people doing the rowing while the rest sit around watching. So you help church members become crew rather than passengers – take them through an *Everybody Welcome* course (Jackson and Fisher, 2009)[1] or the *Growing Leaders* course (Lawrence and Heathfield, 2004)[2]. But make sure you give them oars to enable them to join the rowing team.

You can look for slacker water where the current is not so strong against you. It could be as simple as changing the service time to one suitable for today rather than 100 years ago. The current tends to be particularly fierce during vicar vacancies so prepare to manoeuvre through those choppy waters through using the *Growing through a Vacancy* guide (Jackson, 2013).[3]

You can generate better momentum by jettisoning excess weight. Is the church carrying too much baggage from the past in its programme of activities? You will make better progress when the load is lightened.

But at the end of the day you are still in a rowing boat trying to cross an ocean of cross currents by dint of human effort alone.

So, naturally, your mind turns to the prospect of hoisting a sail. Can your boat, your church, be driven forward not just by human effort but by the power of the wind, the breath, the ruach, the Spirit of God? How can we grow a sail and catch the wind of the Spirit? We'll need the courage to go where the wind blows us and we'll need to grow in spiritual depth in order to develop a keel that will stop the sailing sloop from capsizing in the breeze. Because the sloop can tack at an angle to the wind, it has to be controlled by a human hand on the rudder as well as by the wind's strength and direction. However, the crew can work as hard as they like but they will never make progress directly against the wind, against the Spirit of God.

So, sailing is a harder, more skilful, art to master than rowing but it is so much less effort and takes us so much further! Of course if we can align the sails and the oars together then even better progress can be made through the roaring forties and the doldrums alike. The growth of the church comes best from the combined forces of God and humans.

What is going on where you are?

If we are to prophecy to the breath as well as the bones, to hoist a sail as well as weald an oar, to grow through the power of the Spirit as well as human endeavour, we need to cultivate spiritual awareness. The Holy Spirit is not inactive. The very survival of the Church of England, despite its own shortcomings in a hostile environment, is all the proof I need of the Spirit's activity. So what is the Holy Spirit doing where you are? The wind blows where it wills and it varies in strength, but there is usually some evidence blowing around of God's wind in the sails of the church. Mission is seeing what God is doing and joining in. So let church members pray, talk through and discover what God the Holy Spirit is already doing today where they are.

In our village at the moment God seems to be doing at least two connected things. He is bringing together an exceptional group of people to the staff and congregation of the church. And he is stirring early responses to him in many young parents and families. We have been given a large mission capacity and a clear mission field. The wind of the Spirit is blowing. Whether we can rise to the opportunity presented to us by the Holy Spirit we will have to see! But what is the Holy Spirit currently up to where you are? If you get a sense of that then you will know where to put your main mission effort, joining in with what God is doing.

The wind is not in the same direction or of the same power in every place. Prophesying to the breath and hoisting a sail will look different in different places. But here are some general principles and national trends to help us catch the wind of the Spirit and sail into a growing future. Their common feature is that they are demanding. Sailing where the Spirit blows usually means service and sacrifice. Where faith is just a leisure-time pursuit the church withers, where faith is serious, in earnest about the whole of life, the church blossoms. In Chapter 17 I said we catch the wind of the Spirit through prayer. Other keys include:

Repentance

The Church of England has accumulated a lot of stuff over the years it needs to repent of. The weight of the unconfessed baggage of the Church's sin is a handicap it needs freeing from by the power of repentance, forgiveness and new life. This is a process we well understand as individual Christians from the weekly routine of confession and absolution. But the Church also needs its representatives to confess the corporate sins of an inward-looking preoccupation in a world needing a Saviour, of disunity handled gracelessly, of failure to change with the times, of complacency and resignation in the face of a nation starting to reject it. In *Hope for the Church* (Jackson, 2001, p. 32)[4] I called for a national process of repentance, a call quoted and taken up by the report *Mission-Shaped Church* (Williams, 2004, p. 13): 'But this is also a moment for repentance. We have allowed our culture and the Church to drift apart, without our noticing. We need the grace of the Spirit for repentance if we are to receive a fresh baptism of the Spirit for witness.'[5] But I am not sure the call to repent of the ways and weaknesses, the culture and condition of the Church of which we are part has been properly heeded. 'Godly sorrow brings repentance that leads to salvation' (2 Corinthians 7.10). Godly sorrow is not an easy or comfortable starting point but it needs to be ours. Sorrow leads to repentance, forgiveness, restoration, new life and new growth.

Renewal

The charismatic and renewal movements from the 1970s onwards brought much progress. However, they also failed to deliver much of what was promised. Renewal of church life and worship has not led to the hoped-for revival as measured by conversions. Partly this is because we turned something intended for mission into something for ourselves. Renewal gave us experiences of God, made us feel better, livened up our music and worship, and offered some of us inner and physical healing. The spiritual renewal, the fresh baptism in the breath of the Holy Spirit, needed today is not a new dose of what we made it before, but new power for mission. This is the promise of Jesus:

> 'You will receive power when the Holy Spirit comes on you; and you will be my witnesses in Jerusalem, and in all Judea and Samaria, and to the ends of the earth.' (Acts 1.8)

So we ask for the power of the Holy Spirit to make us witnesses in and around our familiar church home (Jerusalem and Judea), among people who have some relationship to the Church (Judea) and to the increasing numbers of effective aliens to the Church (the ends of the earth). Baptism in the Holy Spirit is not a badge of God's favour but an equipping for witness. We should seek our own renewal in the power of the Spirit not for our own sakes but for the sake of those we can then reach with the good news of Jesus Christ. This is a costly and sacrificial renewal in the service of the kingdom of heaven. But when we have the courage to ask for it then we must expect the God of mission to equip his Church to share his mission.

Revival

Mass movements of peoples turning to Christ and transforming the churches have usually happened in cohesive communities like Welsh mining villages a century ago. Simply to expect God to bring about revival today is to misread the times and escape our obligations. We live in one of the least cohesive communities in history. Individualism is king. God is not going to do everything while the Church does nothing. So many people have so far to travel from their current world view to a Christian faith, so many hang-ups to sort out along the way, that God is more than ever relying on faithful local churches to accompany myriads of them on their journeys towards him. God is not about to bypass the Church, instead he is calling the Church to costly renewal in order to make it into the effective witness and evangelist it was always meant to be.

Sacramentalism

Sacramentalism, it is said, has done evangelism no favours through its emphasis on the insiders' service that is Holy Communion to the exclusion of more accessible styles. But we now need a new sacramentalism driven by people passionate about baptizing new believers. This is the primary sacrament. The Eucharist feeds members of the body of Christ but baptism creates them. Repetition of the eucharistic feeding of the people of God is the easy bit. The baptism of infants is not that difficult either, even if infants do cry. But baptism of the newly believing is the primary sacramental challenge to the priestly calling of the Church.

Numbers of infant and child baptisms have been going down for many years because they had a large element of social rather than religious motivation. Adult baptisms, however, have been going up (Figure 18.1).

Renewed sacramentalism will be passionate about driving up that total over time so that 20,000 or 50,000 newly believing adults and teenagers are being baptized each year. The Holy Spirit will need to drive us out of our comfort zones to find the people he is preparing. Baptism will be accompanied by serious initiation into the faith of the Church and the commitment of believers, so driving its future spiritual and numerical growth.

Figure 18.1 Adult (13+) baptisms in the Church of England

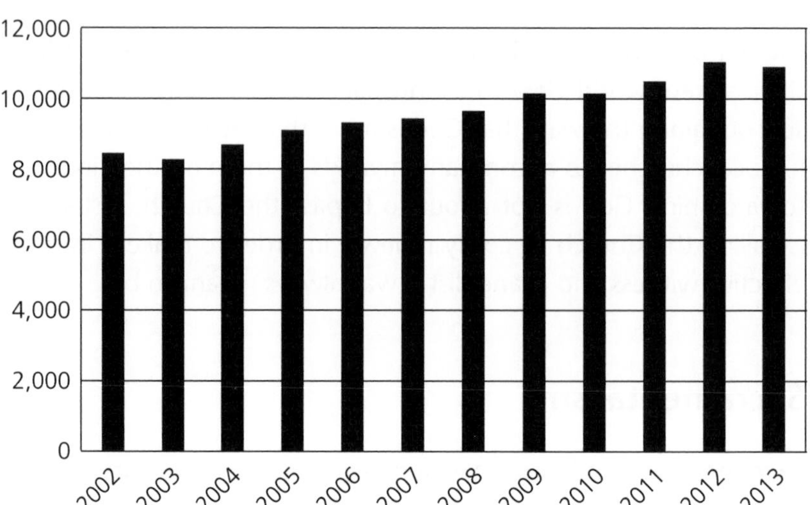

Confidence in the Church

The prime minister recently spoke of his own Christian faith in a Britain he still saw as a Christian country, and he got heavily criticized for it. In a multi-religious and partly secular country it was apparently wrong for a politician to 'do' God. The Church is too thinly supported to be anything other than a fringe activity – so of course Britain is no longer a Christian country. The attorney general claimed that Christians were increasingly afraid to express their beliefs because the rise of militant religious fundamentalism was making non-believers intolerant of all religious people. Although the Christian faith still underpinned the laws and culture of the country, practising Christians were being driven out of the public arena into a privatized religious observance by a hostile secularizing agenda.

Meanwhile, many ordinary Anglicans, assailed by constant media stories about the shrinking Church, its outdated and no longer acceptable views on public morality, the dangers of religious fundamentalism, batty vicars, disunity and rows at Synod, do not have the confidence to talk openly about their faith. We Anglicans get it coming both ways – we can be ridiculed for being wishy-washy if we don't make strong faith-claims, or fundamentalist bigots if we do. Anglicans are fair game for satire and ridicule in a way that other faiths and denominations never would be.

This background climate can make it harder for local churches to gain credibility in their own communities. And Anglicans embarrassed about their church are unlikely to be the best evangelists.

So what is the best way for the Church to recover confidence in itself and respect in the chattering classes? The old Christendom is unlikely to reassert itself sometime soon. So do we accept our new position towards the edge of society where the Church was for its first 300 years before Constantine? It can be a good place in which to grow, away from the public spotlight. Or do we connect in the public sphere not as the establishment voice directing public morality but as the alternative voice to the secular establishment? An established episcopal Church with archbishops as major public figures can hardly choose not to engage. Once again, this is the difficult route. Life is much easier out of the public gaze, away from public controversy, than it is in the rough and tumble of a sometimes hostile world.

However good the Church's public representatives, however positive their profiles, the respect they are afforded and the power they have to influence, critically depend on the progress of the Church they lead. When the Church of England is seen by the media and political classes to be growing numerically it will gain new respect. And when the people of the churches know they are gaining ground numerically their confidence will grow again. In recent years the growth of the Church has been hindered by the image of the Church. Now we are looking for the image of the Church to be changed by the growth of the Church. Then a new benevolent cycle of growth can begin.

We have seen throughout this book that much of the new growth in the churches is happening at grass-roots level under the radar of many observers, statisticians and even dioceses. This is surely a strategy of the Holy Spirit – generating a quiet, almost underground, growth out of which new confidence and respect will come, from which further growth will result so that a stronger Church can take a new and better place in the public arena. Let's have confidence in this strategy of the Holy Spirit and join in with it!

Confidence in the gospel

Even more important than confidence in the Church is confidence in the faith.

Does the Church stand more chance of attracting new generations with a message trimmed and tailored to the susceptibilities of the age or with a no-compromise theologically conservative message that is unashamedly countercultural? It looks as though the theologically liberal strands have probably suffered faster decline than the more conservative ones. Evangelicals and charismatics have formed an ever increasing proportion of the people and clergy. We can see something similar in other denominations – the more conservative Baptist and Pentecostal churches tend to have done better numerically than the more liberal Methodist and United Reformed Churches. But the strident and the simplistic have not made a lot of headway either.

Perhaps the key is to hold the historic faith with confidence, teach it with authority and proclaim it with discretion. It may not work to frighten people into churches by threatening them with hell-fire but that need not stop Christians believing in conditional salvation. The gospel is not one single line of argument, it is a many-faceted diamond that can be turned to show different faces to different people at different times. When I was young, Lucozade was sold in chemists' shops as a pick-me-up for sickly children. It was a treat when I was feeling a little better. Now it is sold everywhere except the chemists' shop as an energy drink for the fit and healthy. But it is exactly the same stuff inside the bottle. We have gone on a similar journey in the way we present the Christian faith – from a remedy for the sickness of sin to the offer of life in all its abundance. We have turned the diamond around but it is the same diamond and we can still have confidence in every aspect of it. It is still the remedy for sin, but new Christians might need to develop a concept of sin before they can begin to see the need for a remedy.

The Church of England is a broad church! We do not all express our theology and worship in the same way. When we respect and learn from each other this breadth becomes a strength. When we don't, disunity undermines us. But, on the whole, Anglican breadth is a strength for church growth. Far more people can find a home in the Church of England than if every church was the same. And it means we have a chance to learn from each other. Its rich internal variety together with its national reach make the Church of England a flexible tool in the hands of the Holy Spirit. Though naturally this leads to all sorts of complications and difficulties – a uniform church would be much easier to lead!

And there are boundaries beyond which a rich breadth of theological understanding strays into heresy. Different Anglicans draw those boundaries in different places. The sharp issues come in relation to the practical outworking of our theological and biblical understanding. For example our approach to same-sex marriage will – or should be – determined by our theological and scriptural understanding. Confidence in the gospel means standing on what we believe this tells us, whether or not this coincides with current cultural norms. And then, of course, we need the wisdom of the Spirit to communicate well.

Resurrection hope

Christians believe in 'the Holy Spirit, the holy catholic Church, the communion of saints, the forgiveness of sins, the resurrection of the body, and the life everlasting' (Apostles' Creed). A Church without a resurrection hope is not Christian and has no future. The resurrection hope is the heart of the good news we have to offer so it should be up-front and central in church life.

For 2,000 years the Church has witnessed to the resurrection of Jesus Christ. But the resurrection hope for the human race generated by the physical resurrection of Jesus is not about a detachable, disembodied soul floating away to a spiritual heaven. It concerns the restoration of the whole created order, including ourselves, to the perfection God always intended. And so our resurrection hope is for the whole of ourselves – body, mind, spirit, soul, everything – to become perfectly and fully functioning in the image of our creator within a fully functioning and perfected created order.

Tom Wright in his book *Surprised by Hope* (2007, p. 247)[6] explains that in the Gospel accounts the resurrection of Jesus is not presented as a piece of supernatural proof that God can raise the dead and take us to heaven. It is not our escape route out of this wicked world into the ethereal heavenly one. Rather it launches the kingdom he had taught about, a kingdom of heaven designed to take over the kingdom of this world. The resurrection is not about escaping from the world, but about mission to the world based on Jesus' lordship over it. Jesus' resurrection is the trigger for a new world order in which his followers are sent to the whole world with a gospel of redemption hope for the whole world. It is so much more than the hope that 'our souls go to heaven when we die'. It is both 'now' as outposts of the kingdom of heaven spring up today, and 'not yet' as we await the return and reign of Christ over a redeemed, resurrected creation.

So evangelism and the growth of the Church are about more than saving the souls of some individuals from the fate of the world – they are about the redemption and destiny of the whole created world. This is much more the sort of gospel likely to grip the idealism and imagination of the young – 'You are invited by God to share in transforming the destiny of his creation, including your own destiny. Be part of the kingdom of heaven breaking in to the kingdom of this world. In so doing you will make the world a better place today and prepare both it and yourself for eternity.'

This is also a gospel understanding that unites soul-saving and social-gospelling Christians, for these are both aspects of the same authentic gospel diamond.

And it is a gospel for a kingdom-community not just for individuals. It is the whole Church community that bears witness to the resurrection and models the community of a redeemed humanity in a redeemed creation, the first fruits of the kingdom of heaven. The Church corporately is the key witness to the resurrection and the key evangelist for the kingdom of heaven.

If at Easter Jesus commissions his followers for the task of transforming the world, at Pentecost he equips them to accomplish it with the gift of his Holy Spirit. What is primarily needed for this task is not just belief about Jesus' resurrection but love for the resurrected Jesus. What is the question Jesus keeps throwing at Simon Peter after the miraculous catch of fish? It is not, 'Do you believe me?', it is 'Do you love me?' Only when Peter responds with 'You know that I love you' does Jesus commission him for the mission ahead – 'Feed my sheep' (John 21.16–17). And when Thomas finally met the risen Christ he didn't mutter intellectually 'Ah, now I believe', he cried out in awed and joyful commitment, 'My Lord and my God' (John 20.24–28).

So it is not believers in Jesus who will evangelize the world, it is lovers of Jesus. If the Church is to grow seriously in depth, in numbers and in its transformation of society its people have to grow in their love for the risen Jesus. Church leaders, pastors and teachers can do their best to inspire the people of God to be lovers of Jesus, to inspire the Bride of Christ truly to love her husband. The best tool they have within themselves for this, of course, is example. You can't teach love but you can show it, model it. However, ultimately, the one indispensable source of the love that is needed for the mission and growth of the Church is the Holy Spirit. 'The fruit of the Spirit is love, joy, peace …' (Galatians 5.22). We rely on the Holy Spirit to grow in us our love for the living Jesus and for the world he came to redeem. That is the motive and the power source for the whole mission of the Church, enabled and measured by its growth in depth, numbers and vitality.

One reason why the Pentecostal strand of the Christian faith has grown so fast in recent decades may be its emphasis on a relationship with and experience of Christ rather than simply beliefs about him. The resurrection is a living reality rather than simply a point in a creed. A Christian who, from the Holy Spirit, has caught a love for Jesus and the world of which he is Lord should thereafter possess a faith as infectious as influenza.

Of course it does not matter what strand of the Christian Church you come from – if your faith is infectious your church will grow.

Solid, sacrificial faith

Every so often I take the service in a small village church where the churchwarden's husband is allergic to lilies. He attends church every Sunday right up to Good Friday but then stays away until around Ascension Day when the Easter lilies bought in memory of loved ones have been removed. In Roger's world it is always Lent and never Easter. He may be an extreme example, but generally in the Church of England we do 40 days of sackcloth for Lent, a Holy Week of suffering and crucifixion, then one day of resurrection before the clergy all go off on holiday to recover. In many churches Easter Sunday morning is not even much of a party. Yes, every Sunday is resurrection day but surely a Church whose faith is truly centred upon the resurrection would have the time proportions more balanced. That might be one of the keys to our future growth.

Perhaps resurrection is not the only element of theology to take more seriously. There is clearly some truth in the charge that churches have been slimming down on their theological content. Just compare the content of contemporary worship songs with traditional hymns. Or look at the collapse of the Christian book market! (Thank you for bucking the trend and buying this one.) Personally I'm very pleased that liturgies have been slimmed down and simplified – but there is a cost.

In a way all this has been natural and inevitable as people have become more interested in experience and authenticity than in doctrinal details. The old charge of the liberation theologians that the Church in the West was too interested in orthodoxy (right belief) and too little interested in orthopraxis (right living) has tended to stick. Not many of us actually want to sit and listen to the vicar's 45-minute lecture on some arcane piece of theological academia. We want help to live as Christians in our daily lives.

But perhaps this pendulum now needs to start swinging back the other way again. Churches without a serious theological underpinning all too easily swallow the latest piece of political correctness. A sailing sloop without a solid keel is likely to capsize. Christians who don't really know their Bibles can hardly know what they are supposed to believe.

And then there is the culture in some churches in which the faith has become the dream topping on the comfortable trifle of consumer living. This is not quite prosperity theology but it is all too easy to turn the Jesus who has come to give us life more abundantly into the Jesus whose role is to make us feel good. This might have a superficial attraction in the short term and a congregation in that culture might grow for a while. But as soon as trouble comes and people don't feel so good any more there is nothing to fall back upon. Solid growth is more likely to come where the prevailing culture is not only joy in the resurrection but also sacrifice for the sake of the kingdom of heaven. The risen Jesus is not there to make us feel comfortable but to demand that we take up our cross and follow him. A full and balanced Easter faith involves both the sacrifice of the old life and the gift of a new one. We will always need the whole of the creed. If we live the creed we will grow the Church.

Notes

Introduction

1. Bob Jackson, *Hope for the Church*, Church House Publishing, 2002.
2. Bob Jackson, *The Road to Growth*, Church House Publishing, 2005.
3. Bob Jackson and George Fisher, *Everybody Welcome*, Church House Publishing, 2009.
4. Bob Jackson, *Growing through a Vacancy*, CPAS, 2013, www.cpas.org.uk/church-resources
5. Bob Jackson, *Leading your Church into Growth – Local*, LyCig, 2014.

Chapter 1 Growth in numbers

1. Church of England Mission and Public Affairs Council, *Mission-Shaped Church*, Church House Publishing, 2004, page vii.

Chapter 2 Measuring growth in depth and vitality

1. Christian Schwarz, *Natural Church Development Handbook*, BCGA, 1996.
2. Robert Warren, *The Healthy Churches' Handbook*, Church House Publishing, 2012.
3. Robert Warren, *Developing Healthy Churches*, Church House Publishing, 2012.
4. Mark Yaconelli, *Contemplative Youth Ministry*, SPCK, 2006.
5. Mike Starkey, *Ministry Rediscovered: Shaping a unique and creative church*, BRF, 2011.
6. Robert Warren, *Developing Healthy Churches*, Church House Publishing, 2012.

Chapter 3 Growth initiatives

1. Bob Jackson, *Hope for the Church*, Church House Publishing, 2002.
2. Bob Jackson, *The Road to Growth*, Church House Publishing, 2005.
3. Bob Jackson and Alan Piggot, *Another Capital Idea*, Diocese of London, 2011.

4. Bob Jackson and George Fisher, *Everybody Welcome*, Church House Publishing, 2009.
5. David Banbury, Robin Gamble and Bob Jackson, *Leading your Church into Growth – Local*, LyCig, 2014.

Chapter 4 Growth in patterns

1. David Goodhew (ed.), *Church Growth in Britain*, Ashgate, 2012.
2. Peter Brierley, *London's Churches are Growing*, London City Mission, 2013.
3. Bob Jackson, *The Road to Growth*, Church House Publishing, 2005, page 58.

Chapter 5 Growth in total?

1. Bob Jackson, *Hope for the Church*, Church House Publishing, 2002.

Chapter 6 Intending to grow

1. Bob Jackson, *The Road to Growth*, Church House Publishing, 2005.
2. Mike Chew and Mark Ireland, *Mission Action Planning*, SPCK, 2009.
3. Mike Chew and Mark Ireland, *Mission Action Planning*, SPCK, 2009.

Chapter 7 Leading to grow

1. J. Obelkevich, *Religion and Rural Society: South Lindsey, 1825–75*, Oxford University Press, 1976, page 120.
2. Bob Jackson, *The Road to Growth*, Church House Publishing, 2005, pages 125–6.
3. Robert Warren, *The Healthy Churches' Handbook*, Church House Publishing, 2012.
4. Bob Jackson, *The Road to Growth*, Church House Publishing, 2005.
5. Bob Jackson, *Growing through a Vacancy*, CPAS, 2013, www.cpas.org.uk/church-resources
6. Robin Gamble, *Leading your Church into Growth*, LyCiG.
7. David Banbury, Robin Gamble and Bob Jackson, *Leading your Church into Growth – Local*, LyCiG, 2014.

Chapter 8 Training to grow

1. Bob Jackson, *The Road to Growth*, Church House Publishing, 2005, pages 141ff.
2. Bob Jackson and George Fisher, *Everybody Welcome*, Church House Publishing, 2009.

3. Bob Jackson, *Growing through a Vacancy*, CPAS, 2013, www.cpas.org.uk/church-resources
4. David Banbury, Robin Gamble and Bob Jackson, *Leading your Church into Growth – Local*, LyCiG, 2014.
5. Bob Jackson, *Growing through a Vacancy*, CPAS, 2013, www.cpas.org.uk/church-resources

Chapter 9 Inviting to grow

1. Bob Jackson and George Fisher, *Everybody Welcome*, Church House Publishing, 2009.
2. Michael Harvey, *Unlocking the Growth*, Monarch, 2012.
3. 'From anecdote to evidence', www.churchgrowthresearch.org.uk, page 40.
4. Bob Jackson and George Fisher, *Everybody Welcome*, Church House Publishing, 2009.

Chapter 10 Families to grow

1. 'From anecdote to evidence', www.churchgrowthresearch.org.uk
2. Bob Jackson and Alan Piggot, *Another Capital Idea*, Diocese of London, 2011.

Chapter 12 Changing to grow

1. Bob Jackson, *The Road to Growth*, Church House Publishing, 2005, page 58.
2. Bob Jackson, *The Road to Growth*, Church House Publishing, 2005, chapter 6.
3. Bob Jackson, *The Road to Growth*, Church House Publishing, 2005, page 49.
4. You can find this quote in a well-known and helpful book on change-management, William Bridges, *Managing Transitions*, NB Publishing, 1995, page 37.

Chapter 13 Spending to grow

1. 'Giving Insight', Network, November 2011, available online: www.parishresources.org.uk/wp-content/uploads/Giving-Insight
2. Bob Jackson, *The Road to Growth*, Church House Publishing, 2005, chapter 13.
3. Bob Jackson, *The Road to Growth*, Church House Publishing, 2005, chapter 13.
4. *Investing in the Church's Growth*, Church Commissioners, 2008.

Chapter 14 Cathedrals to grow

1. 'From anecdote to evidence', www.churchgrowthresearch.org.uk
2. Leslie Francis and Emry Williams, 'Not all cathedral congregations look alike', *Rural Theology* 8.1, 2010, pages 39–40.
3. Church Commissioners: report of the Resourcing Mission Group, *Resourcing Mission for a 21st Century Church*, Church House Publishing, 2006.
4. Bob Jackson and Alan Piggot, *Another Capital Idea*, Diocese of London, 2011.

Chapter 15 Dioceses to grow

1. Bob Jackson, *Growing through a Vacancy*, CPAS, 2013, www.cpas.org.uk/church-resources

Chapter 16 The angel of the church

1. Robert Warren, *The Healthy Churches' Handbook*, Church House Publishing, 2004.

Chapter 18 The Holy Spirit and growth

1. Rob Jackson and George Fisher, *Everybody Welcome*, Church House Publishing, 2009.
2. James Lawrence and Simon Heathfield, *Growing Leaders*, CPAS, 2004.
3. Bob Jackson, *Growing through a Vacancy*, CPAS, 2013, www.cpas.org.uk/church-resources
4. Bob Jackson, *Hope for the Church*, Church House Publishing, 2002, page 32.
5. Rowan Williams, *Mission-Shaped Church*, Church House Publishing, 2004, page 13.
6. Tom Wright, *Surprised by Hope*, SPCK, 2007, page 247.

Index

Act Concerning Peter's Pence and Dispensations, 1534 92
Acts of the Apostles
  1.8 274
  1.15 8
  2.41 8
  2.42 3
  2.42-47 10
  4.4 8
  5.14
  6.8 10
  9.31 6
  11.28 264
  13.2 256
  13.3 265
  15.6, 7 264
  15.13, 19 265
  15.19 73
  44 3
  45 3
  47 3
age
  church attendance and 50–1, 69
  see also children and youth
St Albans 230
Alpha courses
  discipleship 31
  spiritual maturity and 23
St Alphege Seasalter 136–9
Anecdote to Evidence programme 99
angels 247–8, 253, 254
Another Capital Idea (Jackson and Piggot) 146, 221
Apostles' Creed 279
Aquila and Priscilla's church 159–60
Astley Abbotts 113
Aston Eyre 112
Australia
  National Church Life Survey 13–15

Back to Church Sunday 34–5, 36, 37
baptisms
  numbers of 69
  sacramentalism 275–6
  statistics of 52
Baptist Church 41, 278
Barnabas 256
Bath 230
belonging, as core quality 14
Birmingham 224
  Transforming Church strategy 226, 242
Blackburn
  growth 78–9, 224, 230, 242
  schools and church 157
Book of Common Prayer 142
Bosch, David 224
Bradford
  Cathedral 212, 217
  growth of 230
Brierley, Peter
  London's churches are growing 40
Bristol 224, 230, 242
British Social Attitudes survey
  age of firm beliefs 237
  church attendance 61, 141

Canterbury 229, 230
  Cathedral 212

Capital Vision 226
Carey, Archbishop George
 Decade of Evangelism 28–30
 Springboard initiative 33
Carlisle 229, 230
cathedrals xiv
 attraction of 215–18
 civic profile and special services 217
 difference in locations 211–12
 diversity of congregation 212–13, 214–15
 and Greater Churches 219–21
 growth of attendance 44, 206, 209–13
 in the Netherlands 208–9
 services 210–11, 213–14
 threats to 218–19
Catholic Church
 frequency of church attendance 62
 lay ministry and 116
 numbers of churches 105
 UK membership 41
Centre for Youth Ministry 30, 52
Chadwick, Mike 132
change xiv, 17, 186
 categories of 185
 Christian meaning of 177
 Church of England and 179–81
 combining with tradition 182
 as a constant 177–8
 desire for stable 'truth' 178–9
 endings and losses 191–2
 as growth factor 45–6
 process of 193–5
 relation to attendance 183–90
 resistance to 189–90
charismatic movement 31–2
Chelmsford 224, 230
Chester 230
Chew, Mike
 Mission Action Planning (with Ireland) 78
Chichester 230
children and youth
 baptisms 53
 cathedral visits 218
 change and 185–6
 Fresh Expressions and 166–7
 Messy Church and 35–6, 149–50
 paid staff for 156–7
 passing on through generations 140–1
 proportion of churches and 50–1
 responsiveness of 146
 seasonal events 158
 Sunday schools 142–4, 154–5
 toddler groups 152
 ways to bring back 151–8
 working with schools 157
 see also Messy Church
Church Army Research Unit 36, 163–4
church attendance/growth
 assessing progress of 20–1, 68–70
 cathedrals and 44
 changing patterns of xiv
 children and 140–4, 146–51
 decline narrative 40, 48
 depth and vitality 10–13
 Easter and Christmas 57–8, 62, 69
 effect of training 123–4
 failure of Decade of Evangelism 29
 frequency 61–4
 God's hand in 258–60
 identifying weaknesses 21–2
 increments of 221
 joiners and leavers 8–9, 64–5, 69, 150–1, 242
 journey of leadership 24
 large-scale surveys of 66–8, 69
 listening and guidance 256–7
 measuring 3–9, 11–12, 20, 241, 260–2
 new focus and xiii–xiv
 October counts 59–61, 69
 patterns of 39–46
 relation to change 183–90
 single/multi-church clergy effects 94–100
 small churches and 42–4
 Spirit and strategy 37–8
 stimulating vitality 21–5

uniqueness of churches 262
usual Sundays 58–9, 69
ways to bring back the young 151–8
see also Church of England; congregations; Messy Church; mission; planting
Church Census, UK 40–4
Church Commissioners
Investing in the Church's Growth 206
mission development 52
'Mission Development Funding' 30
Resourcing Mission for a 21st Century Church 219
single/multi-church clergy and 99
Church Growth Fund 206
Church Growth in Britain (ed. Goodhew) 40
Church Growth Research Programme 99, 164
cathedral growth 213–4
large-scale surveys 66
'The Church Health Review' (Truscott) 19–20
Church Life survey 21, 34–5
Church of England
active clergy and churches 107
ages and 50–1
assessing size of 68–70
cathedrals and 209
change and 179–81
clergy of 51–2, 69
confidence in the Gospel 278–9
confidence within society 276–8
diocese and finances 206–7
ecumenical projects 164
electoral rolls of 56–7, 69
number of churches 49–51, 69
parish allocations 201–3
PCC income 56, 69
renewal 274
repentance 273
resurrection hope 279–83
revival 274–5
rites statistics 52–5, 69
theology of 279, 282–3
UK membership 41
website statistics 48
see also church attendance/growth; churches; clergy
Church Times
on inviting churches 129
survey 66
churches
angels and 247–8, 253
as community 4–5
core qualities of 14
eight quality characteristics of 15–16
fitting to members 23–4
Greater 219–21
growing through vacancies 121–2
healthy 32, 36
incarnational 181–2
income 56
joining with other churches 153
as learning organizations 86
local budgeting 196–201
MAP and 87–91, 118–19
New Testament ekklesia 5–6
paid workforce of 30
planting 159–63
the power of the past 248–51, 254–5
pruning activities and 90
sacraments and 164
smallest 42–4
'Statistics for Mission' 7
see also church attendance/growth; congregations
churches as buildings
appeal of cathedrals 215–18
functional structures 15
Greater Churches 219–21
improving 185
numbers of 94–5, 105–6
physical facilities 154
see also cathedrals
Churches Together Stewardship Network
'Giving Insight' 201
Clarke, Paul 129–30

clergy
bishops and MAP 84–6
change and 179, 184
church-wide planning 87
diocese strategy and 228
financial cuts and 222–3
focal ministry 108–13, 188
gift-oriented ministry 15
inviting 129–30
leadership 100–1, 263
Mission Action Plans and 76
mission over promotion 117–18
multi-church benefices 92–6, 101–3
ordination of women 30
pastoral care 185, 186
professional role of 115
recruitment of 106–8, 236
restructuring ministry 102–8
seeking advice 264
single/multi-church effects 96–100
staffing cathedrals 219
statistics of 51–2, 107
tasks and responsibilities 90
team approach and 104–5, 235
vacancies 105, 121–2, 240
voluntary ministry and 108
communication
diocese and local 238
electronic invitation 131–2
reaching younger age groups 152
community
of cathedrals 215–18
churches as 4–5
diocesan support 236–7
healthy churches and 17
hurdles to invitation 251
local needs 25
numbers of 69
Old Testament concepts of 5–6
resurrection 281
size of 65
training and 120–1
village churches 44, 180–1
see also congregations; Fresh Expressions
Compassionate vision 226
confession 254–5
Confident vision 226
confirmations 55, 69
congregations
active mission of 36–7
ages of 45, 50–1, 69
cathedrals 212–18
clergy vacancies and 105
cultural transformations and 233–4
diversity 212–15
individual members and 25
initiatives from 37, 233–4
lapsed members 28
numbers of 69
nurturing the mature 22–3
planting 159–63, 185, 205
tasks and responsibilities 90
see also children; church attendance/growth
consumerism 283
Contemplative Youth Ministry (Yaconelli) 25
control, MAP and 86
coordination, MAP and 86
Corinthians, First Letter to
3.1-9 259
9.16 260
16.1 6
16.19 159
Corinthians, Second Letter to
1.1 114
7.10 273
Coventry
growth of 230
NCD strategy 16
Creative vision 226

St David's 45
change and 46, 183, 186–7
children and young people 147
focal ministry 108, 111, 120
Growing Hope 226
MAP and growth 82–3
prayer bookmark 232–3
responsiveness of children 146
restructuring ministry 102–3
Derby 81–2, 230

Deuteronomy
- 6.6, 7 140

Developing Healthy Churches (Warren) 26
Dewsbury Minster 220
dioceses xv
- church-planting 239
- clergy and 236, 238
- collective wisdom of 225
- communication and 238
- crisis of 222–3
- effectiveness of strategy 242–3
- financial matters and 240–1
- growth possibilities 229–31
- listening 226–7
- ministry models 238
- mission 223–5, 239
- priority needs/opportunities 237–8
- strategies 223–5, 227–9, 231–41
- support whole community 236–7
- teamwork and 235
- use of research 241
- vacancies and 240
- vision 225–6

discipleship
- courses 31
- strategy and theology 234
- Yaconelli on 25

Durham 230
- Cathedral 212

St Ebbs 230
Ecclesfield 159
ecumenicalism 164
Elizabeth I, Queen 20
Ely 229, 230
English Heritage 39
Ephesians, Letter to
- 1.1 6
- 2.19-22 128
- 4.11-13 10
- 6.1 6–7

ethnicity
- cathedral congregations 214–15
- London churches and 40

European Foundation for Quality Management 19
European Values survey 62
evangelism
- Billy Graham and 27–8
- Decade of 28–30
- need-orientated 15
- in a secular society 276–8
- the young and 144–5

Evangelism Task Force 37
Everybody Welcome (Jackson and Fisher) 130–1
Everybody Welcome course xiv, 121, 135–6, 137, 271
Exeter 224, 230
Eyam, Derbyshire xv
Ezekiel
- 37.4, 8, 9, 10, 11 269–70

faith
- as core quality 14
- energizing 17
- sharing 14
- through the generations 140–1

families xiv
- loving parents and children 152
- Messy Church initiative 35–6
- monthly family services 155
- *see also* children and youth

financial matters xiv
- applying for funds 204–5
- budgeting for families 154
- cathedrals and 216–17, 218–19
- decisions about capital 203–5
- dioceses and 206–7, 222–3, 237–8, 240–1
- giving and 198–201
- in the Gospels 196
- grants for MAP 86
- means and ends 119
- Mission Development Funding 241
- money and happiness 11
- parishes and the diocese 201–3
- PCC income 56, 69
- planting congregations 205
- strategy and 228

Fisher, Archbishop Geoffrey 225, 231–2

Fisher, George
Everybody Welcome (with Jackson) 130–1
Francis, Leslie 66, 215
Fresh Expressions 33–4, 36
cathedrals and 214–15
children and families 148–9, 156
church growth and 45
congregations and 165–6
definition of 163–4
diocese and 239
frequency of church attendance 63
lay leaders 106
leadership and 100–1, 167–9
Leicester and 119
Liverpool and 148–9
mortality rates of 169
numerical growth in 169–71
planting 167–9, 205
qualifications for 165
training and 114, 119–20
types of 166–7
voluntary ministry 108
see also Messy Church
friendship and 251–3
funerals 54–5, 69

Galatians, Letter to
3.28 128
5. 22 281
St George's, Leeds
'Way In/Way Out' groups 22
giving
Gift Day 199–200
trends and attitudes 198–201
Gladstone, William E. 92, 98
Gloucester 230
God
giving hope to churches xv
guidance 264–6
has 'top copy' 25–6
healthy churches and 19–20, 26
intercessory prayer 266–8
invitation of the Trinity 127–8
joining in with 272–3
making things grow 258–60
of mission 224–5
mystery tour of 257–8
seeking what He wants 17
Going for Growth course 147, 226
good practice, sharing 85
Goodhew, David
Church Growth in Britain 40
Graham, Billy 27–8, 29, 130, 257
grants, MAP goals and 86
Greater Churches Network 219–20
Green, Michael 28
groups
holistic 15
small 185
Growing Hope 226
Growing Leaders course 271
Growing through a vacancy course xiv, 105, 121–2, 240
Guildford 230
Gumbel, Nicky 31

Harvey, Michael 134
Unlocking the Growth 132–3
healthy churches
characteristics 16–17
Truscott's marks of 19–20
The Healthy Churches' Handbook (Warren) 101, 253
Hebrews, Letter to
10.24-25 6
Hereford 229
Holmes, John 213–4
Holy Spirit
breath of God 269–70
movement of spiritual renewal 31–2
renewal and 274
repentance and 273
revival 274–5
sailing with wind of 270–3
Hope, Bishop David
growth strategy 242
Mission Action Plan 33, 76
Hope for the Church (Jackson) xiii, 32, 273
on the trends 47–8
Hosea
11.1 5

incarnational churches 181–2
inclusion and welcome
  as core church quality 14
  healthy churches and 17
  hurdles to 251–2
  making change and 193
  proportion of churches and 50–1
innovation 14
intentionality xiv
  cathedrals and 217
  child attendance and 152
  mission and growth 73–6
Investing in the Church's Growth (Church Commissioners) 206
invitation xiv
  cathedrals and 217
  churches and 129
  clergy and congregations 129–31
  electronic 131–2
  improving 134–6, 135–6
  Philip and 127
  problems with 132–3, 251–3
  Trinity and 127–8
  welcome teams 136–9
  see also inclusion and welcome
Ireland, Mark
  Mission Action Planning (with Chew) 78
Isaiah
  42.9 27
  46.9 92

Jackson, Bob
  Another Capital Idea (with Piggot) 146, 221
  Everybody Welcome (with Fisher) 130–1
  Growing Through a Vacancy 105
  Hope for the Church xiii, 32, 47–8, 273
  see also The Road to Growth (Jackson)
Jeremiah
  29.11 xiii
  30.1, 2 258
Jesus Christ 177–8
  invitation of 128
  John the Baptist and 39
  love and 281–2
  money and 200
  resurrection 279–80
  stages of spirituality and 17–18
John, Gospel of
  1.45-46 127
  3.30 39
  20.24-28 281
  21.16-17 281
John the Baptist 39
St John's College Durham 213–4
St John's Nottingham Centre for Church Growth 205
Judges, Book of
  14.14 222

Kautzer, Ben 213–4

laity
  Fresh Expressions initiative 119
  increasing involvement 185
  training and 115–17
Lambeth Conference, 1998 88
leadership xiv
  child and youth ministry 153
  as core church quality 14
  effecting change 190–1
  empowering 15
  Fresh Expressions initiative 167–9, 170–1
  healthy churches and 19
  importance of 100–1
  journey of 24
  training and 114
Leading your Church into Growth course xiv, 32, 47, 121–2
  clergy and community 236–7
  development and content of 123, 125–6
  effectiveness of 115, 123–5, 126
  focal ministry and 111
  missionary congregations and 36–7
  sponsorship 206
Leicester
  access to capital 204
  children and families 147–8

Fresh Expressions 119, 171
joiners and leavers 64
Statistics for Mission and 9
strategy 224, 230, 242–3
Lichfield
Back to Church Sunday 34
children and youth ministers 156–7
focal ministry 112
Going for Growth 226, 266–7
growth of 230
guidance for Growth Fund 237–8
joiners and leavers 64
MAP and growth 80–1
Messy Churches and 175
numbers of churches 50
single/multi-church clergy 99
Statistics for Mission and 9
strategy 4, 224, 242–3
Lincoln 102, 230
Lincolnshire 92
Lings, George 164
listening 256–7
Liverpool
fresh expressions 148
growth of 224, 230, 242
London
Capital Vision 239
growth of 40–2, 78, 229, 230, 242
MAP and 33, 78
strategies of 226, 242
London's churches are growing report (Brierley) 40
loss, change and 191–3
love
of Christ 281–2
church relationships and 15
Luke, Gospel of
8.1-3 196
15 128
Lunn, Bishop David 223–4

Macmillan, Harold 231–2
Magic Roundabout (television) 74–5
Manchester 34, 230
Mar Thomas Church, Kerala 73
St Mark's Grenoside 159
marriages 54, 69
Marshall, Bishop Michael 28
St Mary and Holy Apostles Scarborough 159, 160, 199–200
St Mary, Haughley 129–30
Matthew, Gospel of
25, 34, 35, 40 128
mentoring
MAP and 85
spirituality and 18
Messy Church xv, 35–6, 37, 149–50
child attendance and 151, 156
community wishes and 153
development of 171–3
growth of 40, 50, 173–5
joiners 64–5
in Lichfield 238
schools and 157
Methodist Church 175, 278
Fresh Expressions initiative 33–4
UK membership 41
Ministry Rediscovered (Starkey) 25–6
mission
Bishop's Mission Orders 239
of congregations 36–7
diocesan strategies 223–5
focal ministry 110
growth with 73–6
Mission Development Funding 241
strategy and 228
Mission Action Planning (MAP) 16, 37
acting on 89
Bishop Hope's initiative 33
broad understanding of 88
change and 194–5
churches' use of 87–91
dioceses' use of 84–6, 237
effectiveness 77
as growth factor 46
guidance checklist 262–6
history of 76–7
missionary congregations 36–7
numerical growth and 77–83
PCC and 268
persuasion over demand 84
priorities 89
SMART 89–90

tasks and responsibilities 90
training churches for 118–19
understanding and application of 83–4
writing and reviewing 90–1
Mission and Pastoral Measure 2011 239
Mission Development Funding 204, 206
Mission-Shaped Church (Williams) 4–5, 273
'Mission-Shaped Ministry' 168
money *see* financial matters
Monkhopton 112
Moore, Lucy 35, 171
music, cathedrals and 215–16, 217

National Church Life Survey (NCLS) 13–15
Natural Church Development 36
Natural Church Development Handbook (Schwarz) 15–16
The New Testament
confidence in 278–9
see also individual books and letters of
Newcastle 230
Norwich 224, 230, 242

Orthodox churches 41
outward outlook
healthy churches and 17, 19
Oxford 230

Parochial Church Councils (PCC)
financial matters and 197–8, 207
MAP and 87
prayer and 268
vacancies and training 122
Paul
Barnabas and 256
instruction on training 114
in prison 266
St Paul's Cathedral 212
Pentecostal churches 41, 278
Peter, First Letter of
2.9 116
Peter, love and 281
Peterborough 230
Philip 127
Philippians, Letter to
3.13 255
Piggot, Alan
Another Capital Idea (with Jackson) 146, 221
Pilgrim Course 37
planting 159–63, 185, 205
dioceses and 239
teams and leadership 167–9
pluralism
effect of clergy cuts 96–8
historical perspective of 92–3
Pluralities Act, 1838 92
Portsmouth 230
postmodernism 180
prayer
giving hope to churches xv
intercession and growth 266–8
mission and 87–8, 265
strategy initiatives and 231–3
Presbyterian Church 41
prodigal son 128
Proverbs
16.3 266
19.21 265
22.6 144
Psalms, Book of
78.1-8 140
119.105 264

Raikes, Robert 142
Ramsey, Archbishop Michael 231–2
renewal 274
repentance 253–5, 273
Resourcing Mission for a 21st Century Church (Church Commissioners) 219
resurrection 279–82
'Reveal' research 17–19, 22–3
Revelation
2.1, 2, 4 247
3.19, 20 254
5.9, 10 116
writing to angels 249

Ripon 230
The Road to Growth (Jackson) xiii, 32, 76
 change and 183
 clergy cuts 96
 financial matters 201, 203
 Mission Actions Plans and 76
 multi-church situations 101
 service times 186–7
 training programmes 117
Rochester 224, 230, 242
Rublev, Andrei 127–8

sacraments and rites
 sacramentalism 275–6
 statistics of 52–5, 69
 see also baptisms; confirmations; funerals; marriages; worship and services
Salisbury 224, 242
 Cathedral 212
Scarborough 190
 St Mary's 159, 160, 199–200
schools, working with 157
Schwarz, Christian 19
 Natural Church Development Handbook 15–16
 quality practices 32
secular society
 confidence within 276–8
 Decade of Evangelism and 29
 dry bones and 269
Sentamu, Archbishop John 225
services *see* worship and services
Sheffield 230
 impact of Billy Graham 27–8, 257
Silas 266
SMART planning 89–90
Southwark 41–2, 230
Southwell 224, 230, 242
speaking in tongues 31
spirituality
 measuring 10–13
 passionate 15
 renewal of 31–2
 'Reveal' research 17–19
 stages of 17
 stimulating 21–5
Starkey, Mike
 Ministry Rediscovered 25–6
'Statistics for Mission' (Church of England) 7, 41, 67
 child members and 151
 error margins 49
 explaining costs and 202
 use of data 241
Stephen 10
strategy
 celebrating achievements 235
 cultural transformation 233–4
 good theology and 234
 prayer and 231–3
 principles of 227–9
 teamwork and 235
'Stronger as One?' (Tweedie) 99
Sunday schools 154–5
support, healthy churches and 19
Surprised by Hope (Wright) 280

Tasley 113
The Times newspaper 180–1
Timothy, First Letter to
 1.2 114
training xiv
 clergy *versus* laity 115–17
 communities 120–1
 effectiveness of 114–15
 focal ministry 120
 Fresh Expressions and 119–20
 MAP and 85
 for mission 117–18
Transforming Church 226
Trinity, invitation of 127–8
Truro 230
Truscott, John
 Church Health Review 19–20
Twain, Mark 188
Tweedie, Fiona
 'Stronger as One?' 99

United Reformed Churches 278
Unlocking the Growth (Harvey) 132–3

vacancies 121–2

vision
as core church quality 14
then strategy 88
vitality, stimulating 21–5
Vitalize initiative 34
Voas, David 141
'From anecdote to evidence' survey 114–15
growth in dioceses 229
growth with mission 75
on invitation 135
inviting congregations 130
large-scale surveys 66–7

Wakefield 230
Ward, Revd John 112
Warren, Robert 19, 21
Developing Healthy Churches 26
The Healthy Churches' Handbook 16–17, 101, 253
as Springboard Missioner 29
Webb, John 113
Welby, Archbishop Justin
on the growth of the church 3
invitation and 134
St Wilfrid's Cowplain, Portsmouth 35–6
Williams, Archbishop Rowan
Fresh Expressions initiative 33–4
on the growth of the church 3
Mission-Shaped Church 4–5, 273
Williams, Emry 215
Willow Creek Church, Chicago 16, 17–19
Winchester 230
Cathedral 212
Wolverhampton 34
women, ordination of 30
Worcester 230
worship and services
Book of Common Prayer 213–14
cathedrals and 215, 216
changing service times 186–90
as core quality 14
families and 155
inspiring services 15
loosening up 185–6, 186
service times and 155
Wright, Tom
Surprised by Hope 280

Yaconelli, Mark
Contemplative Youth Ministry 25
York 230
Minster 212

Zechariah
8.4, 5 158